Access to History for the IB Diploma

The Second World War and the Americas 1933–45

John Wright

HODDER
EDUCATION
AN HACHETTE UK COMPANY

For MAW – 'Age cannot wither her, nor custom stale her infinite variety.'

The material in this title has been developed independently of the International Baccalaureate®, which in no way endorses it.

The Publishers would like to thank the following for permission to reproduce copyright material:

Photo credits: p11 Wikipedia; **p31** AP/Press Association Images; **p38** Bettmann/Corbis; **p42** Bettmann/Corbis; **p45** Associated Newspapers Ltd/Solo Syndication and supplied by Llyfrgell Genedlaethol Cymru/National Library of Wales; **p56** Getty Images; **p63** Bettmann/Corbis; **p77** Mondadori via Getty Images; **p96** Getty Images; **p100** Getty Images; **p114** AP/Press Association Images; **p115** Getty Images; **p131** AP/Press Association Images; **p139** Popperfoto/Getty Images; **p145** Library of Congress Prints and Photographs; **p165** Getty Images; **p187** Wikipedia; **p204** Time & Life Pictures/Getty Images.

Acknowledgements: p24 Miller Center archive of US presidential speeches (http://millercenter.org); **p25** *Boston Herald*, 6 October 1937; **p26** *The USA from Wilson to Nixon 1917 to 1975*, by Harriet Ward, Collins Educational, UK, 1998; **p27** The American Presidency Project (www.presidency.ucsb.edu); **p37** *St Louis Post Despatch*, 4 September 1940; **p40** The American Presidency Project (www.presidency.ucsb.edu); *Roosevelt and the United States*, by D.B. O'Callaghan, Longman, UK, 1966; **p41** US National Archives and Records Administration (www.archives.gov); **pp42, 43** *Modern America*, by J. Vick, Collins Educational, UK, 1985; **p46** *Peace and War: United States Foreign Policy, 1931–1941*, by the US Department of State, US Government Printing Office, USA, 1983; **p55** *Department of State Bulletin*, Vol. V, No. 129, 13 December 1941; **p57** US National Archives and Records Administration (www.archives.gov); *Time*, 15 December 1941; **p62** Nuclear Files, Nuclear Peace Foundation (www.nuclearfiles.org); *Memoirs: 1945 Year of Decisions*, by Harry S. Truman, Doubleday, USA, 1955; **p63** *Speaking Frankly*, by James Byrne, Harper Brothers, USA, 1947; **p66** *Harper's Magazine*, February 1947; National Council of Churches (USA) (www.ncccusa.org); **p67** *Mandate for Change 1953–1956*, by Dwight Eisenhower, Doubleday, USA, 1963; *I Was There*, by Admiral William Leahy, Whittlesey House, USA, 1950; *Nippon Times*, 10 August 1945; **p68** *The Roots of European Security*, by V. Nekrasov, Novosti Press Agency Publishing House, Russia, 1984; **p72** *A Democracy at War*, by W. O'Neill, Harvard University Press, USA, 1993; **pp87, 88** *Traitor To His Class*, by H.W. Brands, Anchor, UK, 2009; **p89** *Churchill: A Life*, by Martin Gilbert, Heinemann, UK, 1991; **p92** TeachingAmericanHistory.org; **p98** Temple University, USA (http://isc.temple.edu); **p99** *A History of the United States*, by Hugh Brogan, Pelican, UK, 1987; **p103** *A Prime Minister Remembers*, by Francis Williams, Heinemann, UK, 1961; **p105** *New York Times*, 2 May 1942; **p115** *Six Armies in Normandy*, by John Keegan, Pimlico, UK, 2004 and *Citizen Soldiers*, by Stephen Ambrose, Touchstone, USA, 1997; **p120** *The Penguin History of Canada*, by R. Bothwell, Penguin, Canada, 2006; **p128** US National Archives and Records Administration (www.ourdocuments.gov); **p129** Smithsonian National Museum of American History (www.americanhistory.si.edu); **p132** Canadian Japanese Internment Camps (http://canadianjapaneseinternmentcamps.wordpress.com/); Canadian Broadcasting Corporation (www.cbc.ca); **p136** *Los Angeles Times*, 9 June 1943; **p139** *Reader's Digest*, January 1944; **p140** *Rosie the Riveter Revisited*, by Sherna Gluck, Twayne, USA, 1987; **p143** *Mr. Black Labor*, by D. Davis, E.P. Dutton, USA, 1972; **p147** *Baltimore Afro-American*, 16 January 1943; **p148** *Citizen Soldiers*, by Stephen Ambrose, Simon & Schuster, UK, 1997; **p162** George S. Messersmith Papers, University of Delaware Library, Newark, Delaware, USA; **pp163, 165, 167** *Roosevelt and the Holocaust*, by R. Beir and B. Josepher, Barricade Books, USA, 2006; **p168** Holocaust Survivors and Remembrance Project (http://isurvived.org); **p171** American Presidency Project (www.presidency.ucsb.edu); **p173** *The Encyclopaedia of World War II: A Political, Social and Military History*, by Spencer Tucker and Priscilla Roberts (editors), ABC-CLIO, USA; **p174** Jewish Virtual Library (www.jewishvirtuallibrary.org); *Oregonian*, 20 April 1945; **p179** Teachingamericanhistory.org; **p193** *Hiroshima Diary*, by Michihiko Hachiya, University of North Carolina, USA, 1995; *The Good War*, by Studs Terkel, Pantheon Books, USA, 1984; **p202** Bureau of Labor Statistics (www.bls.gov); **p204** *War, Economy, and Society, 1939–1945*, by Alan S. Milward, University of California Press, USA, 1979; **p206** *Major Problems in American History*, by C. Gordon (editor), Houghton & Mifflin, USA, 1999; **p209** Bits of News (www.bitsofnews.com); **p210** History Matters (http://historymatters.gmu.edu); An excerpt from *War, Economy, and Society, 1939–1945*, by A. Milward, University of California Press, USA, 1979; **p214** *Conversations with Stalin*, by Milovan Djilas, Harcourt Brace International, USA, 1963; *Pelican History of the United States of America*, by Hugh Brogan, Penguin Books, UK, 1987; **p221** *Hamilton Spectator*, 22 November 1945.

Every effort has been made to trace all copyright holders, but if any have been inadvertently overlooked the Publishers will be pleased to make the necessary arrangements at the first opportunity.

Although every effort has been made to ensure that website addresses are correct at time of going to press, Hodder Education cannot be held responsible for the content of any website mentioned in this book. It is sometimes possible to find a relocated web page by typing in the address of the home page for a website in the URL window of your browser.

Hachette UK's policy is to use papers that are natural, renewable and recyclable products and made from wood grown in sustainable forests. The logging and manufacturing processes are expected to conform to the environmental regulations of the country of origin.

Orders: please contact Bookpoint Ltd, 130 Milton Park, Abingdon, Oxon OX14 4SB. Telephone: +44 (0)1235 827720. Fax: +44 (0)1235 400454. Lines are open 9.00a.m.–5.00p.m., Monday to Saturday, with a 24-hour message answering service. Visit our website at www.hoddereducation.co.uk

© John Wright 2013

First published in 2013 by
Hodder Education,
An Hachette UK Company
338 Euston Road
London NW1 3BH

Impression number 10 9 8 7 6 5 4 3 2
Year   2017 2016 2015 2014

Cover photo: United We Win Poster by Howard Liberman © Corbis
Illustrations by Gray Publishing
Produced and typeset in 10/13pt Palatino by Gray Publishing
Printed in Dubai

A catalogue record for this title is available from the British Library

ISBN 978 14441 56560

Contents

Dedication

Keith Randell (1943–2002)

The original *Access to History* series was conceived and developed by Keith, who created a series to 'cater for students as they are, not as we might wish them to be'. He leaves a living legacy of a series that for over 20 years has provided a trusted, stimulating and well-loved accompaniment to post-16 study. Our aim with these new editions for the IB is to continue to offer students the best possible support for their studies.

Introduction

This book has been written to support your study of HL option 3: Aspects of the history of the Americas: The Second World War and the Americas 1933–45 of the IB History Diploma Route 2.

This introduction gives you an overview of:

✪ the content you will study for The Second World War and the Americas 1933–45
✪ how you will be assessed for Paper 3
✪ the different features of this book and how these will aid your learning.

 What you will study

This book focuses on how the Americas region responded to a deteriorating world order in the 1930s. Each country took a different path as it confronted the new challenges posed by the rise of totalitarian governments in Europe and Asia. Some countries such as the USA remained neutral while Canada entered the war in 1939. Other nations would only join the war as it was drawing to a close. The lead-up to the Second World War, the impact of the war on both the home front and on the battlefield, and the diplomatic and economic effects of this global conflict on the Americas are examined here.

● The book begins by discussing the period from the end of the First World War to the onset of the Great Depression. Special attention is paid to the growing attraction of an isolationist foreign policy in the face of increased global instability (Chapter 1).
● How the region reacted to events in Asia and Europe from 1933 to 1940 is examined in detail. Increased hemispheric co-operation and co-ordination, including President Roosevelt's 'Good Neighbor' policy, are explored (Chapter 2).
● The military role of the USA during the Second World War is detailed. How the country brought its enormous industrial might to bear on winning the conflict is explained. President Truman's decision to drop atomic bombs on Japan in August 1945 is also investigated (Chapter 3).
● The diplomatic role of the USA once it went to war in December 1941 is analysed. The various wartime conferences held among the major allies and their results are detailed (Chapter 4).
● The military and diplomatic roles of Canada and Brazil during the Second World War are assessed. Both countries made significant contributions in assisting the effort to defeat Germany in particular (Chapter 5).

- The social impact of the war on minorities and women is discussed. All groups were significantly affected by the war, some positively (African Americans) and some negatively (Americans and Canadians of Japanese descent) (Chapter 6).
- The region's reactions to the destruction of the European Jewish communities are analysed. The extent to which governments responded is explored (Chapter 7).
- The impact of new technologies developed during the war is investigated. How this assisted in the Allied victory is also detailed (Chapter 8).
- The war's economic and diplomatic effects on the Americas and how the USA and Canada, in particular, emerged stronger than ever are examined (Chapter 9).

 # How you will be assessed

The IB History Diploma Higher Level has three papers in total: Papers 1 and 2 for Standard Level and a further Paper 3 for Higher Level. It also has an internal assessment which all students must do.

- For Paper 1 you need to answer four source-based questions on a prescribed subject. This counts for 20 per cent of your overall marks.
- For Paper 2 you need to answer two essay questions on two different topics. This counts for 25 per cent of your overall marks.
- For Paper 3 you need to answer three essay questions on two or three sections. This counts for 35 per cent of your overall marks.

For the Internal Assessment you need to carry out a historical investigation. This counts for 20 per cent of your overall marks.

HL option 3: Aspects of the history of the Americas is assessed through Paper 3. You must study three sections out of a choice of 12, one of which could be the Second World War and the Americas 1933–45. These sections are assessed through Paper 3 of the IB History diploma which has 24 essay questions – two for each of the 12 sections. In other words, there will be two specific questions that you can answer based on the Second World War and the Americas 1933–45.

Examination questions

For Paper 3 you need to answer three of the 24 questions. You could answer either two on one of the sections you have studied and one on another section, or one from each of the three sections you have studied. So, assuming the Second World War and the Americas 1933–45 is one of the sections you have studied, you may choose to answer one or two questions on it.

The questions are divided into the 12 sections and are usually arranged chronologically. In the case of the questions on Emergence of the Americas in global affairs 1880–1929, you should expect numbers 15 and 16 to be on this particular section. When the exam begins, you will have five minutes in which to read the questions. You are not allowed to use a pen or highlighter during the reading period. Scan the list of questions but focus on the ones relating to the sections you have studied.

Remember you are to write on the history of the Americas. If a question such as, 'Discuss the economic impact of the Second World War on one country in the region' is asked do **not** write about the impact the war had on Germany or Japan. You will receive no credit for this answer. It is also important to keep in mind that you should be writing about countries in the Americas from 1933 to 1945. Be sure to stick to this time frame. If you write about the impact of the First World War, for example, your score will be seriously affected.

Command terms

When choosing the three questions, keep in mind that you must answer the question asked, not one you might have hoped for. A key to success is understanding the demands of the question. IB History diploma questions use key terms and phrases known as command terms. The more common command terms are listed in the table below, with a brief definition of each. More are listed in the appendix of the IB History Guide.

Examples of questions using some of the more common command terms and specific strategies to answer them are included at the end of Chapters 2–4, 6 and 9.

Command term	Description	Where exemplified in this book
Analyse	Investigate the various components of a given issue	Page 49
Assess	Very similar to evaluate. Raise the various sides to an argument but clearly state which are more important and why	Page 106
Compare and contrast	Discuss both similarities and differences of two events, people and so on	Page 224
Examine	Look closely at an argument or concept from a variety of perspectives	Page 155
To what extent	Discuss the various merits of a given argument or opinion	Page 82

Answering the questions

You have two-and-a-half hours to answer the three questions or 50 minutes each. Try to budget your time wisely. In other words, do not spend 75 minutes on one answer. Before you begin each essay, take five to seven minutes and compose an outline of the major points you will raise in your essay. These you can check off as you write the essay itself. This is not a waste of time and will bring organization and coherency to what you write. Well-organized essays that include an introduction, several well-supported arguments and a concluding statement are much more likely to score highly than essays that jump from point to point without structure.

The three essays you write for Paper 3 will be read by a trained examiner. The examiner will read your essays and check what you write against the IB mark scheme. This mark scheme offers guidance to the examiner but is not comprehensive. You may well write an essay that includes analysis and evidence not included in the mark scheme, and that is fine. It is also worth remembering that the examiner who will mark your essay is looking to reward well-defended and well-argued positions, not to deduct for misinformation.

Each of your essays will be marked on a 0–20 scale, for a total of 60 points. The total score will be weighted as 35 per cent of your final IB History. Do bear in mind that you are not expected to score 60/60 to earn a 7: 37–39/60 will equal a 7. Another way of putting this is that if you write three essays that each score 13, you will receive a 7.

Writing essays
In order to attain the highest mark band (18–20), your essays should:

- be clearly focused
- address all implications of the question
- demonstrate extensive historical knowledge
- demonstrate knowledge of historical processes such as continuity and change
- integrate your analysis
- be well structured
- have well-developed synthesis.

Your essay should include an introduction in which you set out your main points. Do not waste time copying the question but define the key terms stated in the question. The best essays probe the demands of the question. In other words, there are often different ways of interpreting the question.

Next, you should write an in-depth analysis of your main points in several paragraphs. Here you will provide evidence that supports your argument. Each paragraph should focus on one of your main points and relate directly to the question. More sophisticated responses include counter-arguments.

Finally, you should end with a concluding statement.

In the roughly 45 minutes you spend on one essay, you should be able to write three to six pages. While there is no set minimum, you do need explore the issues and provide sufficient evidence to support what you write.

At the end of Chapters 2–4, 6 and 9, you will find IB-style questions with guidance on how best to answer them. Each question focuses on a different command term. The more practice you have writing essays, the better your results will be.

The appearance of the examination paper

Cover

The cover of the examination paper states the date of the examination and the length of time you have to complete it: 2 hours 30 minutes. Please note that there are two routes in history. Make sure your paper says Route 2 on it. Instructions are limited and simply state that you should not open it until told to do so and that three questions must be answered.

Questions

You will have five minutes in which to read through the questions. It is very important to choose the three questions you can answer most fully. It is quite possible that two of the three questions may be on the Second World War and the Americas 1933–45, especially after mastering the material in this book. That is certainly permissible. After the five minutes' reading time is over, you can take out your pen and mark up the exam booklet:

- Circle the three questions you have decided to answer.
- Identify the command terms and important points. For example, if a question asks, 'With reference to **two** countries in the region, analyse the economic impact of the Second World War', underline <u>analyse</u> and <u>economic impact</u>. This will help you to focus on the demands of the question.

For each essay take five to seven minutes to write an outline and approximately 43–45 minutes to write the essay.

 # About this book

Coverage of the course content

This book addresses the key areas listed in the IB History Guide for Route 2: HL option 3: Aspects of the history of the Americas: the Second World War and the Americas 1933–45. Chapters start with an introduction outlining key questions they address. They are then divided into a series of sections and topics covering the course content.

Throughout the chapters you will find the following features to aid your study of the course content.

Key and leading questions

Each section heading in the chapter has a related key question which gives a focus to your reading and understanding of the section. These are also listed in the chapter introduction. You should be able answer the questions after completing the relevant section.

Topics within the sections have leading questions which are designed to help you focus on the key points within a topic and give you more practice in answering questions.

Key terms

Key terms are the important terms you need to know to gain an understanding of the period. These are emboldened in the text the first time they appear in the book and are defined in the margin. They also appear in the glossary at the end of the book.

Sources

Throughout the book are several written and visual sources. Historical sources are important components in understanding more fully why specific decisions were taken or on what contemporary writers and politicians based their actions. The sources are accompanied by questions to help you dig deeper into the history of the Second World War and the Americas 1933–45.

Key debates

Historians often disagree on historical events and this historical debate is referred to as historiography. Knowledge of historiography is helpful in reaching the upper mark bands when you take your IB History examinations. You should not merely drop the names of historians in your essay. You need to understand the different points of view for a given historiographical debate. These you can bring up in your essay. There are a number of debates throughout the book to develop your understanding of historiography.

Theory of Knowledge (TOK) questions

Understanding that different historians see history differently is an important element in understanding the connection between IB History Diploma and Theory of Knowledge. Alongside some of the debates is a Theory of Knowledge-style question which makes that link. Each question is followed by a list of possible tie-ins with other areas of knowledge and ways of knowing.

Summary diagrams

At the end of each section is a summary diagram which gives a visual summary of the content of the section. It is intended as an aid for revision.

Chapter summary

At the end of each chapter is a short summary of the content of that chapter. This is intended to help you revise and consolidate your knowledge and understanding of the content.

Examination guidance

At the end of chapters are:

- Examination guidance on how to answer questions, accompanied by advice on what supporting evidence you might use, and sometimes sample answers designed to help you focus on specific details (Chapters 2–4, 6 and 9).
- Examination practice in the form of Paper 3 style questions (Chapters 1, 5, 7 and 8).

End of the book

The book concludes with the following sections.

Timeline

This gives a timeline of the major events covered in the book, which is helpful for quick reference or as a revision tool.

Glossary

All key terms in the book are defined in the glossary.

Further reading

This contains a list of books and websites which may help you with further independent research and presentations. It may also be helpful when further information is required for internal assessments and extended essays in history. You may wish to share the contents of this area with your school or local librarian.

Internal assessment

All IB History diploma students are required to write a historical investigation which is internally assessed. The investigation is an opportunity for you to dig more deeply into a subject that interests you. This gives you a list of possible areas for research.

CHAPTER 1

The Americas from peace to the Depression 1919–32

This chapter looks briefly at the impact of the First World War on the USA and its role in the peace settlement in 1919. It then considers how the USA began to pursue a policy of isolation, yet found it was unable to avoid economic involvement with global affairs. It also considers the period of prosperity the USA experienced in the 1920s, followed by the Wall Street Crash and its impact, on both the USA and Latin America.

You need to consider the following questions throughout this chapter:

✪ How did US foreign policy develop during 1919–32?

✪ How did the global economy affect the Americas during 1919–32?

 # US involvement and isolation

▶ *Key question: How did US foreign policy develop in the years 1919–32?*

The USA entered the First World War in April 1917. President Wilson had tried to keep the USA out of the conflict, but sympathy for the Allies and Germany's aggressive submarine warfare made the USA's neutral stance difficult to maintain. Wilson stated that the USA was going to war to 'maintain democracy'.

The end of the First World War

President Wilson's 14 Points

In January 1918, in a speech to **Congress**, President Wilson put forward **14 Points** which he wanted to become the basis of any peace settlement. He sought to create a new world order and hoped that the USA could offer leadership and guidance. Wilson's fourteenth point proposed the establishment of a League of Nations and it was Wilson's hope that this body would offer peaceful solutions to any future international problems. When the ceasefire or armistice was agreed in November 1918, the Allies accepted Wilson's proposals as a blueprint, but these were modified during the subsequent peace talks in Paris.

When negotiations began in Paris, President Wilson realized that he would have to compromise with the European leaders and deviate from his 14 Points. The French Prime Minister, Georges Clemenceau, in particular,

←··········
What part did the USA play in the Peace Settlement at the end of the First World War?
··········

 **KEY TERM**

Congress USA legislature consisting of the Senate and the House of Representatives.

14 Points The principles drawn up by President Wilson for ending the war.

sought huge **reparations** from Germany. Wilson was able to negotiate the final figure, but even then, the amount was so high (£6.6 billion) that Germany considered it too punitive. There were many Americans who demanded swift repayment of the loans the USA had provided to the Allies to help finance the war, and were dismayed when some of the Allies asked for the loans, amounting to almost $10.3 billion, to be repudiated. This made many Americans want to abandon involvement with Europe completely.

Why did the USA adopt a policy of isolationism after 1919?

The move to isolationism

When the USA entered the First World War in 1917, Wilson indicated that it was not to be viewed as a marker for future entanglements in European and world affairs. Indeed, when war was declared, Wilson was careful to call the USA an associated power (in keeping with **isolationism**), rather than an ally.

The USA and the League of Nations

President Wilson helped to draw up the Covenant of the League and it was this which showed his naivety. He expected countries to adhere to the Covenant and assumed that the threat of economic or military sanctions would deter any warlike intentions.

However, Congress refused to **ratify** the **Treaty of Versailles** and refused to join the League of Nations, pushing the USA towards isolation. There were some Republicans who called themselves the 'irreconcilables' because they could never agree to join the League of Nations. These politicians viewed that involvement with Europe would mean entanglements in future wars. Another group, the 'reservationists', supported the League but sought to amend Article 10 of the Covenant.

Article 10 was interpreted by the 'reservationists' as meaning that if conflicts arose between members of the League, it would determine the level of participation of the other members. For the USA this would mean that Congress would no longer have the final say in declaring war and this attacked the very heart of the constitution. Many US politicians also felt that becoming a member of the League undermined the **Monroe Doctrine**. The League of Nations was severely weakened by the absence of the USA.

The 1922 Washington Conference and 1928 Kellogg–Briand Pact

Although it was US government policy to follow isolationism, the Republican governments of the 1920s made distinct efforts to maintain world peace and prevent war. President Harding oversaw the Washington Conference for the Limitation of Armaments in November 1921. Agreements were reached at the Washington Conference in February 1922 to limit the number of **capital ships** and to stop constructing new warships for ten years.

The next major involvement for the USA came in 1928 when the Kellogg–Briand Pact was signed. Aristide Briand, the French Foreign Minister, visited

SOURCE A

'The gap in the bridge.' A cartoon published in December 1919 in the British magazine *Punch*, shortly after the USA had refused to join the League of Nations.

How useful is Source A to a historian studying the USA and the League of Nations?

Washington, DC to try and make an alliance with the USA. US Secretary of State Frank Kellogg followed the policy of isolation and he saw an opportunity to create an international treaty which would outlaw war. The USA saw such an agreement as a clear way out of involvement in military entanglements. Eventually, more than 60 countries signed the pact and Kellogg won a Nobel Peace Prize in 1929.

US involvement and isolation

Involvement
- President Wilson's 14 Points basis of peace
- Wilson compromised on reparations
- Wilson helped to set up the League of Nations
- 1922 Washington Conference limited number of capital ships
- USA helped to draw up 1928 Kellogg–Briand Pact that outlawed war as national policy

Isolation
- Wilson called USA an associated power not an ally
- Congress refused to ratify the Treaty of Versailles
- USA refused to join League of Nations, feared Monroe Doctrine was challenged and the USA was losing sovereignty

SUMMARY DIAGRAM

US involvement and isolation

The USA and the global economy in the 1920s

▶ **Key question:** *How did the global economy affect the Americas in the years 1919–32?*

As the USA had become by far the world's strongest economic power during the First World War, it was impossible for it not to be linked to other nations via trade and commerce because of the wartime loans (see page 10). After the war ended, the Allies had problems repaying these loans as a result of an economic downturn.

The economic boom in the USA

Why did the US economy boom after the war?

Economic problems

World trade markets had altered during the war. European nations had lost out to the USA and Japan because the UK and France had geared industry to war production. President Wilson had suggested that the world should try to have low **tariffs** in order to stimulate trade. However, this suggestion was not followed by some countries because they feared competition. The 1920s became a decade of economic contradictions for the USA because its Republican governments led by President Harding (1920–3), Coolidge (1923–9) and Hoover (1929–33) wished to follow a policy of *laissez-faire*. However, because of a flood of cheap European imports, they found themselves following **protectionist** policies, by increasing tariffs and by making financial loans to Europe. On a background of rising unemployment, which reached ten per cent in 1921, President Harding lowered taxes and reduced government spending in the hope of stimulating the economy.

Growing prosperity

After 1922, the USA began to experience an economic boom. There was a rapid growth in newer industries and as industry grew profits increased, so did wages, although at a much slower rate. Between 1923 and 1929, the average wage in the USA rose by eight per cent and this enabled some workers to buy – often on credit – the new consumer goods such as cars, vacuum cleaners, washing machines, radios and refrigerators. The growth of credit made it much easier for people to buy goods even though they did not have enough cash to pay for them immediately. This was due to the development of hire purchase whereby goods were paid for by instalments.

The stock market

In the 1920s, the **stock market** seemed to be the link to the prosperity of the USA. The values of stocks and shares rose steadily throughout the decade until they climbed dramatically in 1928 and 1929.

KEY TERM

Tariffs Duties or taxes imposed on items of overseas trade.

Laissez-faire The theory that an economy should be run without government interference.

Protectionist A policy which placed tariffs/taxes on imports to protect US industry from foreign competitors.

Stock market A place where stocks and shares are bought and sold.

The amount of buying and selling of shares also grew substantially until it was a common occurrence for ordinary working people to become involved.

Most companies' shares seemed to rise, and so people were prepared to risk their money on buying shares and began to speculate: **buying on the margin**, fuelling speculation and borrowing. Share prices continued to rise and by the summer of 1929, investors had borrowed $8.5 billion to buy on the margin – a figure that had risen from $3.2 billion in 1926. In 1929, more than 1.1 billion shares were sold and about 25 million Americans became involved in the frenzy of buying shares.

 **KEY TERM**

Buying on the margin
Purchasing stocks and shares by putting up only a part, or a margin, of the purchase price and borrowing the remainder.

There was such confidence about the economy in the USA that Herbert Hoover won the 1928 presidential election promising to maintain prosperity for all US people using such phrases as 'A chicken in every pot and a car in every garage.'

President Hoover and the Great Depression

How did President Hoover deal with the Great Depression?

The Wall Street Crash

Because the boom of the 1920s had been largely based on credit and speculation, the US economy was not in a position to cope with any severe jolt to the system. Moreover, any loans that US banks had made abroad and at home would have to be recalled in order to maintain their solvency. When this happened, ordinary people, foreign banks and companies found themselves going bankrupt.

In October 1929, the American stock market on Wall Street crashed. People suddenly began to sell shares – in their millions – and confidence in the stock market was lost. The value of shares plummeted. The impact of the crash was quite spectacular in the USA. Many stockbrokers were unable to repay their debts to the banks. Many banks were bankrupted and thousands of people who had savings in failed banks were also bankrupted. Credit, which had been so easy to access, collapsed and anyone who had taken out a loan had to repay it quickly. Moreover, those banks that survived were unwilling to make further loans – the time of speculation and risk-taking was over. Allied with all the other problems of the US economy, an economic depression developed.

Unemployment

By the end of 1929, there were about 2.5 million unemployed in the USA, although this was only five per cent of the workforce. Unemployment began to gather pace as fewer consumer goods were purchased and the number of goods sold in retail stores halved in the years 1929–33. People stopped buying goods and employees were laid off.

From the boom time of the 1920s, the USA became a land of unemployment, tramps, bread queues and soup kitchens. People were evicted from their homes and lived on the streets.

President Hoover's reaction to the Wall Street Crash and ensuing depression (the 'Great Depression') was to continue to balance the budget. He followed the Republican ideas of *laissez-faire* and '**rugged individualism**' but he did ask business leaders not to cut wages or production levels.

Government help for farmers

Farmers suffered because many had taken out mortgages during the war to buy land – now they could not sell their goods and hence could not maintain mortgage repayments. Congress passed the Hawley–Smoot (Hawley and Smoot were Republican members of Congress) Tariff Act in 1930 to protect US farmers by increasing import duties. Hoover gave further assistance to US farmers with the Agricultural Marketing Act of 1930 which tried to stabilize prices and sought to ensure that produce was sold at a profit.

The Reconstruction Finance Corporation

As the Depression worsened, government intervention won approval from Congress and it approved the Reconstruction Finance Corporation (February 1932) which made $2 billion in loans for ailing banks, insurance companies and railroads. The RFC was established to 'strengthen confidence' and stimulate industry and create jobs. By 1932, the federal government was spending $500 million per year more than it had done in 1928. Despite government interference, the economic situation did not improve and, by 1932, there was increasing opposition to Hoover from many quarters in the USA. The people of the USA showed their dissatisfaction with Hoover by electing Franklin Roosevelt, a Democrat, as president in 1932.

> **How was Latin America affected by economic changes after 1919?**

→ # The economies of Latin America

US trade and Latin America

By the end of the First World War, the USA had tremendous influence in most of the economies of South and Central America as well as the Caribbean. **Latin America** was an area where the USA could buy raw materials cheaply. The USA invested heavily in Latin America after 1918, especially in Cuba where, by 1928, US-owned refineries produced 75 per cent of the country's sugar. Brazil became increasingly dependent on the North American market for a large proportion of its exports, from 32.2 per cent in 1913 to 47.1 per cent in 1927 and, by this time, the USA was the largest single buyer of Brazilian goods. In addition, Brazil began to borrow heavily from the USA. The US United Fruit Company expanded its huge banana plantations in Central America and, in Peru, the USA became the biggest buyer of its sugar production and also non-precious metals, especially copper.

The Depression and Latin America

The Depression had a catastrophic effect on Latin America. The weak economies of the USA and Europe meant that markets shrank for Latin American nations. Exports of meat, coffee, sugar and metals were greatly reduced and there were no replacement markets for these goods. The value of Latin America's exports in the years 1930–4 was just under half of what it had been in the preceding five years. In addition, US tariffs only served to exacerbate the situation.

The result of the Depression for Latin America meant that countries either tried to maintain links with their trading partners by special agreements or decided to follow a policy of industrialization so that there would be less reliance on the USA and Europe.

There were also crucial political ramifications for Latin America as a result of the Depression. It acted as a catalyst for change and, by October 1930, Argentina, Brazil, Chile, Peru, Guatemala, Honduras and El Salvador had seen the military take over the country or attempt to do so. In these countries there was a willingness to accept the solutions of the military, who offered stability and structure amid the uncertain economic chaos. Rising unemployment and the demise of key industries meant that groups looked for a change to the political *status quo.* Argentina and Brazil exemplify this.

Events in Argentina

Argentina saw the value of its exports drop from $1537 million in 1929 to $561 million in 1932. As unemployment soared after 1929, the government of President Yrigoyen was challenged by some of the ***estancieros*** and the military. The army had developed as an independent body which did not always look favourably on the politicians in the country.

Yrigoyen was overthrown by the military in 1930, ushering in what is known as the **'Infamous Decade'**. Initially, General Uriburu led the country but, in 1932, General Justo became president and created a coalition called the *Concordancia*, a broad national government which had distinct right-wing leanings.

Events in Brazil

In Brazil, the Depression brought political issues to a head. Rivalry between the two leading states – São Paulo (a coffee-producing state) and Minas Gerais (essentially a milk-producing state) – created a political grouping called *café com leite* ('coffee with milk'). These two states dominated Brazilian politics. During the 1920s, there had been some discontent in the army and ***tenentes*** were unhappy with President Bernardes and the São Paulo bloc. The Depression led to a **balance of payments** crisis and coffee growers could not sell their produce. There was a growing feeling that the *café com leite* system was preventing any industrialization of Brazil. It was thought that the coffee élite of São Paulo did not want change and ignored the interests of Brazil. In the election of 1930, there were accusations of vote-fixing and, following unrest, the military stepped in and replaced President Luís with Getúlio Vargas, who had been the runner-up in the election. His rule ended the *café com leite* period of dominance.

KEY TERM

Estancieros The large landowners who were the élite of the nation.

Infamous Decade The period following Uriburu's coup which was characterized by rural decline, electoral corruption and economic dislocation.

Tenentes Army lieutenants in Brazil.

Balance of payments The difference in value between total payments made to a country and total payments received from that country in a given period.

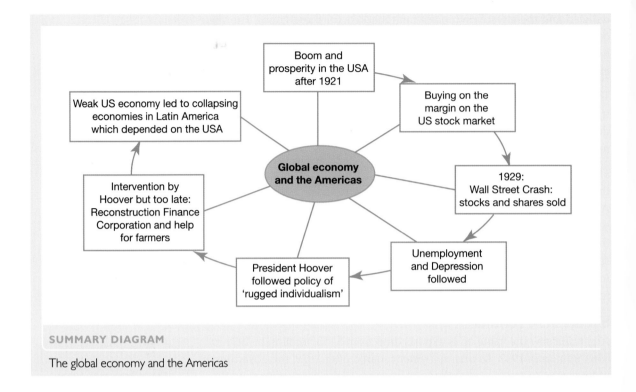

SUMMARY DIAGRAM

The global economy and the Americas

Chapter summary

The Americas from peace to the Depression 1919–32

After the First World War, the USA was successful in avoiding foreign entanglements and enjoyed a period of economic growth and prosperity. However, it could not avoid completely the economic woes of the world.

When the Wall Street Crash occurred, the USA drifted into the Great Depression and could find no panacea. Latin America was not immune to the economic vagaries of the 1920s and early 1930s. It was heavily dependent on the US market for the export of its raw materials and agricultural produce. When this market began to dry up, Latin America experienced the Depression, suffering unemployment, contracting markets and even military takeovers.

 Examination practice

Below are two exam-style questions for you to practise on this topic.

1 Assess the economic impact of the Great Depression on **two** countries in the region. (For guidance on how to answer 'Assess' questions, see page 106.)

2 To what extent were the economies in the Americas connected to one another? (For guidance on how to answer 'To what extent' questions, see page 82.)

CHAPTER 2

Hemispheric reactions to the events in Europe and Asia 1933–41

This chapter looks first at how US foreign policy developed during the 1930s and then at how the USA reacted to the early stages of the war in Europe and Asia. It includes an analysis of President Roosevelt's foreign policy before 1940, and then looks at the presidential election of 1940 in the context of the war. It also discusses the gradual erosion of the Neutrality Acts and the USA's growing assistance to the UK and the USSR via Lend–Lease. Finally, it analyses Roosevelt's role in defining war aims in the Atlantic Charter in 1941.

You need to consider the following questions throughout this chapter:

✪ In what ways did inter-American diplomacy develop during the 1930s?
✪ How did the USA's policy of neutrality change?
✪ How did US relations with Japan develop during the 1930s?
✪ To what extent was Roosevelt's foreign policy isolationist during the 1930s?
✪ What was the initial response of the USA to the war in Europe?
✪ Why was the 1940 presidential election important for the USA?
✪ How did the US Navy become increasingly involved in the defence of the USA?

① US foreign policy in the 1930s: the 'Good Neighbor' policy

▶ **Key question:** *In what ways did inter-American diplomacy develop during the 1930s?*

When Roosevelt became president in 1933, the majority of members of Congress were isolationists. Roosevelt did not intend becoming involved in European affairs. He wanted the USA to follow a policy of friendship towards other countries and thought the USA could act as a 'moral force' for good in the world, especially to his American neighbours.

> Why did Roosevelt adopt the 'Good Neighbor' policy?

The introduction of the 'Good Neighbor' policy

Overcoming the economic crisis facing the USA was President Roosevelt's foremost task. He encouraged economic and diplomatic co-operation through the idea of the '**Good Neighbor**' policy which was in a sense a continuation of Hoover's policies of persuasion and economic pressure to exert influence on Latin America. Roosevelt saw his policy as transforming the Monroe Doctrine into arrangements for mutual **hemispheric** action against aggressors.

> **KEY TERM**
>
> **Good Neighbor** Foreign policy adopted by Roosevelt to mend and improve relations with Latin America.

SOURCE A

Excerpt from President Roosevelt's inaugural speech, 4 March 1933.

In the field of world policy I would dedicate this nation to the policy of the good neighbor, the neighbor who resolutely respects himself and, because he does so, respects the rights of others – the neighbor who respects his obligations and respects the sanctity of his agreements in and with a world of neighbors.

> **?** What can you learn about Roosevelt's attitude to foreign affairs from Source A?

Roosevelt appointed Cordell Hull as his Secretary of State to carry out his 'Good Neighbor' policy. Roosevelt and Hull were aware that the Smoot–Hawley Tariff Act of 1930 (see page 14) had damaged the economies of Latin America and that amendments were needed to restore improved trading relations in the Americas. However, Hull was more inclined to free trade than Roosevelt, who wanted to follow protectionist policies. Roosevelt did not agree with the decisions made at the world economic conference in London because he did not like the **internationalist** approach that was suggested.

> **KEY TERM**
>
> **Hemispheric** Relating to the western or eastern or northern or southern part of the world. In this case, it refers to North and South America.
>
> **Internationalist** An advocate for co-operation and understanding between nations.

The Inter-American Conference at Montevideo 1933

At the Inter-American Conference at Montevideo, Uruguay, the USA and all Latin American states agreed that no country had the right to intervene in the internal or external affairs of another.

> How did relations between the USA and Latin America change?

Relations between the USA and Latin America

In accordance with the 'Good Neighbor' policy, US troops left Haiti, the Dominican Republic and Nicaragua. In 1934, Congress signed a treaty with Cuba that nullified the **Platt Amendment**, which had authorized the US occupation of Cuba. The USA did retain one naval base at Guantánamo. By 1938, the 'Good Neighbor' policy had led to ten treaties with Latin American countries, resulting in huge trade increases for the USA. Hull's policies of low tariffs improved the economies of the Latin American countries, especially in Cuba when the tariff on Cuban sugar was reduced and trade increased accordingly.

To show continued goodwill to his neighbours, Roosevelt passed the Reciprocal Trade Agreement Act in 1934. This repealed several of the 1920s

> **KEY TERM**
>
> **Platt Amendment** The amendment added to the Cuban constitution of 1901, which affected Cuba's right to negotiate treaties and permitted the USA to maintain its naval base and intervene in Cuban affairs for the preservation of Cuban independence.

isolationist trade policies so the USA could compete better in foreign trade. The 1934 act began the historic move towards lower trade barriers and greater global engagement. However, it was tempered by the Johnson Act of the same year. After the failure of European nations to honour their war debts to the USA, Congress forbade government loans to any foreign country that had defaulted. By mid-June 1934, when the USA was owed over $22 billion, all foreign countries except Finland had defaulted. There was no recognition that a major reason why Europeans could not honour their debts was the Hawley–Smoot Tariff's exclusion of their exports from US markets.

In 1936, the USA renegotiated the Panama Canal Treaty. Panama and the USA signed the General Treaty of Friendship and Cooperation whereby the USA forfeited the right to participate in Panamanian politics, giving greater independence to the country. The USA also yielded its right to seize additional land for its administration or defence of the canal. The annual rent to Panama was raised to $430,000. For Roosevelt, this treaty was a sound example of his 'Good Neighbor' policy whereby the USA was clearly trying to conciliate Latin America and not act like an acquisitive imperialist nation. Although, at the same time, the USA used economic influence to dominate several Latin American economies.

Buenos Aires Conference 1936

Following Japan's attacks on China in 1931 and Italy's attacks on Abyssinia in 1935, the beginning of the **Spanish Civil War** in 1936, and the spread of fascism in Europe, President Roosevelt called for a peace conference to be held in the Americas to discuss the issues of arms limitations, neutrality and foreign intervention. The result was the Conference for the Maintenance of Peace held in Buenos Aires, Argentina, in December 1936.

> 🔑 **KEY TERM**
>
> **Spanish Civil War** The war (1936–9) in which the Nationalists, led by General Franco, overthrew the Republican government.

Roosevelt deemed the conference so important that he spent a month visiting South America. He was met by huge, friendly crowds in Brazil, Argentina and Uruguay before the conference. He made several speeches promoting his 'Good Neighbor' policy and hemispheric solidarity.

> **Mexico and the Spanish Civil War**
>
> President Lázaro Cárdenas of Mexico offered support to the Republicans in the Spanish Civil War. He saw similarities between their struggle and the Mexican Revolution, noting especially the quest for freedom and social justice. Cárdenas sent arms and ammunition in the fight against the Spanish fascists. At the end of the war, he allowed thousands of Republican refugees to settle in Mexico. His support brought him into open conflict with Germany and Italy, who sent large amounts of aid to their fellow fascists.
>
> As part of his leftward leanings, Cárdenas offered asylum to Leon Trotsky, the exiled Bolshevik leader. Trotsky lived in Mexico from 1936 until his assassination in 1940 by an agent of the USSR.

On the first day of the conference, President Roosevelt outlined his plan for an American peace programme. All American nations agreed to consult each other if there was a security threat within the hemisphere. This was the first time that the US government accepted the principle of consultation with other American countries in the event that the peace of the hemisphere was threatened. The USA proposed a neutrality pact for American nations in the **Western Hemisphere**. The delegates drew up a convention that called for all to follow a common policy of neutrality in the event of conflict. This Non-Intervention Protocol was signed on 16 December 1936. Roosevelt was keen to keep Latin American countries close to the USA and was concerned about the spread of fascism to the hemisphere. This was seen in Brazil with the formation of the Integralist Movement, founded by Plínio Salgado, which shared some characteristics of the fascism taking hold in Europe at that time.

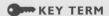 **KEY TERM**

Western Hemisphere The part of the world containing North and South America.

? According to Source B why was Roosevelt keen to emphasize the idea of the New World to his audience?

SOURCE B

Excerpt from President Roosevelt's speech to the delegates at the Buenos Aires Conference, 1936.

Three years ago, recognizing that a crisis was being thrust upon the New World, with splendid unanimity our twenty-one Republics set an example to the whole world by proclaiming a new spirit, a new day, in the affairs of this Hemisphere. You who assemble today carry with you in your deliberations the hopes of millions of human beings in other less fortunate lands. Beyond the ocean we see continents rent asunder by old hatreds and new fanaticisms. We hear the demand that injustice and inequality be corrected by resorting to the sword and not by resorting to reason and peaceful justice … Can we, the Republics of the New World help the Old World to avert the catastrophe which impends?

Yes; I am confident that we can.

Eighth Pan-American Conference, Lima 1938

As war clouds gathered in Europe, Roosevelt wanted to avoid any entanglements there. He convened the Eighth Pan-American Conference in Lima, Peru, in 1938 to develop collective security in the Americas. The decisions made there are testimony that each state sought to avoid war and any actions which might lead to war.

Declaration of the Solidarity of America

The 21 American republics agreed on a Declaration of the Solidarity of America, which stated they would continue to co-operate, work to defend each other against all foreign intervention and allow their foreign ministers to meet whenever it was deemed desirable.

Declaration of American Principles

The 21 republics also issued a Declaration of American Principles which resolved to support the following principles as essential:

- The intervention of any state in the internal or external affairs of another is inadmissible.
- All differences of international character should be settled by peaceful means.
- The use of force as an instrument of national or international policy is forbidden.
- International co-operation should be used to ensure the maintenance of the agreed principles.

Roosevelt's foreign policy

Latin America

In 1938, Roosevelt showed that he would keep his promise of the Montevideo Conference (see page 18) when Mexico **nationalized** US-owned oil companies. He took no aggressive action and did not intervene despite pressure from the powerful US oil companies. Although the Mexican government compensated them, the US oil companies restricted the development of the Mexican oil industry for several years by encouraging a boycott of Mexican oil. The USA wanted to show Latin America the detrimental consequences of nationalizing US interests.

The 'Good Neighbor' policy was viewed as successful for a range of reasons, not just for how it strengthened Latin American relations during the troubled 1930s. The Reciprocal Trade Agreements (see page 18) with many Latin American countries were testimony to this. The breadth of the policy allowed the US government to promote a cultural exchange programme. In 1938, Roosevelt created the Cultural Division of the State Department, with Latin America as a special focus. There were four conferences that covered education, art, music, publications and libraries. Additionally, Hollywood filmmakers agreed to change the stereotypical image of Latin Americans in their films and *Time* magazine started publishing in Spanish and Portuguese for the Latin American readership in the USA.

However, the policy also directly and indirectly supported pro-US dictatorships such as Somoza in Nicaragua, Trujillo in the Dominican Republic and Batista in Cuba. Roosevelt was happy to support these leaders because they brought stability to their country after uprisings, and secured their friendship by acknowledging them as legitimate authorities.

←------ **What was the impact of Roosevelt's foreign policy?**

 **KEY TERM**

Nationalized Placed under state control.

```
                        ┌─────────────────────────┐
                        │    'Good Neighbor' policy │
                        └─────────────────────────┘
                    ┌───────────────┴───────────────┐
```

Improved security	Improved trade and general relations
• 1933 Montevideo Conference • USA and all Latin American states agreed that no country had the right to intervene in the internal or external affairs of another • 1936 US–Panama Treaty: USA forfeited the right to participate in Panamanian politics, giving greater independence to Panama • 1936 Buenos Aires Conference: called for all to follow a policy of neutrality in the event of conflict • 1938 Lima Conference	• US troops left Haiti, the Dominican Republic and Nicaragua • 1934 Reciprocal Trade Agreement Act between USA and Latin American countries • 1938 Declaration of American Principles • 1938, Roosevelt created the Cultural Division of the State Department for cultural exchanges

SUMMARY DIAGRAM

US foreign policy in the 1930s: the 'Good Neighbor' policy

2 The USA's policy of neutrality

▶ **Key question:** How did the USA's policy of neutrality change?

**KEY TERM**

Matériel Military equipment.

Totalitarianism When political regimes suppress political opposition and control all aspects of people's lives.

The widespread feeling that involvement in the First World War had been a mistake continued in the USA throughout the 1930s. It was made evident when Congress passed a series of Neutrality Acts which intended to keep the USA out of future wars. It was felt that the USA had unnecessarily lost men and *matériel*, and that Europe was drifting towards further conflict as a result of the growth of **totalitarianism**.

The rationale behind neutrality

What did the Nye Committee do?

The Nye Committee
A major influence on public opinion and attitudes to war in the early part of Roosevelt's first administration was the Special Committee on Investigation of the Munitions Industry. It was chaired by the Republican Senator Gerald Nye, a committed isolationist. The committee was established to examine the causes of the USA's involvement in the First World War. It reported that between 1915 and January 1917, the USA had lent Germany $27 million and, in the same period, it had loaned the UK and its allies $2.3 billion. Many people suggested that the USA therefore had a vested interest in helping the

UK to win and that this was a key reason for entering the conflict. Additionally, the committee looked into the huge profits made during the war by such companies as Dupont Chemicals and J.P. Morgan Banking. The committee's findings raised public awareness and added weight to the non-interventionist movement.

The Neutrality Acts

The first Neutrality Act 1935

The first **Neutrality Act** gave the president the power to prohibit US ships from carrying US-made munitions to countries at war. The Neutrality Act could also prevent US citizens from travelling on ships of those countries at war except at their own risk. This was to avoid situations like the *Lusitania* incident (1915) when 128 US citizens were killed in the sinking of the British passenger ship by a German submarine.

The Ludlow Amendment

There were many people opposed to the USA's involvement in a future war. Congressman Ludlow suggested there should be a national referendum on any declaration of war, except in cases when the USA had been attacked first. He introduced the amendment several times in Congress during 1935–40 and it was defeated each time. The 50,000 veterans who took part in the peace march in Washington, DC on 6 April 1935 (the eighteenth anniversary of the American entry into the First World War) gave a clear indication of the anti-war feeling in the USA.

The 1936 presidential election campaign showed Roosevelt to be wary about foreign affairs because he made only one speech on the issue. Indeed, Alf Landon, his chief opponent, made only two.

The second Neutrality Act 1936

The second Neutrality Act banned loans or credits to countries at war. The act set no limits on trade in materials useful for war and US companies such as Texaco, Standard Oil and Ford were thus able to sell such items on credit to General Franco in the Spanish Civil War.

The third Neutrality Act 1937

A third Neutrality Act forbade the export of munitions for use by either of the opposing forces in Spain. It did, however, permit nations involved in a war to buy goods other than munitions from the USA, provided they paid cash and used their own ships. This became known as 'cash and carry'.

The fourth Neutrality Act 1937

This authorized the US president to determine what could and could not be bought, other than munitions, to be paid for on delivery, and made travel on ships of countries at war unlawful.

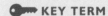

How did the Neutrality Acts affect the USA's involvement in the war?

KEY TERM

Neutrality Act An act passed to limit US involvement in possible future wars.

The problems with neutrality

US neutrality and the Sino-Japanese War

It soon became clear that following a policy of neutrality was not straightforward. When there was an outbreak of fighting between Japan and China in July 1937, it was decided not to invoke the Neutrality Acts because neither Japan nor China had officially declared war. Roosevelt supported China and sent arms there. There were many in Congress who were outraged by Roosevelt's stance and said it threatened the US policy of isolation. The **Sino-Japanese War** created a range of problems for the USA, not least the worsening of relations with Japan. In December 1938, Roosevelt extended commercial credits worth $25 million to China without incurring the displeasure of the isolationists.

The 'Quarantine Speech'

In the 1930s, the totalitarian and militaristic states of Germany, Italy, Japan and Spain openly built up large armed forces. Roosevelt despised the spread of totalitarianism in Germany and Italy and, by 1937, began to see that the USA might need to become involved in European affairs. His views differed from those of Congress and, most importantly, the majority of the American people. For some, the idea of US involvement in others' problems was completely abhorrent. For others, going to war would end the reforms of the **New Deal**.

In 1937, a **Gallup poll** indicated that almost 70 per cent of Americans thought that US involvement in the First World War had been a mistake and 95 per cent opposed any future involvement in war. Although Roosevelt was aware of public opinion, in October of that year he made a speech in Chicago, warning the people of the USA about the situation in Europe and the Far East and the consequent dangers of war. It became known as the 'Quarantine Speech'. He had been appalled by the Nationalist bombing of civilians in Spain and the aggressive nature of Japan in declaring war on China in 1937. He had to tread a delicate path and his speech warned the USA not only of the horrors of war but also the problems with neutrality. Roosevelt suggested a quarantine (see Source C) of the aggressors but was careful not to mention specific countries.

KEY TERM

Sino-Japanese War War between China and Japan from 1937 to 1945.

New Deal The domestic policies of Franklin Roosevelt for economic and social reform.

Gallup poll A public opinion poll originated by Dr George Gallup in the 1930s.

? What does Source C show about Roosevelt's attitude to world events?

SOURCE C

Excerpt from Roosevelt's 'Quarantine Speech', 5 October 1937, from the Miller Center archive of US presidential speeches (http://millercenter.org/president/speeches/detail/3310).

Without a declaration of war and without warning or justification of any kind, civilians, including vast numbers of women and children, are being ruthlessly murdered by bombs from the air … If those things come to pass in other parts of the world, let no one imagine that America will escape, that America may expect mercy, that this Western Hemisphere will not be attacked … It seems to be unfortunately true that the epidemic of world lawlessness is spreading …

Innocent peoples, innocent nations are being cruelly sacrificed to a greed for power and supremacy which is devoid of all sense of justice and humane considerations. … War is a contagion, whether it be declared or undeclared. It can engulf states and peoples remote from the original scene of hostilities. We are determined to keep out of war, yet we cannot insure ourselves against the disastrous effects of war and the dangers of involvement. We are adopting such measures as will minimize our risk of involvement, but we cannot have complete protection in a world of disorder in which confidence and security have broken down … There must be positive endeavors to preserve peace.

Roosevelt wanted to impose economic pressure on Japan but the *Chicago Tribune* suggested that such action might only increase Japan's militant tendencies. Some newspapers, such as *The Oregonian* and *Baltimore Sun*, supported his views but the newspapers owned by publisher Randolph Hearst opposed the speech. When a journalist pressed Roosevelt to explain what he meant by his comments in the speech, Roosevelt refused to say. He replied, 'I was just looking for some way to peace; and by no means is it necessary that that way be contrary to the exercise of neutrality.'

Shortly after delivering the speech, Roosevelt said to his speechwriter, Sam Rosenman: 'It is a terrible thing to look over your shoulder when you are trying to lead, and find no one there.'

SOURCE D

Excerpt from the *Boston Herald*'s editorial, 6 October 1937, the day after Roosevelt's 'Quarantine Speech'.

The mantle of Woodrow Wilson lay on the shoulders of Franklin Roosevelt when he spoke yesterday in Chicago. It may be true that 'the very foundations of civilization are seriously threatened.' But this time, Mr. President, Americans will not be stampeded into going 3,000 miles [5000 km] across water to save them. Crusade, if you must, but for the sake of several millions of American mothers, confine your crusading to the continental limits of America!

What are the values and limitations of Source D for a historian studying US neutrality?

Roosevelt and the mounting European crisis

Having won some praise from a few US politicians for his views in the speech, Roosevelt did not follow it up and offered no real action. He was concerned that many citizens disagreed and was concerned to have been called an alarmist and a warmonger. However, the rapid deterioration of relations in Europe and Hitler's increasing power began to force a change in attitude. Many Americans began to realize that the security of their country was at stake.

Roosevelt began to express his strong support for the Western democratic states. After the **Munich Agreement**, Hitler announced further rearmament and so did Roosevelt with a further $300 million granted to the defence budget. In October 1938, Roosevelt opened secret talks with the French on

KEY TERM

Munich Agreement
Agreement between the UK, Germany, France and Italy, September 1938, which ceded the Sudetenland to Germany.

how to bypass US neutrality laws and allowed the French to buy US aircraft. After tortuous negotiations in 1939, the French government placed large orders with the US aircraft industry.

The USA censured Germany in March 1939, and recalled its ambassador for breaking the Munich Agreement and seizing parts of Czechoslovakia. As tensions heightened in Europe, Roosevelt called on Germany and Italy to give assurances that they would not attack any European country over a period of ten years. He proposed discussions about armaments reductions and the restoration of world trade but his suggestions were rejected and Hitler said he had no aggressive intentions. Roosevelt suggested arbitration during the **Danzig crisis** but again his proposals were rejected by Germany.

War in Europe, September 1939

What was the impact of the outbreak of war on the USA?

SOURCE E

Excerpt from Roosevelt's 'fireside chat' to the USA, 3 September 1939. This was the day that the UK declared war on Germany.

We have certain ideas and certain ideals of national safety, and we must act to preserve that safety today, and to preserve the safety of our children in future years. That safety is and will be bound up with the safety of the Western Hemisphere and of the seas adjacent thereto. We seek to keep war from our own firesides by keeping war from coming to the Americas … It is our national duty to use every effort to keep them [wars] out of the Americas … This nation will remain a neutral nation, but I cannot ask that every American remain neutral in thought as well. Even a neutral has a right to take account of facts. Even a neutral cannot be asked to close his mind or his conscience.

? According to Source E what was the purpose behind this 'fireside chat'?

? How would someone against the policy of isolation have countered the argument shown in Source F?

SOURCE F

An excerpt from a speech by Charles Lindbergh, made on 15 September 1939, two weeks after the war between the UK and Germany broke out. Quoted from *The USA from Wilson to Nixon 1917 to 1975*, by Harriet Ward, published by Collins Educational, UK, 1998, page 36. Lindbergh became a leading member of the isolationist America First Committee (see page 36).

We must not be misguided by foreign propaganda to the effect that our frontiers lie in Europe. One need only glance at a map to see where our true frontiers lie. What more could we ask than the Atlantic Ocean on the East and the Pacific on the West?

Two days after the outbreak of the war in Europe, the US government announced its neutrality and, under the Neutrality Act of 1937, Roosevelt prohibited the export of arms and munitions to all **belligerent** powers. At the Pan-American Conference in October 1939, a 300-mile (500-km) security zone off the coasts of the Americas was established, within which all hostile action by the belligerent powers was forbidden. It became known as the **Hemisphere Neutrality Belt** and it was hoped that it would insulate the Americas from the European conflict.

Roosevelt had to accept the position of neutrality but sought ways to assist the UK and France. He began a regular secret correspondence with the First Lord of the Admiralty, Winston Churchill (later the prime minister), in 1939 to discuss ways of supporting the UK.

In a **fireside chat** in 1939, Roosevelt said the USA would not become involved. A Gallup poll showed that although 94 per cent of Americans approved of Roosevelt's statement, some 80 per cent wanted the Allies to win. Indeed, more than 50 per cent wanted to send aid to the UK and France provided there was no risk to the USA.

The fifth Neutrality Act 1939

The USA then made further amendments to the Neutrality Act in November 1939. The fifth Neutrality Act meant that the president could authorize the 'cash and carry' export of arms and munitions to countries at war, but they had to be transported in the countries' own ships. In addition, the president could specify which areas were theatres of war in time of war, through which US citizens and ships were forbidden to travel, and proclaimed the North Atlantic a **combat zone**. He did this because German **U-boats** were attacking British ships and bringing the war close to the USA. Roosevelt ordered the US Navy to patrol the western Atlantic and reveal the location of the German submarines to the British.

SOURCE G

Excerpt from President Roosevelt's speech to Congress asking for amendments to the Neutrality Act, 21 September 1939. Quoted from the American Presidency Project (www.presidency.ucsb.edu/ws/index.php?pid=15813).

Let no group assume the exclusive label of the 'peace bloc'. We all belong to it … I give you my deep and unalterable conviction, based on years of experience as a worker in the field of international peace, that by the repeal of the embargo the United States will more probably remain at peace than if the law remains as it stands today … Our acts must be guided by one single, hard-headed thought – keeping America out of the war.

Neutrality and US rearmament

The reduction of US armed forces

With the USA pursuing a foreign policy of isolation and non-involvement after the end of the First World War and working on the assumption that war could be avoided, the US army was reduced to about 19,000 officers and 205,000 enlisted men. This created a force which could defend the USA, its overseas territories and possessions. In January 1921, Congress reduced the

> 🔑 **KEY TERM**
>
> **Hemisphere Neutrality Belt** Roosevelt declared that the Atlantic, 300 miles (500 km) out from the eastern US coast, was part of the Western Hemisphere and therefore neutral.
>
> **Fireside chat** Informal talks that President Roosevelt made on the radio. They were so called because it was intended that people could sit at home and listen to the president.
>
> **Combat zone** An area of military fighting.
>
> **U-boats** German submarines.

What does Source G suggest about President Roosevelt's view of the USA and the war in Europe?

> **To what extent did the USA rearm in the 1930s?**

Regular army The permanent standing army of a nation or state.

NIRA The National Industrial Recovery Act, part of Roosevelt's New Deal. It aimed to increase productivity in US industry.

Munich crisis The crisis over the Sudetenland in Czechoslovakia. Hitler demanded this German-speaking area and was awarded it after the conference in Munich, September 1938.

Flying Fortress The Boeing B-17 bomber aircraft which had so many machine guns it was given this name.

army to 175,000 and a year later it limited the **regular army** to 12,000 commissioned officers and 125,000 enlisted men. The size of the army remained at about that level until 1936. The budget for the War Department was fixed after the early 1920s at around $300 million per year. US naval expansion was restricted by agreements made in the Washington Naval Conference (see page 10) and the Kellogg–Briand Pact (see pages 10–11). The latter outlawed the use of war as a means of policy and gave the USA a clear rationale for limiting the other branches of its armed forces. Until the mid-1930s, only the navy increased in size, within the terms of international agreements.

Growth of the navy

The navy was seen as the mainstay of the country's defence but the USA had never built to the naval limits permitted in the Washington agreements (see page 10) and in 1934, the **NIRA** provided the navy with $237 million for warship construction. The navy then ordered 20 destroyers, four submarines, four light cruisers and two aircraft carriers. The expenditure could be justified on grounds of national defence and the creation of jobs.

Further improvements to the navy came following the Vinson–Trammel Act of 1934. This allowed the construction of 102 new warships over the next eight years and still kept the USA within the terms of the Washington agreements. The act ensured that as US ships became obsolete, they were replaced. By 1937, the US Navy had aircraft carriers, cruisers, destroyers and submarines under construction, and by 1939 possessed 15 battleships.

Increasing military budgets

From 1935, the armed forces' budget was increased because it was felt that existing forces would find it difficult to defend the USA as a result of years of lack of investment. Roosevelt was able to expand the US Navy following the Naval Expansion Act of 1938. One billion dollars was allocated over the next seven years for the continued development of the navy. The air force had about 1600 planes by the late 1930s.

In October 1938, after the **Munich crisis**, Roosevelt said that he would spend another $300 million on armaments and told reporters that he would probably ask Congress for $500 million. Three months later, Roosevelt asked Congress for $552 million for defence expenditure to prepare the country for war. The US government planned to expand fortifications in the Pacific and the Caribbean. Part of the military budget was put towards the development of the **Flying Fortress**, indicating that the air force was to be seen as both offensive and defensive. Despite all the increase in budgets, the USA was not adequately prepared for war by the late 1930s.

USA's policy of neutrality

- 1934: Nye Committee – questioned US motives for involvement in First World War
- 1935: Ludlow Amendment – sought to have a referendum to determine any US involvement in a war
- 1937: Sino-Japanese War – Roosevelt extended commercial credits worth $25 million to China
- 1937: Roosevelt made the Quarantine Speech
- 1939: Roosevelt censured Hitler's actions and in October established the Hemisphere Neutrality Belt (300 miles (500 km) out into the Atlantic) to insulate USA from the European conflict
- Late 1930s: Roosevelt increased defence spending

- 1935: first Neutrality Act – US president given power to prohibit US ships from carrying US-made munitions to countries at war
- 1936: second Neutrality Act – banned loans or credits to countries at war
- 1937: third Neutrality Act – warring nations allowed to buy goods other than munitions from the USA provided they paid cash and used their own ships. This became known as 'cash and carry'
- 1937: fourth Neutrality Act – US president to decide what could be bought and made travel on ships of countries at war unlawful
- 1939: fifth Neutrality Act – US president could authorize the 'cash and carry' export of arms and munitions to countries at war, but they had to be transported in the countries' own ships

SUMMARY DIAGRAM

The USA's policy of neutrality

The USA and Japan in the 1930s

▶ **Key question:** *How did US relations with Japan develop during the 1930s?*

The relationship between the US and Japan deteriorated throughout the 1920s and 1930s. There had been some ill-feeling at the Paris Peace Conference in 1919 because the Japanese government felt that the Allies treated it and its people as inferiors. Although there was agreement about naval limitations at the Washington Conference (see page 10), relations worsened following the passing of the Immigration Act of 1924 which ended Japanese migration to the USA.

The Immigration Act 1924

What was the effect of the Immigration Act on relations between the USA and Japan?

The Immigration Act limited the annual number of people who could be admitted from any country but completely prevented Asian immigration. The act was introduced 'to preserve the ideal of American homogeneity' and was often known as the Japanese Exclusion Act. It stopped the growth of the Japanese community in the USA. The Japanese government protested strongly at the introduction of the act, which it felt violated the 1907 **Gentlemen's Agreement** between the USA and Japan, and one Japanese citizen committed ritual suicide outside the US embassy in Tokyo in protest in 1924. The Japanese government declared the day it came into action as a day of national humiliation. The antipathy that Japan had felt towards the Western powers at the Peace Conference was increased.

Economic rivalry

How did economic rivalry between the USA and Japan develop?

In the late 1920s and 1930s there was increasing concern in the USA over the rising economic and imperial power of Japan. The Japanese needed extra land and resources for their fast-growing population and to stimulate further economic expansion. They also lacked oil, rubber and other key natural resources. During the 1930s, 80 per cent of Japan's imported oil came from the USA and as the main competitor of the USA in the Pacific region, it was imperative for Japan to move away from US oil dependence by securing new oil and energy sources. Japan looked to China and South-east Asia's natural resources, such as oil, tin and rubber – resources which the USA also relied on.

However, Japan's aspirations in China conflicted with the **open-door policy** which sought to keep China's natural resources and markets free from control by Japan or any other nation.

Japan and Manchuria

US anxieties about foreign influence in China increased in 1931 when Japan invaded the Chinese province of Manchuria. Within a year, Japan had captured and renamed it Manchukuo. The new name meant that it was the home of the Manchu people and was now the Manchu state. Manchukuo became a **puppet state** of Japan. President Hoover strongly disapproved of the invasion and morally condemned it, but did not support the idea of **sanctions** against Japan. Later, Roosevelt did not recognize the Japanese puppet state but did little else. He followed the policy of President Hoover and hoped to deal with the issue of Japan at a later date. The open-door policy was allowed to lapse. The League of Nations condemned the invasion but was unable to force Japan to leave Manchuria. Japan left the League, claiming it had taken Manchuria because it was essential for its economic and military security.

KEY TERM

Gentlemen's Agreement Whereby the USA would not impose restrictions on Japanese immigration and Japan would not allow further emigration to the USA.

Open-door policy The practice by which one country grants opportunities for trade to all other nations equally.

Puppet state Nominally a sovereign state but controlled by a foreign power.

Sanctions Punishments against a country for breaking international law.

Six years after the invasion of Manchuria, Japan invaded northern China and bombed Shanghai and other Chinese cities into submission. At first, the USA simply supported the League of Nations in calling the Japanese an aggressor and gave financial aid to the Chinese. Roosevelt did not begin trade sanctions and, though he condemned Japan's actions, he merely asked Americans to boycott Japanese silk.

USS *Panay* incident 1937

Relations between the USA and Japan were tested in December 1937 when Japanese bombers sank the USS *Panay* and three tankers belonging to the US Standard Oil Company on the Yangtze river at Nanking. The USS *Panay*'s role was to patrol the river to protect US lives and property in China, and had just rescued American citizens in Nanking. Two Americans were killed and 30 were wounded. The US government demanded an apology, compensation and a guarantee that there would not be a repeat of such an incident. The Japanese did as they were asked and paid $2,214,000 of compensation on 22 April 1938, officially closing the incident. Roosevelt was

← **What was the impact of the USS *Panay* incident on relations between the USA and Japan?**

What effect would the photograph in Source H have had on US public opinion at the time?

SOURCE H

The sinking of the USS *Panay* after a Japanese air attack, 12 December 1937.

criticized for not invoking the Neutrality Act and allowing US vessels to be in a warzone. Roosevelt said that the conflict was an undeclared war and thus not covered by the Neutrality Acts (see pages 23–4). He did not take military action because he knew the US Navy was unprepared for war and above all, there would be no support in Congress.

(see pages 23–4)

The sinking of the USS *Panay* did not lead to war but it did harden attitudes towards Japan in the USA. Many Americans contributed to relief funds to assist China. Importantly, the *Panay* incident led to greater awareness of the militaristic nature of the fascist regimes around the world.

Following the bombing of Chinese civilians by the Japanese air force in 1937, there was outrage in the USA. The US State Department openly stated that it did not look favourably on aircraft companies that supplied countries with equipment for use against civilians. This was the beginning of the US **moral embargo**. It was extended after the USA ended its commercial treaty with Japan, resulting in the cessation of arms exports.

> ◉━ **KEY TERM**
>
> **Moral embargo** The partial or complete prohibition of commerce and trade in goods with a particular country based on the notion that trading in those goods does not accord with accepted humanitarian standards.

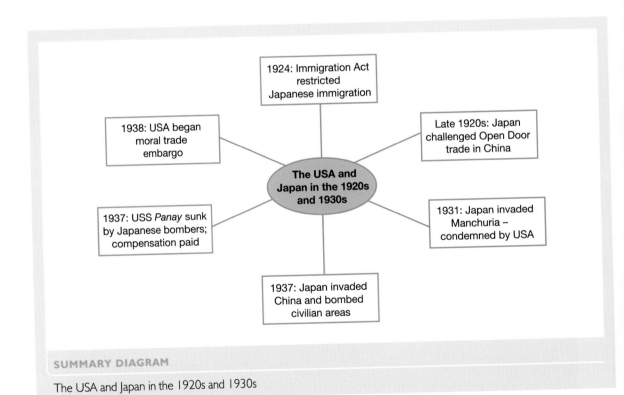

SUMMARY DIAGRAM

The USA and Japan in the 1920s and 1930s

④ Key debate

> ▶ **Key question:** *To what extent was Roosevelt's foreign policy isolationist during the 1930s?*

During the 1930s, the USA passed five Neutrality Acts and yet the armed forces' budget substantially increased. Roosevelt also increased trade links and drew closer to Latin America. He made comments about events in Europe but was always wary about challenging the American people's wish to avoid involvement in a war. When he became president in 1933, Roosevelt was faced with extremely serious economic problems and these dictated his foreign policy. Although Roosevelt was personally appalled by the growth of **militarism** and totalitarianism, both Congress and public opinion were opposed to any future US entanglements in international conflicts.

Historians tend to consider Roosevelt and his foreign policy from three viewpoints: isolationist, gradualist and pragmatist.

 **KEY TERM**

Militarism The tendency to regard military efficiency as the supreme ideal of the state and to subordinate all other interests to those of the military.

The main views of the debate

Isolationist

The USA had refused to ratify the Treaty of Versailles in March 1920 and consequently had not become a member of the League of Nations. Its internationalist credentials had been damaged. Its geographical position made it safe from international aggression and helped to foster the idea of being divorced from the problems of Europe. Most importantly, public opinion was against any involvement in war because memories of the First World War were still powerful. Hence, by the time Roosevelt became president, the wish to remain an isolated country had become entrenched in the USA. The Nye Committee (see pages 22–3) convinced many that the USA had gone to war in 1917 so that bankers and arms manufacturers could make profits. There was a strong, pervasive feeling that people had been persuaded to support a just war when in fact they had been duped by the profiteers.

Historian Robert A. Divine in *The Illusion of Neutrality* (1962), when looking at the USA in the 1930s, stated, 'Americans were frightened by the complex forces threatening the peace of the world and sought to escape them by taking refuge in ironclad neutrality.' Historian Daniel Snowman in *America Since 1920* (1978) suggested that the more events became potentially dangerous in the world in the 1930s, the more the US government seemed to want to cut off the USA from the world.

The passing of five Neutrality Acts (see pages 23, 24 and 27) was the clearest indication of Congress's attitude to US involvement in war. Roosevelt's acceptance of these acts was seen as clear evidence of his attitude to US involvement in conflict. Roosevelt did not openly condemn the actions of Hitler or Mussolini or Japanese militarism.

In a speech to Congress on 4 January 1939, Roosevelt urged that the USA 'avoid any action, or lack of any action, which will encourage, assist, or build up an aggressor' and this was seen as his marker for US neutrality.

Despite Roosevelt's love of democracy and hatred of totalitarianism, he did not challenge Congress over the Neutrality Acts and was happy to follow his 'Good Neighbor' policy so that the USA avoided entanglements in the 1930s.

Gradualist

Some historians consider that Roosevelt was gradualist, that is, he believed that changes to public opinion could be brought about in small, discrete increments rather than in abrupt strokes. Robert Dallek in *Franklin Roosevelt and American Foreign Policy* (1979) has pointed out 'Roosevelt's prevailing inclination was to move slowly in foreign affairs.' Emily Rosenberg, in her essay 'The dilemmas of interwar American foreign policy' (1999) views the New Deal as widening Roosevelt's authority over international economic policy, securing his aim to have powers without resorting to Congress. Although he signed the second Neutrality Act of 1937, Roosevelt found various ways to assist China in the Sino-Japanese War because public opinion favoured China. Robert D. Schulzinger in *American Diplomacy in the Twentieth Century* (1983) states that the 'Quarantine Speech' was 'a trial balloon which did not explode' and infers that he was slowly preparing the US public for further action. Indeed, the conferences and naval actions testify to Roosevelt's gradual approach. Historian H.W. Brands in *Traitor To His Class: The Privileged Life and Radical Presidency of Franklin Delano Roosevelt* (2008) sees him as a gradualist and described the declaration of war against Japan as 'after months of stretching his authority and bending the truth in an effort to educate the American people, Roosevelt would receive his mandate …'.

Pragmatist

Historians also suggest that Roosevelt was a pragmatist in foreign affairs, in that his policies were determined by practical consequences rather than by any philosophy. Roosevelt was a consummate politician, always aware of the power of public opinion. Like any politician he wanted to remain in power. William O'Neill in *A Democracy at War* (1993) suggested that Roosevelt could not go to war against Hitler because public opinion blocked him, and Donald R. McCoy in *Coming of Age* (1973) suggested that Roosevelt 'was shackled by public opinion and by Congress's obedient response to it'. Robert Dallek in *Franklin D. Roosevelt and American Foreign Policy, 1932–1945* (1980) also says that Roosevelt would only act when he could be certain of 'an unequivocal popular consensus'.

Daniel Snowman sees the inconsistencies of Roosevelt's actions but argues that he was trying to work out a compromise from the conflicting pressures around him. For example, Roosevelt invoked neutrality in the Italo-Abyssinian War 1935–6 because he did not wish to offend Italian Americans. Roosevelt also realized that intervention in the civil war in Spain 1936–9 would likely have cost the Democrats much of the Catholic vote in elections. Roosevelt opposed the Neutrality Act of 1937 on the grounds that it penalized the victims of aggression such as Ethiopia, and that it restricted his right as president to assist friendly countries, but signed it because public support was so overwhelmingly for it.

Rosenberg suggests that Roosevelt's quiet support of the Johnson Act (see page 19) gave him flexibility and allowed him to offend as few people as possible.

It has also been suggested that Roosevelt was not concerned about US involvement in foreign affairs and that he was, as many politicians are, pragmatic in the pursuit of and retention of power. His speech at Chautauqua, New York, in August 1936 saw him praise the Neutrality Acts but then also seek discretionary powers for the president in foreign affairs. Here, he was trying to please both sides of the involvement/ non-involvement debate.

Even if Roosevelt did advocate intervention in any foreign conflict, he knew that the USA could face defeat because of the poor state of its armed forces.

> **T O K**
>
> To what extent was it reasonable or feasible for the USA to pursue an isolationist policy in the 1930s? (Logic, Social Sciences – Economics.)

⑤ The US response to the European war 1939–40

> ▶ *Key question: What was the initial response of the USA to the war in Europe?*

The first two years of the war for the USA are ones of incremental involvement led by Roosevelt and organized opposition.

Public opinion in the USA

◀ **What was the initial response of the USA to the war in Europe?**

As seen on pages 26–7, following the outbreak of war in Europe in September 1939, President Roosevelt stated on the radio in a 'fireside chat' that the USA would not become involved.

The Committee to Defend America (CDA)

This committee was a political action group formed in May 1940 that supported Roosevelt in wanting to help the UK. It was founded by William White, a Kansas City journalist, and soon established 600 branches across the USA. However, it did not wish to become involved in the fighting and refused to accept any funds from the steel industry, armaments manufacturers or international bankers because they were thought by the public to encourage nations to fight wars.

The America First Committee (AFC)

This was set up in September 1940 and opposed the CDA. The AFC opposed anything that might risk US neutrality. The AFC claimed that the UK only continued to refuse to negotiate with Hitler because it wanted to convince the USA to enter the war on its side so that it could preserve its empire. AFC leaders made it clear that US intervention would result in national bankruptcy and the collapse of the US system of capitalism and free enterprise. Emphasizing these points won much support across the country. At its peak, it had 800,000 members.

In its first public statement on 4 September 1940, the AFC put forward its basic ideas:

- The USA must build an impregnable defence for the country.
- No foreign powers, nor group of powers, should be able to attack the USA successfully if it was fully prepared for war.
- US democracy could only be preserved by keeping out of the European war.
- The idea of aid – 'aid short of war' – weakened national defence at home and threatened to involve the USA in war abroad.

The AFC opposed all of Roosevelt's and Congress's war-related measures (the destroyers-for-bases exchange with the UK, the occupation of Iceland, the Atlantic Charter, aid to the USSR, the extension of conscription and Lend–Lease, see pages 41–3). The AFC ensured that the possibility of entering the war was kept in the public's minds, especially via their many large public meetings, where they refuted the **interventionist** argument that a German victory or Japanese conquest would put the USA at an economic disadvantage or eventually lead to war.

How did the US government react to the outbreak of war in Europe?

Government reaction

As seen on pages 23, 24 and 27, the government made five amendments to the Neutrality Act between 1935 and 1939. It became clear that the Neutrality Act had favoured Germany since Germany had no need to buy armaments, whereas the UK and France desperately required them. By 1939, Roosevelt had ordered the US Navy to reveal the location of German submarines to the British (see page 27). His concerns about Germany were growing and this showed through his actions.

US reaction to German successes in Europe 1940

In July 1940, following the French surrender to Germany, Roosevelt and his advisers were concerned that Hitler might take over the French Caribbean islands of Guadeloupe and Martinique. Roosevelt organized the Pan-American Conference in Cuba that month. The countries of North and South America stated that in the interests of defence, the **American republics** could take over and administer any European possession in the New World which faced aggression (the Havana Act). By this it hoped to prevent any

European colony being captured by Nazi Germany. July also saw Congress approve the Two Ocean Navy Act whereby the USA planned to expand the size of its navy by 70 per cent to address threats around the world. US firms would build 201 new warships, including seven battleships of 55,000 tons at a cost of $5.2 billion.

Although Canada had been at war with Germany since 10 September 1939, Roosevelt only met Canadian Prime Minister Mackenzie King in August 1940. They then agreed to set up a Joint Board of Defence to co-ordinate US and Canadian defence efforts.

US aid to the UK

After the **Dunkirk evacuation** in June 1940, Roosevelt ordered that the USA should send war *matériel* to assist the UK. He circumvented the Neutrality Act by saying that the items were surplus to US requirements. By October, the UK had received 970,000 rifles, 87,500 machine guns and 895 artillery pieces, although the arms were old and had been used during the First World War.

In August 1940, Prime Minister Churchill asked the USA once again (the first request had been in May) for 40–50 destroyers to bolster the British navy. Roosevelt was keen to oblige but the Neutrality Acts prevented this.

It was then suggested by US government lawyers that the Neutrality Acts could be circumvented if there was a deal for having US naval and air bases on British territory in the Americas in exchange for the ships. The deal was announced on 3 September, whereby the USA would supply 50 destroyers in return for bases. The USA was granted land on 99-year rent-free leases on:

- Newfoundland
- the eastern side of the Bahamas
- the southern coast of Jamaica
- the western coast of St Lucia
- the west coast of Trinidad
- Antigua
- British Guyana.

When the deal was announced, Roosevelt had to endure tremendous criticism because he had bypassed Congress by making an **executive decision**. Some of his opponents pointed out that if the UK were to be defeated, then Hitler would be able to use the ships against the USA in a future war. The deal did bring the USA closer to entering the war, if not as an active participant, then at least as an arms supplier.

SOURCE I

Headline from the *St Louis Post Despatch* about the destroyers for bases deal. It was published on 4 September 1940, the day after the deal was announced.

Dictator Roosevelt Commits an Act of War.

 KEY TERM

Dunkirk evacuation The evacuation of British and some French forces from mainland Europe.

Executive decision A decision made by the president without consulting Congress.

What does Source I reveal? ?

SOURCE J

Photograph of some of the destroyers sent to the UK in 1940.

? Look at Source J. How did President Roosevelt justify giving so many warships to the UK?

KEY TERM

Peacetime draft
The selection of people for service in the military. The draft had been compulsory in the First World War but this was the first time the USA had had conscription in peacetime.

Closer co-operation with the UK continued in November when US Secretary of War Henry Stimson and British Minister of Supply Sir Walter Layton agreed to a partial standardization of British and US military weapons and equipment. The agreement established a general policy of sharing British and US technical knowledge for weapons production.

The peacetime draft

Following the deal with the UK, Congress increased the US budget for defence spending by $173 million on the previous year to $669 million and passed the Selective Training and Service Act. This required all men between the ages of 21 and 35 to register. It meant that the USA had a **peacetime draft** for the first time in its history and was recognition that the USA might face foreign aggression in the near future. The men who were conscripted had to serve for 12 months, no more than 900,000 men could be in training for service at one time, and the servicemen had to stay in the USA or in US territory while serving. If needed, soldiers could also fight for the USA or its allies.

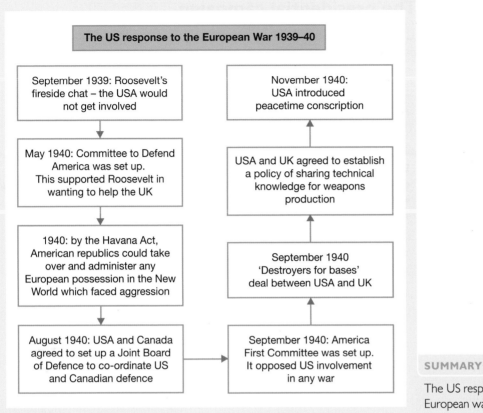

The US response to the European War 1939–40

September 1939: Roosevelt's fireside chat – the USA would not get involved

↓

May 1940: Committee to Defend America was set up. This supported Roosevelt in wanting to help the UK

↓

1940: by the Havana Act, American republics could take over and administer any European possession in the New World which faced aggression

↓

August 1940: USA and Canada agreed to set up a Joint Board of Defence to co-ordinate US and Canadian defence

→

September 1940: America First Committee was set up. It opposed US involvement in any war

↑

September 1940 'Destroyers for bases' deal between USA and UK

↑

USA and UK agreed to establish a policy of sharing technical knowledge for weapons production

↑

November 1940: USA introduced peacetime conscription

SUMMARY DIAGRAM

The US response to the European war 1939–40

⑥ The 1940 presidential election

▶ **Key question:** Why was the 1940 presidential election important for the USA?

As a result of the growing world crisis, Roosevelt decided to run for a third term as president. This was, in itself, an issue because presidents were expected to honour the precedent set by George Washington (president from 1789 to 1797) of standing down after two terms, to show that the office was more important than the man. On top of this, by now Hitler had conquered the western part of Poland, Norway as well as much of Western Europe. Roosevelt had to tread a delicate path between assisting the UK and taking the USA into war, while keeping the public on his side.

What was Roosevelt's
attitude to the war
during the election
campaign?

The presidential campaign

The campaign naturally focused on the USA's neutrality and isolationist policies. The AFC was vehement in its opposition to involvement in the war and consistent in its attacks on Roosevelt. It accused Roosevelt of deliberately creating a situation whereby the USA was being pulled into the war. During the campaign, Roosevelt always made the point that he was against any US involvement in the conflict in Europe (see Source K).

? How useful is Source K as evidence of Roosevelt's attitude towards US involvement in a future war?

SOURCE K

Extracts from some of Roosevelt's speeches during the presidential campaign from the American Presidency Project (www.presidency.ucsb.edu/ws/index.php?pid=15813).

Boston on 30 October: 'I have said this before, but I shall say it again and again and again: Your boys are not going to be sent into any foreign wars.'

Brooklyn on 1 November: 'I am fighting to keep our people out of foreign wars. And I will keep on fighting.'

Rochester, New York, on 2 November: 'Your national government ... is equally a government of peace – a government that intends to retain peace for the American people.'

Buffalo on 2 November: 'Your President says this country is not going to war.'

Cleveland on 3 November: 'The first purpose of our foreign policy is to keep our country out of war.'

Roosevelt's Republican opponent, Wendell Willkie, was a former Democrat who agreed with much of Roosevelt's New Deal and foreign policies. However, Willkie accepted the advice of some Republicans and attacked Roosevelt during the presidential campaign, accusing him of secretly planning to take the USA to war. The accusation did win Willkie some support and importantly pushed Roosevelt into making pronouncements about the USA's neutrality (see Source L). However, as historian William O'Neill states, both candidates for the presidency 'knew that the chances of avoiding war were between slim and non-existent'.

? What are the values and limitations of Source L?

SOURCE L

Excerpt from President Roosevelt's 'fireside chat' of 29 December 1940. Quoted in *Roosevelt and the United States*, by D.B. O'Callaghan, published by Longman, UK, 1966, page 96.

This is not a fireside chat on war. It is a talk on national security ... The people of Europe who are defending themselves do not ask us to do their fighting. They ask us for the implements of war, the planes, the tanks, the guns, the freighters which will enable them to fight for their liberty and for our security. Emphatically, we must get these weapons to them, get them to them in sufficient volume and quickly enough so that we and our children will be saved the agony and suffering of war which others have had to endure ... We must be the great arsenal of democracy.

Consequences of the election

Roosevelt won the election but saw his share of the vote fall from the 60.8 per cent of 1936 to 54.7 per cent. Nevertheless, he interpreted the victory as strong public support for a programme of military preparedness and giving aid to the UK, yet acknowledged that there was no overwhelming desire to take the USA into war. However, in his address to Congress on 6 January 1941, he made a powerful speech which seemed to set down his aims for a post-war world. This became known as the 'Four Freedoms speech'.

> **What were the consequences of Roosevelt's victory for the USA?**

SOURCE M

An excerpt from Roosevelt's speech to Congress, 6 January 1941. Quoted from the US National Archives and Records Administration (http://www.archives.gov/exhibits/powers_of_persuasion/four_freedoms/four_freedoms.html).

We look forward to a world founded upon four essential human freedoms. The first is freedom of speech and expression – everywhere in the world. The second is freedom of every person to worship God in his own way – everywhere in the world. The third is freedom from want … – everywhere in the world. The fourth is freedom from fear … – anywhere in the world. That is no vision of a distant millennium. It is a definite basis for a kind of world attainable in our own time and generation. That kind of world is the very antithesis of the so-called new order of tyranny which the dictators seek to create with the crash of a bomb.

> Why was Roosevelt keen to emphasize the ideas of freedom in Source M?

US involvement in the European war 1941

After the presidential election campaign, it was clear that attitudes in the USA were changing. The defeated Wendell Willkie called for all Americans to support Roosevelt's policy to aid the UK against the fascists. Roosevelt increased *matériel* aid to the UK, and the German invasion of the **USSR** in June offered him another opportunity to broaden US involvement (see below). He also extended US naval and military defences.

The British sought continued help from the USA and in March 1941 Congress passed 'The Act Further to Promote the Defence of the United States'. It became known as the Lend–Lease agreement. This gave Roosevelt the power to 'transfer or lend' arms and other goods to any country 'whose defense was necessary to US defense'. The UK was able to defer payment for the goods which amounted to $31.4 billion during the course of the war. However, before the UK was allowed any goods, it had to pay any outstanding debts to the US in gold. Moreover, the UK was forbidden from re-exporting any Lend–Lease goods and could not export manufactured goods containing materials similar to those obtained under Lend–Lease. Hence, initially, the USA acquired money and markets from the scheme.

> **How did US involvement in the European war increase during 1941?**

> 🔑 **KEY TERM**
>
> **USSR** The Union of Soviet Socialist Republics was the name given to Russia after the Bolshevik Revolution. It was also known as the Soviet Union.

SOURCE N

**Photograph of newly manufactured Liberator bombers ready to be sent
to the UK as part of Lend–Lease, August 1941.**

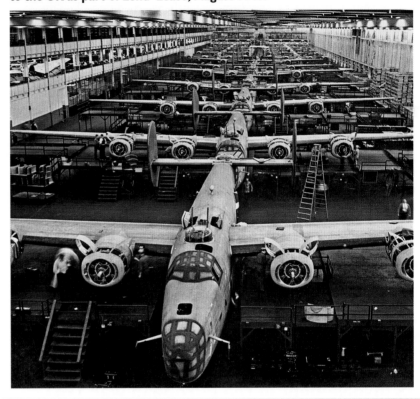

The extension of Lend–Lease

Lend–Lease was extended in July 1941 after the German invasion of the
USSR. Roosevelt offered the Soviet leader, Stalin, goods to the value of
$1 billion via the Lend–Lease scheme. As soon as the decision to aid the
USSR was made, the AFC issued a strong statement opposing the aid,
illustrating how there was still antagonism from ordinary citizens against US
involvement in the European conflict, especially with assisting the USSR.

SOURCE O

**Excerpt from a speech by Charles Lindbergh following the extension of
Lend–Lease to the USSR, 1941. Quoted from 'The reluctant belligerent'
by R.A. Divine, in *Modern America*, by J. Vick, published by Collins
Educational, UK, 1985, page 80.**

*I would a hundred times rather see my country ally herself with England, or
even Germany with all her faults, than with the cruelty, the Godlessness, and the
barbarism that exists in the Soviet Union. An alliance between the United States
and Russia should be opposed by every American, by every Christian, and by
every humanitarian in this country.*

Opposition to Lend–Lease

SOURCE P

Excerpt from a speech by Philip La Follette, a leading Republican and member of AFC, to a group of America First supporters, 1 November 1941. Quoted in 'America First, the battle against intervention 1940–1' by W.S. Cole, in *Modern America*, by J. Vick, published by Collins Educational, UK, 1985, page 79.

Two years ago the President and the War Party launched us on a course of action labeled 'steps short of war' to 'keep us out of war'. That was the most cunning of the many deceitful phrases employed in the propaganda campaign to get us into the war … The sin of the War Party is not that they advocate war. The sin of the War Party is that their only answer to the menace of Hitlerism on Europe is step by step to create Hitlerism in the United States. Every step taken in the past two years has been put over on us by the same fraudulent methods practiced by the European dictators.

How does Source P suggest that Roosevelt was being deceitful about pushing the USA towards war?

The AFC continued to put pressure on Roosevelt after the decision to help the USSR and it added a fifth principle (see page 36): 'The America First Committee advocates a national advisory referendum on the issue of peace or war.' Opponents of the AFC quickly pointed out that people would always vote for peace and that such a reduction of the argument did not engender broad discussion of the issues. Gallup polls in early 1941 showed that 90 per cent of the people surveyed favoured giving more aid to the UK but only 12 per cent were prepared for the USA to go to war.

The erosion of neutrality

Roosevelt allowed British and US military staff members to meet secretly from January to March 1941, to co-ordinate military strategy in case the USA was to go to war against Germany. They developed the ABC-1 Plan which determined that Germany would be defeated first, while US military strategy would be defensive, rather than offensive, towards Japan, should there be any conflict in the Pacific.

In March 1941, Roosevelt extended the combat zone (see page 27) to include Iceland and the Denmark Strait between Iceland and Greenland. This extended the area east in which the US Navy was authorized to escort convoys to the UK, which meant that the USA was more likely to come into conflict with German ships. The US ships would now be able to defend themselves if attacked. This extension cut into the German submarine warfare zone and many saw this as bringing the war closer to the USA.

Indirect involvement in the European war continued to grow in 1941, although Roosevelt was always able to say that his actions were purely for the defence of the USA.

- May–December: the British were allowed to repair one of their **aircraft carriers**, HMS *Illustrious*, in the docks at Norfolk, Virginia.

🗝 **KEY TERM**

Aircraft carrier A warship with an extensive flat deck space for the launch and recovery of aircraft.

- May: Roosevelt gave permission for six British Flying Training Schools to be built. By the end of August, there were some 8000 British pilots being trained on US soil.
- July: 4000 US marines were stationed in Iceland to prevent any German takeover. Additionally, the Danish **government-in-exile** placed Greenland under US protection and authorized the construction of air and naval bases there.

The Atlantic Charter 1941

The German invasion of the USSR in June 1941, altered the nature of the European war. It was imperative that Roosevelt and Churchill met to work out a strategy to help Stalin. In August 1941, they met on a ship off Newfoundland and issued what became known as the **Atlantic Charter**. The meeting lasted four days and the two leaders established a set of goals for the post-war world. The Charter put forward the idea of an international organization to protect the security of all countries, the origin of the **United Nations**. By the end of September, 15 other countries were also signatories.

> **The eight points of the Atlantic Charter, 14 August 1941**
> 1. The USA or the UK would not seek territorial gains.
> 2. Territorial adjustments must be in accord with the wishes of the peoples concerned.
> 3. All peoples had a right to self-determination.
> 4. Trade barriers were to be lowered.
> 5. Global economic co-operation and advancement of social welfare.
> 6. Freedom from want and fear.
> 7. Freedom of the seas.
> 8. Disarmament of aggressor nations and post-war common disarmament.

Reactions to the Atlantic Charter

Germany, Italy and Japan saw the Atlantic Charter as a potential alliance against them. In Tokyo, the Atlantic Charter rallied support for the militarists in the Japanese government, who pushed for a more aggressive approach against the USA and the UK. Yet in the USA, Congress had only a tiny majority in August when it voted to extend conscription from one year to two and a half. On his return from Newfoundland, Roosevelt announced that the USA was no nearer to war than when he had left. Roosevelt pledged no military support for the war in Europe but the Atlantic Charter was a clear sign that the USA was moving towards an alliance with the UK.

What was the Atlantic Charter?

KEY TERM

Government-in-exile
A political group which claims to be a country's legitimate government but is unable to exercise legal power and instead resides in a foreign country.

Atlantic Charter The joint declaration issued by Roosevelt and Churchill which set down the principles to guide a post-war settlement.

United Nations Originally, those countries that had signed the Atlantic Charter. The term was later used for the international organization of nations replacing the League of Nations from 1919. It would promote peace, international co-operation and security.

SOURCE Q

A cartoon published in the British newspaper the *Daily Mail* shortly after the publication of the Atlantic Charter, August 1941. The two men in the middle are Roosevelt and Churchill.

> According to Source Q, what did Roosevelt hope a post-war world would be like?

Impact on USA	The 1940 presidential election	Consequences for the USA and its involvement in the war
• Roosevelt campaigned to maintain US neutrality • Roosevelt made Four Freedoms Speech, January 1941 • Roosevelt gained confidence to assist UK further in the war against Germany		• March 1941: Lend–Lease offered to UK • June 1941: Lend–Lease offered to USSR • July: US troops occupied Iceland • August 1941: Roosevelt signed the Atlantic Charter that set down the principles to guide a post-war settlement

SUMMARY DIAGRAM

The 1940 presidential election

7 The US Navy

▶ Key question: How did the US Navy become increasingly involved in the defence of the USA?

Roosevelt had to couch his military actions in terms of safeguarding the USA. It was not always easy to help the UK. Increasing the size of the US Navy and extending the naval combat zone were examples of helping the UK in the war while keeping the USA out of it.

What happened to make the USA engage in the war?

US Naval action 1940–1

Convoy support

In early 1941, Roosevelt and his advisers could see the damage that German U-boats were wreaking on the British **merchant fleet**. By late spring, losses of approximately 400,000 tons (363,000 tonnes) of ships per month were recorded. Roosevelt ordered the mobilization of the US Atlantic Fleet and, during the summer of 1941, US assistance to the UK grew. In September, US destroyers escorted convoys of British merchant ships as far as Iceland and, in addition, some British ships were being repaired in US shipyards.

The *Robin Moor* incident 1941

Despite the US extension of the combat zone (see page 43) and the mobilization of the fleet, still US ships were attacked and even sunk by German U-boats. On 21 May 1941 the US merchant vessel *Robin Moor* was sunk and its crew was left in the lifeboats. No one was killed. The US reaction was to close down all German and Italian **consulates** in the USA and Roosevelt then **froze all assets** owned by Germany and Italy and the countries that they currently occupied. Some senators claimed that Roosevelt's comments to Congress (see Source R) were designed to inflame public opinion and push the USA into the European war.

> **KEY TERM**
>
> **Merchant fleet** The ships engaged in a nation's commercial shipping.
>
> **Consulates** The premises of officials appointed by countries to protect their interests and citizens in a foreign city.
>
> **Freezing assets** The suspending of access to property, money and investments.

? What point was Roosevelt making to Congress in Source R?

SOURCE R

Excerpt from Roosevelt's message to Congress about the sinking of the *Robin Moor*, 20 June 1941. Quoted in *Peace and War: United States Foreign Policy, 1931–1941*, by the US Department of State, published by the US Government Printing Office, US, 1983, pages 673–6 (also on www.usmm.org/fdr/robinmoor.html).

In brief, we must take the sinking of the Robin Moor *as a warning to the United States not to resist the Nazi movement of world conquest. It is a warning that the United States may use the high seas of the world only with Nazi consent. Were we to yield on this we would inevitably submit to world domination at the hands of the present leaders of the German Reich. We are not yielding and we do not propose to yield.*

The 'shoot on sight' policy

On 4 September 1941, a German submarine attacked the US destroyer *Greer* in the US combat zone, after which Roosevelt ordered the US navy to 'shoot on sight' at German or Italian warships. This policy was virtually an undeclared naval war on German and Italian fleets in the western Atlantic. Roosevelt then asked Congress to revise the 1939 Neutrality Act to permit arming US merchant vessels.

The amended Neutrality Act

As Roosevelt's request was being debated, there was a skirmish between some US destroyers, escorting a British convoy, and some German U-boats. The destroyer *Kearny* suffered a torpedo explosion and 11 sailors were killed. In October, USS *Reuben James* was sunk with the loss of 115 lives. There was little outcry from the US public following these two incidents and any hopes Roosevelt had of using such events as a ***casus belli*** came to nothing.

On 17 November, after repeated confrontations with German submarines in the North Atlantic and the *Reuben James* incident, Congress amended the Neutrality Act, permitting merchant vessels to arm themselves and to carry cargoes to belligerent ports.

War with Germany

By the end of November 1941, Roosevelt had the authority to do almost everything to aid the UK except send US forces. Yet Americans were still not prepared for an actual declaration of war. When the USA declared war on Japan following the attack on Pearl Harbor on 7 December 1941, there was no reason to think that the USA should go to war with Germany. However, the decision was made when Hitler himself declared war on the USA on 11 December.

There are two final points to note about the USA before it became involved in hostilities. First, in October, Roosevelt privately proposed to Churchill that their countries pool their resources and research facilities into developing what became known as the atomic bomb. Second, by early December 1941, some 15,000 Americans had enlisted in either the Canadian or British armed forces.

> **KEY TERM**
>
> ***Casus belli*** The Latin phrase for an event or act which is used to justify a declaration of war.

> ← **How did the USA find itself at war with Germany?**

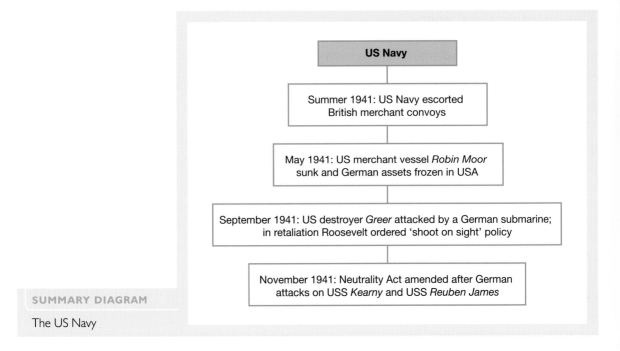

Chapter summary

Hemispheric reactions to the events in Europe 1933–41

The idea of isolationism was extremely strong in the 1930s and for much of the decade many Americans believed the world balance of power had nothing to do with them. It was very difficult to pursue a coherent national security policy. There was a constant dichotomy between Roosevelt's actions and the views and wishes of the US people. Although Roosevelt won the election of 1940, it was not won on a mandate to go to war. Once war broke out in Europe in 1939, Roosevelt gradually increased assistance to the UK by offering destroyers, help with convoy duty and Lend–Lease. Moreover, he was able to offer Lend–Lease to the USSR after June 1941. He was careful to use the guise of protecting the USA to ensure that the public saw a rationale behind his actions, such as extending the Atlantic combat zone and freezing the assets of Germany and Italy.

In Latin America, events in Europe caused concern because of the many commercial and trading links. Brazil flirted with Nazi Germany and by 1937, Vargas (see page 15) had established his own dictatorship. In Argentina, the military sought stability if war were to break out beyond Europe, and Mexico did not see itself as a natural ally of the USA but wanted to maintain close ties with Western Europe.

When US participation in the war finally came, it was the USA that declared war on Japan and Germany that declared war on the USA.

Examination advice

How to answer 'analyse' questions

For questions with the command term <u>analyse</u>, you should try to identify key elements and their relative importance. You need to explain why and how various factors were involved.

Example

<u>Analyse</u> the application and effects of the 'Good Neighbor' policy.

1 To answer this question successfully you should think of all the possible examples of how the 'Good Neighbor' policy was used in Latin America, and the effects for each example.

2 Take several minutes to write down the various examples of how the 'Good Neighbor' policy was used. Try to order them in terms of importance. There is no one correct answer. You will be judged on how you structure your essay and the degree to which you offer supporting historical evidence, as well as the analysis you provide. You are not expected to analyse each and every application of Roosevelt's policy but do try to provide at least three to five examples. You might choose to make a chart of this to refer to when you are writing, so you don't miss an important item. Finally, try to list the key applications in order of importance.

Application	Effects
Haiti, Dominican Republic, Nicaragua	US troops left; direct and indirect support. Dictators: Somoza (Nic.); Trujillo (D.R.); Batista (Cuba)
Mexican nationalization of foreign petroleum companies (1937)	FDR resisted companies' demands for severe retaliation
Reciprocal Trade Agreement Act (1934)	Repealed several isolationist trade policies, lowered tariffs
By 1938, ten trade treaties with Latin America	Increased trade, lowered tariffs
Renegotiation of Panama Canal Treaty	Increased rent to $430,000, USA forfeited rights to participate in Panamanian politics
Nullified Platt Amendment which had authorized US occupation (1934)	Better Cuban–US relations. USA kept one base at Guantánamo
Buenos Aires Conference for Maintenance of Peace (1936)	Discussed neutrality, arms limitations, hemispheric defence. FDR warmly welcomed

3 Be sure in the introduction to define Roosevelt's 'Good Neighbor' policy. You should also briefly discuss why and how the policy was applied and its effects. An example of a good introductory paragraph for this question is given overleaf.

In President Franklin Roosevelt's inaugural speech in 1933, he made clear that he hoped to establish better relations with the neighbours of the USA. By neighbours, he meant in particular Latin American and Caribbean nations. He sought to allay the fears of many in the Americas that the USA would continue to occupy and interfere in the internal affairs of their nations. Roosevelt hoped that this new policy, known as the 'Good Neighbor' policy, would increase trade between American states and be beneficial for all. The policy did result, overall, in better relations between the USA and other countries and was often the basis of US foreign policy. However, in several instances the USA supported dictatorships which oppressed their own people.

4 In the body of the essay, you need to discuss each of the points you raised in the introduction. Devote at least a paragraph to each one. It is a good idea to order these in terms of importance. Be sure to connect the points you raise with the major thrust of your argument. An example of how one of the points could be addressed is given below.

One of Roosevelt's goals in espousing friendlier relations with the USA's neighbours was to increase trade in order to boost employment in a country in the midst of a global depression. In 1934, the Reciprocal Trade Agreement Act was enacted. This was meant to decrease the high tariffs many nations had erected to protect their own industries. Roosevelt felt that if countries agreed to mutually lower tariffs on imported goods, all would benefit. The act was also an indication that Roosevelt and Congress hoped to repeal isolationist trade policies because they held back exports and they knew that the domestic market in the USA was not large enough to get people back to work and factories manufacturing again. By 1938, ten treaties had been signed with Latin American countries. Trade was also a major issue with Mexico. In 1937, the President of Mexico, Lázaro Cárdenas, approved the nationalization of all foreign-owned petroleum companies because they had refused to grant substantial increases in oil workers' pay. US and British companies were the most affected by the seizures and called on Roosevelt to take action against Mexico. Although the USA had had a long history in involving itself in the internal affairs of Mexico, whether politically or militarily, in this instance Roosevelt essentially took a hands-off approach. This was partially due to Cárdenas's promises to pay for the seized companies and partially due to Roosevelt not wishing to antagonize an important ally as war clouds gathered in Europe. Roosevelt did suspend the importation of silver and this hurt the Mexican economy. He wanted to apply pressure on Mexico but that was a far different approach from threatening invasion, which his predecessor might have done.

5 In the conclusion, summarize your findings. This is your opportunity to support your thesis. Remember not to bring up any evidence that you did not discuss in the body of your essay.
6 Now try writing a complete answer to the question following the advice above.

 # Examination practice

Below are two exam-style questions for you to practise on this topic.
1 To what extent were hemispheric meetings successful in the Americas from 1933 to 1940?
   (For guidance on how to answer 'To what extent' questions, see page 82.)
2 Assess the effectiveness of Roosevelt's neutrality policies.
   (For guidance on how to answer 'Assess' questions, see page 106.)

CHAPTER 3

The military role of the USA during the Second World War

As US relations with Germany deteriorated alarmingly during 1939–41, so they became ever more fraught with Japan. This chapter looks at the worsening of relations between the USA and Japan and the aggrandisement of Japan's empire in South-east Asia and China. It considers how war between Japan and the USA broke out and how the USA became involved in the war in Europe, helping the UK in the West and then the USSR on the Eastern Front. The chapter then considers the military role of the USA in the Pacific War and then in the European theatre.

You need to consider the following questions throughout this chapter:

✪ Why did relations between the USA and Japan deteriorate in the years 1939–41?

✪ What was the strategy of the USA in the Pacific War?

✪ Why did President Truman decide to use the atomic bomb?

✪ Why was the role of the USA crucial in the war against Hitler?

① The USA and Japan 1939–41

▶ **Key question:** *Why did relations between the USA and Japan deteriorate in the years 1939–41?*

KEY TERM

Indochina The region of South-east Asia which was a colony of France.

In the late 1930s, Japan edged closer to alliances with the fascist dictators in Europe. The US government became alarmed as it watched Japan's military encroachments into **Indochina**. Roosevelt showed his displeasure by pressuring Japan economically in the hope that such actions would end Japanese activities. The Japanese military held such power in government that it dictated foreign policy. Its key aim was to destroy any chance of the USA interfering with imperial and economic expansion.

> **Why did Japanese activities in China concern the USA?**

→ Japan's imperial and economic expansion

In the later years of the nineteenth century, Japan experienced an industrial revolution. Japan's leadership sought to emulate the great powers of Europe and build a large territorial and trading empire. The Japanese invasion of Manchuria in 1931 and further incursions into China in 1937 created tremendous tension with the USA. The USA had many investments in China, had developed close trading and commercial links with it, and looked on the country as a close friend. Roosevelt wanted to help China but at the same time did not wish to enter into war with Japan. His advisors gave conflicting advice; Cordell Hull (Secretary of State) thought that trade sanctions would push Japan to become more aggressive yet Henry L. Stimson (Secretary of War) and Henry Morgenthau (Secretary of the Treasury) thought that sanctions would cripple Japan and prevent further actions. Roosevelt knew that sanctions against Japan would damage the USA's economy. US investments in Japan were double those in China and 50 per cent of US exports to Asia went to Japan.

The **1911 trade treaty** between the USA and Japan expired on 26 January 1940 and Roosevelt informed the Japanese government that trade would rest on a day-to-day basis. There was a public opinion poll directly after this and 81 per cent of Americans approved of Roosevelt's action. However, Roosevelt did not begin an arms embargo or even a trade boycott of Japanese goods.

US public opinion
Public opinion in the USA sympathized with China. The Japanese massacre in Nanking in 1937 increased antipathy against Japan and Japanese bombing of Chinese civilians in Shanghai aroused great anger in the USA, not only among the people but also among its government. On 1 July 1938, the US Department of State notified aircraft manufacturers and exporters that the US government was strongly opposed to the sale of aircraft and allied equipment to countries that attacked civilian populations. Roosevelt thought that this 'moral embargo' would push Japan towards peace in China.

The Greater East Asia Co-prosperity Sphere
In July 1940, there was a change of government in Japan and the new, militaristic cabinet announced a plan to achieve 'a new order in Greater Asia'. This new order, the 'Greater East Asia Co-prosperity Sphere', was Japan's attempt to create a bloc of Asian nations free of influence from Western nations and provide living space for Japan's growing population. It was also a response to the defeat of France and the Netherlands by Nazi Germany in 1940, which placed their empires in the Far East in a precarious position. Japan hoped to capitalize on this.

The US retaliated with the Export Control Act of July 1940, which authorized the president to stop the export of basic war materials in the interest of national defence. Licences were refused for exporting aviation gasoline and most types of machine tools to Japan. Existing trade agreements with Japanese companies were cancelled, stopping the sale of planes, chemicals and iron.

Japan's foreign agreements
Japan then became a member of the **Three Power Pact** of September 1940 with Germany and Italy. Each country promised to help the others in the event of war with the USA. On 22 September 1940, Japan agreed with the French government of Indochina to grant Japan the right to station 6000 troops there, and to move troops and supplies through northern French Indochina.

🔑 **KEY TERM**

1911 trade treaty A treaty to improve trade and commerce between the USA and Japan.

Three Power Pact This pact, between Germany, Italy and Japan, was signed on 27 September 1940. It is also called the Tripartite Pact.

US General Staff The senior officers who advise in the planning and execution of military policy.

Axis The alliance of Germany, Italy and Japan.

The Russo-Japanese Non-aggression Pact was signed in April 1941. Each country said that it would remain neutral if the other went to war. This gave Japan confidence in its desire to increase its empire in South-east Asia. In response, the **US General Staff** began to increase the number of troops in the Philippines and sent additional aircraft there, from June 1941, such as the B-17 Flying Fortress bombers.

US–Japanese trade conflict

Japan seized the French colonies in Indochina in July 1941. The USA responded by cutting off all supplies of oil, iron and rubber to Japan. As Japan imported more than 85 per cent of its oil from the USA, the ban was a crippling blow. Roosevelt's executive decision stated that the ban was 'to prevent the use of the financial facilities of the USA and trade between Japan and the USA in ways harmful to national defense and American interests'. The Japanese complained that their economy would collapse without oil. The USA insisted they would only lift the ban if the Japanese held peace talks with the Chinese. Japan retaliated by freezing US assets. Trade between the two countries came to a halt. Roosevelt closed the Panama Canal to Japanese shipping, which meant that any trade for countries on the Atlantic seaboard would have to go round Cape Horn. This would not only slow trade but also make it more expensive. Roosevelt then indicated that the USA would take steps to protect US interests if there were any further Japanese encroachments into Asia.

Why did US–Japanese negotiations fail?

US–Japanese negotiations 1941

Japanese aggression

When General Tojo replaced Prince Konoye as Japanese premier on 18 October 1941, the Japanese mood hardened. Tojo's appointment showed how the military in Japan were now in full control of foreign policy. (Tojo had directed the negotiations that led to the **Axis** alliance with Germany and Italy. He had also led the Japanese army in occupied China.) Desperate to find a new source of oil, the Japanese planned to attack oil-rich British Malaya and Dutch colonies in South-east Asia (Java and Sumatra). They knew, however, that the USA might act to stop them and that they were not strong enough to fight both the British and US Pacific fleet. Japan then planned to destroy the US Pacific fleet at Pearl Harbor in Hawaii. They would then be able to attack the British and Dutch possessions and gain the raw materials needed to pursue a war with the USA. The Japanese were extremely confident of victory in a war with the USA provided they could use surprise and gain early success.

Despite mounting tension, the Americans and Japanese met many times during 1940–1 to discuss Japanese aggression in China and Indochina, although they did not make any real agreements.

Operation Magic

Roosevelt and his advisers felt some security because they were able to decipher Japanese radio traffic because of Operation Magic, established in the 1920s to break military and diplomatic codes. Operation Magic also gave information about Japanese ship movements, but did not allow them to find their destinations. US intelligence knew that the Japanese had set 25 November as deadline for making diplomatic progress. When Hull addressed the US cabinet on 7 November, he informed them that the USA should anticipate a military attack by Japan 'anywhere, anytime'.

Final negotiations, November–December 1941

The USA demanded the immediate withdrawal of Japanese forces from China. The Japanese indicated that they would withdraw from Indochina and eventually from China if the UK and the USA stopped sending aid to China and if the USA lifted the trade embargo. Neither side would accede immediately to each other's demands. As the crisis between the two countries worsened, Roosevelt and his advisers expected war at any moment, specifically, an attack on the Philippines. On 3 December, Roosevelt told Lord Halifax, British ambassador to the USA, that if the Japanese attacked South-east Asia then he would allow US military action.

The Japanese government was happy to keep negotiating because it allowed more time to hone its plan of attack on Pearl Harbor. On 6 December, Roosevelt appealed directly to the Japanese emperor, Hirohito, to preserve peace.

SOURCE A

Excerpt from Roosevelt's appeal to Emperor Hirohito, 6 December 1941 from the *Department of State Bulletin*, Vol. V, No. 129, 13 December 1941 (also at ibiblio.org/pha/timeline/4112int.html).

During the past few weeks it has become clear to the world that Japanese military, naval and air forces have been sent to Southern Indo-China in such large numbers as to create a reasonable doubt that this continuing concentration in Indo-China is not defensive in its character. None of the people whom I have spoken of above can sit either indefinitely or permanently on a keg of dynamite ... a withdrawal of the Japanese forces from Indo-China would result in the assurance of peace throughout the whole of the South Pacific area. I am confident that both of us, for the sake of the peoples not only of our own great countries but for the sake of humanity ... have a sacred duty to restore traditional amity and prevent further death and destruction in the world.

Looking at Source A, what did President Roosevelt think Japanese intentions were in Indochina?

The irony of Roosevelt's appeal was that the Japanese fleet was already sailing towards Pearl Harbor.

How damaging for the USA was the attack on Pearl Harbor?

The attack on Pearl Harbor

The damage to the US fleet

The attack on Pearl Harbor on 7 December involved the Japanese fleet sailing more than 3000 miles (5000 km) before launching the attack. US intelligence discovered the fleet's movements and decoded its messages but failed to warn Pearl Harbor in time. When the Japanese attacked at 8a.m. they achieved total surprise. Three hundred and sixty torpedo planes and bombers, launched from Japanese carriers 250 miles (400 km) away, attacked the US fleet, resulting in 2345 US servicemen killed and 1240 injured, and 57 civilians killed and 35 wounded.

The Japanese made simultaneous attacks on the British possessions of Hong Kong, Singapore and Malaya and the US possessions of Guam, Midway Island and the Philippines.

? What would have been the impact on the US public of the photo in Source B?

SOURCE B

Crew abandoning USS *California* in Pearl Harbor, 7 December 1941.

The effects of the attack

In two hours, the US Pacific fleet was crippled. The US Navy had no choice but to rely on its aircraft carriers and submarines because of the damage done to its battleships. However, importantly for the US Navy, the *Tennessee* and *Maryland* battleships returned to service in February 1942 and the *Nevada* in October 1942.

The immediate result of the attack was to bring the USA into the war for, on 8 December, the USA and the UK declared war on Japan.

SOURCE C

Part of President Roosevelt's speech to Congress, 8 December 1941. Quoted from the US National Archives and Records Administration (www.archives.gov/education/lessons/day-of-infamy/).

Yesterday, December 7, 1941 – a date which will live in infamy – the United States of America was suddenly and deliberately attacked by naval and air forces of the Empire of Japan. It will be recorded that the distance of Hawaii from Japan makes it obvious that the attack was deliberately planned many days or even weeks ago. During the intervening time the Japanese Government had deliberately sought to deceive the United States by false statements and expressions of hope for continued peace.

Last night Japanese forces attacked Guam.

Last night Japanese forces attacked the Philippine Islands.

Last night the Japanese attacked Midway Island.

Japan has, therefore, undertaken a surprise offensive extending throughout the Pacific area. No matter how long it may take us to overcome this premeditated invasion, the American people in their righteous might will win through to absolute victory.

What can you learn from Source C about Roosevelt's attitude to Japan?

Italy and Germany then declared war on the USA. The attack on Pearl Harbor roused the US people and any doubts about involvement in war soon dissipated. The Senate unanimously approved Roosevelt's resolution to go to war and there was only one member of the House of Representatives who voted against it.

SOURCE D

An excerpt from the US magazine *Time*, 15 December 1941.

The war came as a great relief, like a reverse earthquake, that in one terrible jerk shook everything disjointed, distorted, askew. Japanese bombs had finally brought national unity to the US.

What is the end result of the Japanese attack according to Source D?

The US Army did not have any divisions ready for combat. The US Navy was severely limited. The air force was significantly weakened by the losses at Pearl Harbor and by attacks on the Philippines. It was time for the USA to enter the Pacific War.

```
┌─────────────────────────────────┐
│    The USA and Japan 1939–41     │
└─────────────────────────────────┘
```

US–Japanese trade relations
- USA allowed 1911 Trade Treaty with Japan to lapse
- 1938: USA began moral trade embargo with Japan on certain military goods
- 1940: Japan established the Greater East Asia Co-prosperity Sphere and the US retaliated with the Export Control Act
- July 1941: further US trade restrictions with Japan following Japanese seizure of French Indo-China

Diplomatic relations
- Relations poor because of invasion of Manchuria in 1931 and further invasion in 1937
- Japan joined the Three Power Pact with Germany and Italy
- Nov/Dec 1941: US–Japanese negotiations to try to improve relations
- Dec 1941: Japanese attack on Pearl Harbor; USA declared war on Japan

SUMMARY DIAGRAM

The USA and Japan 1939–41

2 The USA and the Pacific War

▶ *Key question: What was the strategy of the USA in the Pacific War?*

By the early months of 1942, the Japanese Imperial Army had captured Burma, Malaya, the Dutch East Indies, parts of New Guinea and much US territory such as Guam, Wake Island and the Philippines (see the map on page 59). When Japan captured the Philippines, more than 11,000 US soldiers surrendered. Japan had conquered more than 2.5 million square kilometres (1 million square miles) of land and had 100 million people in its empire. Japanese victories had secured the country 75 per cent of the world's natural rubber reserves, 60 per cent of tin reserves, and vital supplies of oil, which meant that the US embargo was now negated.

What were the initial successes of the USA?

Naval battles 1942

In 1942, two battles severely damaged the Japanese fleet and gave the US an advantage in the Pacific theatre of war.

The Battle of the Coral Sea, May 1942

This was the first naval battle in which the opposing sides never sighted one another, but relied on scout aircraft to direct attacks against each other's warships from the air. During the battle, both sides suffered heavy damage but the Japanese lost two aircraft carriers to the USA's one. Furthermore, the

Japanese failed to capture the rest of New Guinea, from which they could have attacked Australia. It was their first setback. Just one month later came an even more serious defeat.

The Battle of Midway, June 1942

The Japanese naval commander, Admiral Yamamoto, decided to attack the key naval base of Midway Island in the hope that the US Pacific fleet would sail there to defend it.

What Yamamoto did not know was that Japanese radio messages had been decoded and passed to Admiral Nimitz, commander of the US Pacific fleet. The Japanese assembled a huge fleet: 11 battleships, eight aircraft carriers, 12 cruisers, 43 destroyers and more than 700 aircraft. The US forces were three carriers, eight cruisers, 15 destroyers and about 350 planes. Yet by the end of the battle, Japan had lost four carriers, 50 per cent of its carrier fleet. The USA lost only one. The battle was a clear US victory and ended Japanese naval superiority. Most importantly, Japan could not keep pace with the USA in replacing ships and training pilots. (See pages 187–8 in Chapter 8 for the importance of aircraft carriers in the Pacific War.)

SOURCE E

Map showing Japan's defeat in the Pacific War 1942–5.

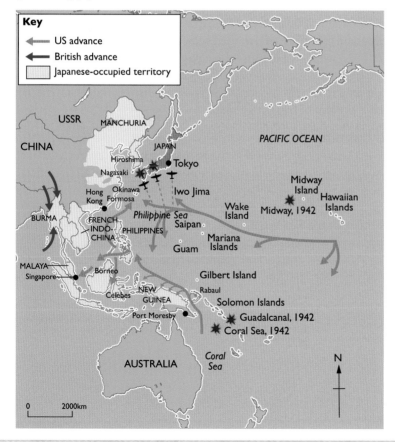

What can you learn from Source E about the defeat of Japan?

What successes did the USA have in 1943–5?

US successes 1943–5

After its successes at sea, the USA focused on regaining some of its lost territory as a first step in the land war against Japan.

The battle for Guadalcanal

The island of Guadalcanal, part of the Solomon Islands, became a key battleground. Japanese troops were constructing an airfield on Guadalcanal which, when operational, could place its aircraft within range of US and Allied territory. US troops attacked the island on 7 August 1942. This was followed by bitter, often close combat fighting over the next five months until the Japanese abandoned the island and evacuated their remaining 10,000 troops in 1943.

SOURCE F

? What does Source F tell you about the Japanese attitude to combat?

An anonymous US soldier speaking about the battle for Guadalcanal.

The Japanese just would not surrender. At Guadalcanal, we surrounded the Japanese in the valleys. They were tough fighters. We cut off the remains of a Japanese regiment. After we had surrounded them we used loud-speakers to try to get them to surrender. But they kept fighting. We had to go in the valleys and kill them. They would not surrender.

The US lost about 7000 men and the Japanese about 31,000. This was the first successful US land battle in the Pacific. Importantly, they had further victories in New Guinea because the Japanese had committed so many troops to the fighting on Guadalcanal. The Japanese began to realize that the USA was able to supply and replace men and *matériel* faster than they could. This was a portent of things to come.

Island hopping

In mid-1943, the US command in the Pacific began Operation Cartwheel, which was designed to isolate the Japanese base at Rabaul, New Guinea (see Source E, page 59). Instead of engaging large Japanese garrisons one after the other, the plan was designed to prevent them from being supplied and let them, in the words of US General MacArthur, 'wither on the vine'. This approach of bypassing Japanese strong points became known as 'island hopping'. US forces moved from island to island, using each as a base for capturing the next. The intention was to recapture the Philippines and then move to Japan.

The following chart gives a chronology of the main events in the Pacific War during 1943–5.

Timeline of US progress in Pacific 1943–5

Date	Key event
1943 Nov	US troops captured the island of Tarawa in the Gilbert Islands. Out of Japanese garrison of 4836 only 17 surrendered
1944 Jan–Feb	US captured Saipan. This gave the USA an airbase within bombing distance of Japan itself
October	The Battle of Leyte Gulf. This was the greatest naval battle in history where the Japanese attempted to prevent the loss of the Philippines. Japan lost 27 major warships to six US warships. At this stage, the Japanese began to send *Kamikaze* pilots against the US fleet. *Kamikaze* means 'Divine Wind' and pilots would deliberately crash their planes on to a US battleship. It was thought an honourable act to commit suicide in this way
1945 Feb–March	US troops landed on Iwo Jima which had Japanese airfields. The losses included 4000 US and 20,000 Japanese. The casualty rate reached 75 per cent in two US marine divisions
March–Aug	US bombing campaign using captured Japanese airfields and new **B-29 Superfortress bombers**. The US air force destroyed a quarter of all Japanese houses in firebomb attacks
April–June	US troops invaded the island of Okinawa

The attack on Iwo Jima and Okinawa

Following the capture of Saipan in mid-1944, the USA began to prepare for the attack on the Japanese mainland. After the capture of Iwo Jima and Okinawa, raids on Japan increased and its air defences crumbled. B-29 Superfortress bombers were able to attack the mainland at will. The most devastating attack, Operation Meetinghouse, happened on 9–10 March 1945 when about 80,000 people died in a raid on Tokyo. It was considered to be the worst single loss of life during one bombing raid.

Japan became a country under siege because it had lost control of the seas and the air. However, despite defeats on land, at sea and in the air, Japan repeatedly refused to the **unconditional surrender** the USA demanded.

When the Allied leaders met at Potsdam in late July 1945, they demanded once again Japan's immediate unconditional surrender or they would face 'prompt and utter destruction'.

The end of the war

President Truman and the atomic bomb

When Harry Truman became president in April 1945, Stimson advised Truman to set up a committee for advice about the future use of atomic weapons. This became the Interim Committee which first met on 31 May 1945.

Truman was faced with certain dilemmas about the war with Japan. Following the Yalta Agreements (see pages 95–7), Truman knew that the USSR would declare war on Japan by 8 August and he was concerned that

KEY TERM

B-29 Superfortress bomber An advanced heavy bomber used in the US campaign to bomb mainland Japan in the final months of the war. It was used to carry out the bombing of Hiroshima and Nagasaki.

Unconditional surrender Surrender without conditions, in which no guarantees are given to the country that is surrendering.

How did the USA end the war?

its power in Asia would grow. He did not want to see the continued spread of communism. In addition, some of his military advisers had warned that the USA needed to invade Japan, something which would cause the deaths of hundreds of thousands of US soldiers. Using the **atomic bomb** offered a chance to end the war quickly.

Truman had various options with regard to the surrender of Japan. The USA could:

- invade Japan
- negotiate surrender on mutually agreeable terms
- assume that the entry of the USSR into the war, linked with Japan's growing inability to wage total war, would bring about surrender
- demonstrate the power of the atomic bomb over the Bay of Tokyo
- use the bomb on Japan itself to immediately end the hostilities.

Truman received the report from the Interim Committee in early June and it stated that the atomic bomb should be used as soon as possible against Japan. Truman accepted its decision and although he heard strong arguments against using the bomb from some military advisors and scientists, he discounted them.

What does Source G show about the attitude of some scientists to the use of the atomic bomb?

SOURCE G

Excerpt from the Franck Report, June 1945. The report was the product of a committee under the chair of James Franck, a member of the Manhattan Project and Director of the Chemistry Division at the University of Chicago (from www.nuclearfiles.org/menu/key-issues/ethics/issues/scientific/franck-report.htm).

If the United States were to be the first to release this new means of indiscriminate destruction upon mankind, she would sacrifice public support throughout the world, precipitate the race for armaments, and prejudice the possibility of reaching an international agreement on the future control of such weapons.

Truman had warned, in the July Potsdam Declaration (see page 101), that it was essential to receive unconditional surrender from the Empire of Japan or Japan would face 'prompt and utter destruction'.

Sources H and I below give some idea of what helped Truman to make his decision about the use of the bomb.

What are the values and limitations of Source H?

SOURCE H

An excerpt from *Memoirs: 1945 Year of Decisions*, by Harry S. Truman, published by Doubleday, USA, 1955, pages 419–23.

Let there be no mistake about it. I regarded the bomb as a military weapon and never had any doubt that it should be used. The top military advisers to the President recommended its use, and when I talked to Churchill he unhesitatingly told me that he favored the use of the atomic bomb if it might aid to end the

...ar ... In deciding to use this bomb I wanted to make sure that it would be used
a weapon of war in the manner prescribed by the laws of war. That meant
...at I wanted it dropped on a military target. I had told Stimson that the bomb
...ould be dropped as nearly as possibly upon a war production centre of prime
...litary importance ...

SOURCE I

**...n excerpt from *Speaking Frankly*, by James Byrne, US Secretary of State
...1945, Harper Brothers, USA, 1947.**

*...'e were losing too many troops 'island hopping' in the Pacific. Any weapon
...hich would bring an end to the war and save a million casualties among the
...merican boys was justified. And we are talking about people who hadn't
...sitated at Pearl Harbor to make a sneak attack. I believed the atom bomb
...ould be successful and would force the Japanese to surrender on our terms.*

> What does Source I tell you
> about Byrne's attitude
> towards the Japanese?

...the same time as Truman was considering the use of the atomic bomb, the
...military were planning to invade mainland Japan (Operation Downfall)
...1 November 1945. The first stage of the operation was the invasion of the
...nd of Kyushu, which would be followed by the invasion of Honshu.

SOURCE J

...roshima after the atomic bomb, 6 August 1945.

> How useful is Source J as
> evidence of the effects of the
> atomic bomb on Hiroshima?

The end of the war

In Japan, the leadership was divided between the 'war group', who wanted to fight to the death, and a 'peace group' led by Prime Minister Suzuki, who wanted to negotiate an end to the war. The government made secret approaches to the USSR to act as a go-between with the USA, without progress.

On 6 August 1945, President Truman ordered the dropping of the atomic bomb on Hiroshima. The bomb killed about 70,000 and wounded about the same number. The Japanese still refused to surrender and faced invasion in Manchuria when the USSR declared war. Failure to surrender led the USA to drop a second atomic bomb on Nagasaki on 9 August. This time, it killed around 40,000. The USA was preparing a third bomb to be ready for 19 August, but the Japanese surrendered on 14 August and signed the Instrument of Surrender on 2 September, officially bringing the Second World War to a close.

Why was the USA victorious in the war?

Reasons for US victory

Ultimately, the USA was able to produce more aircraft, aircraft carriers and weapons than Japan. Additionally, it had a huge workforce and vast natural resources and importantly its industrial centres never came under attack. US air raids badly affected Japanese production. Absenteeism reduced the output of Japanese industry. Steel output, which was 7.8 million tonnes (8.6 million tons) in 1944, fell to 1 million tonnes (1.1 million tons) in 1945. Aircraft production fell by one third. Oil stocks, which were 43 million barrels at the start of the year, fell to just four million by March 1945. By contrast, US industrial production increased on a yearly basis, although it did slow down from late 1944 (see table on page 204 in Chapter 9). Japan's war industries could not compete against the USA; for example, after Pearl Harbor, the USA built 325,000 aircraft and the Japanese 79,000.

The USA gained command of the sea and air after the battles of Coral Sea, Midway and Leyte Gulf. This was essential for successful operations in the Pacific Islands. Through island hopping, US forces were efficient and only secured those islands with strategic airfields or harbours. This tactic also caused thousands of Japanese troops to stay trapped on islands, unable to participate in the fighting.

The Japanese were disadvantaged in more ways:

- Following the capture of Iwo Jima and Okinawa, the USA could use the airfields to bomb Japan at will in 1945.
- After 1943, US submarines sank more than 75 per cent of Japan's merchant ships and after 1944, US bombing destroyed large numbers of Japanese homes and factories.
- In 1945, many people were starving and industrial production collapsed.
- From March to September 1945, 275 square kilometres (105 square miles) of Japan's cities were destroyed by **incendiary bombs**. Twenty-two million people, a quarter of the population, became homeless.

KEY TERM

Incendiary bombs Bombs designed to start fires.

With the war in Europe over, the industrial might of the USA turned against Japan. Attacks on the Japanese mainland could be made at will. The Japanese government's attitude needed to change to end the conflict.

USA and the Pacific War

US naval war
- May 1942: Battle of the Coral Sea – USA prevented capture of New Guinea and assault on Australia
- June 1942: Battle of Midway – major US victory; Japan lost four aircraft carriers
- October 1944: Battle of Leyte Gulf; Japan lost 27 major warships

US land war
- January 1943: USA captured Guadalcanal; Japan lost c.30,000 men
- 1943: US tactic of 'island hopping' began
- March 1945: USA captured Iwo Jima – USA lost 4000 and Japan 20,000 men
- June 1945: USA captured Okinawa – USA lost 12,000 and Japan 100,000 men

US air war
- February 1944: USA captured Saipan – able to use airbase to bomb Japanese mainland
- March 1945: USA bombed Tokyo – c.80,000 killed
- 6 and 9 August 1945: atomic bombs dropped on Hiroshima and Nagasaki

Japan signed the Instrument of Surrender: 2 September 1945

SUMMARY DIAGRAM

The USA and the Pacific War

③ Key debate

▶ *Key question:* Why did President Truman decide to use the atomic bomb?

At the time of the bombings, the orthodox view was that the attacks on Hiroshima and Nagasaki were to bring a swift end to the war. However, revisionist historians have refuted this, arguing that there were several other key reasons why the bombs were used, not least the issue of US–Soviet relations and the USSR's position in Asia. Truman faced many senior advisers and military commanders who offered conflicting advice. He had to consider moral and political issues as well as the possibility of huge US casualties.

The orthodox view
Winston Churchill, then British prime minister, supported Truman's decision to use the bomb, as did Stimson, who stated that the Japanese army was large and powerful and that fighting would not end until late 1946.

? What does Source K suggest about Stimson's attitude to using the bomb?

SOURCE K

Extract from 'The decision to use the bomb', by Henry Stimson, published in *Harper's Magazine*, February 1947.

My chief purpose was to end the war in victory with the least possible cost in the lives of the men in the armies which I had helped to raise. The face of war is the face of death; death is an inevitable part of every order that a wartime leader gives. The decision to use the atomic bomb was a decision that brought death to over a hundred thousand Japanese. The destruction of Hiroshima and Nagasaki put an end to the Japanese war. It stopped the fire raids and the strangling blockade; it ended the ghastly specter of a clash of great land armies.

Historians such as Herbert Feis, writing in *Japan Subdued: The Atomic Bomb and the End of World War II* (1966), put forward the orthodox view that Truman made his decision on purely military grounds in order to ensure a speedy victory. David McCullough, the author of a biography of Truman (1992), also accepted this. William O'Neill in *A Democracy at War* (1993) stated that the Japanese military had no intention of surrendering and meant to fight to the last man, woman and child. He also points out that the Japanese military did not consider surrender even after Hiroshima. In the three months after Truman became president, the USA had sustained nearly half of the casualties inflicted upon it by the Japanese in three years of fighting. Robert J.C. Butow, writing in *Japan's Decision to Surrender* (1954), stressed the crucial importance of Hiroshima and Nagasaki in bringing about surrender. Butow's text is still seen as an important part of the debate.

Alonzo L. Hamby, writing in *Man of the People* (1995), said that Truman was motivated by the thought of more and more US soldiers dying. Richard Frank has argued in *Downfall: The End of the Imperial Japanese Empire* (1999) that the USA would have changed its mind about invading Japan in November 1945 because the latter was still a power to be reckoned with. Frank writes that the bomb's use was better than all existing alternatives, and saved not only Allied lives but Japanese lives as well. Sadao Asada and Professor Barton Bernstein have also argued that there was a possibility that Japan would not have surrendered by November. Hence, using the atomic bomb ended the conflict.

? What does Source L suggest about Truman's character?

SOURCE L

Extract from Truman's letter of 11 August 1945 to the General Secretary of the Federal Council of Churches of the USA (www.ncccusa.org/centennial/augustmoment.html).

Nobody is more disturbed over the use of atomic bombs than I am but I was greatly disturbed over the unwarranted attack by the Japanese on Pearl Harbor and their murder of our prisoners of war. The only language they seem to understand is the one we have been using to bombard them … When you have to deal with a beast you have to treat him as a beast. It is most regrettable but nevertheless true.

The revisionist view

Truman has been criticized on several grounds for his decision. Military advisers told Truman that Japan was a defeated nation and that the US naval blockade of the home islands meant that its war effort would wane quickly. Reportedly there were also three million Japanese soldiers stranded in China who could not return to Japan to defend the homeland.

SOURCE M

Excerpt from *Mandate for Change 1953–1956*, by Dwight Eisenhower, published by Doubleday, USA, 1963, page 380.

I voiced … my grave misgivings, first on the basis of my belief that Japan was already defeated and that dropping the bomb was completely unnecessary, and secondly because I thought that our country should avoid shocking world opinion by the use of a weapon whose employment was, I thought, no longer mandatory as a measure to save American lives. It was my belief that Japan was, at the very moment, seeking to surrender with a minimum loss of 'face.'

> According to Source M, why did Eisenhower not wish to 'shock world opinion'?

Senior commanders from all arms (Eisenhower, MacArthur, Leahy, King, Nimitz, Arnold and LeMay) opposed its use. Admiral Leahy saw the use of the bomb as no different to using poisonous gas or bacteriological weapons. Indeed, some of them saw that the USA was surrendering its moral high ground if it became the first to use such a weapon.

SOURCE N

Extract from *I Was There*, by Admiral William Leahy, published by Whittlesey House, USA, 1950, page 441.

The lethal possibilities of atomic warfare in the future are frightening. My own feeling was that, in being the first to use it, we had adopted an ethical standard common to the barbarians of the Dark Ages. I was not taught to make war in that fashion, and wars cannot be won by destroying women and children. We were the first to have this weapon in our possession, and the first to use it. There is a practical certainty that potential enemies will develop it in the future and that atomic bombs will at some time be used against us.

> What does Source N show about the morality of using the atomic bomb?

SOURCE O

Excerpt from the Japanese newspaper *Nippon Times*, 10 August 1945. This was published the day after the atomic bomb was dropped on Nagasaki.

How can a human being with any claim to a sense of moral responsibility deliberately let loose an instrument of destruction which can at one stroke annihilate an appalling segment of mankind? This is not war; this is not even murder; this is pure nihilism. This is a crime against God and humanity which strikes at the very basis of moral existence. What meaning is there in any international law, in any rule of human conduct, in any concept of right and wrong, if the very foundations of morality are to be overthrown as the use of this instrument of total destruction threatens to do? What more barbarous atrocity

> According to Source O, what distinguished the atomic bomb from other weapons?

can there be than to wipe out at one stroke the population of a whole city without distinction – men, women, and children; the aged, the weak, the infirm; those in positions of authority, and those with no power at all; all snuffed out without being given a chance of lifting even a finger in either defence or defiance!

Revisionist historians have written that the use of the atomic bomb had more to do with keeping the USSR out of Asia and warning them of the military power that the USA now possessed. The publication of the US Strategic Bombing Survey's Report bolstered this view after the war. It concluded that the US blockade would have obliged Japan to surrender by November. Historian Gar Alperovitz in *Atomic Diplomacy* (1965) wrote that Truman *et al.* knew it was unnecessary and there was evidence, by the late summer of 1945, that Truman was engaging in 'atomic diplomacy' by trying to intimidate the USSR. The Soviet historian Vadim Nekrasov in *The Roots of European Security* (1984) stated that the US decision to use the bomb was simply to show its power to the world, especially to the USSR.

How reliable is Source P as evidence of the motives of the USA in using the atomic bombs?

SOURCE P

Extract from *The Roots of European Security*, by V. Nekrasov, published by Novosti Press Agency Publishing House, Russia, 1984.

Officially, the Americans claimed that the bombings on Hiroshima and Nagasaki intended to bring the end of the war nearer and avoid unnecessary bloodshed and casualties, but there were entirely different objectives. The purpose of the bombings was to intimidate other countries, above all the Soviet Union. In other words, the US decision to use atomic energy for military purposes intended to produce a diplomatic and psychological impact, and this has since involved the world in a nuclear arms race.

Tsuyoshi Hasegawa in *Racing the Enemy: Stalin, Truman and the Surrender of Japan* (2006) has written that Truman used the atomic bomb to win the war against Japan without Soviet assistance, thus limiting Soviet expansion in Asia. He argues that it was the anticipated Soviet participation in the war which had the greatest influence on Japan's decision to surrender. These arguments have also been supported by several other historians, especially Martin Sherwin in *A World Destroyed: Hiroshima and Its Legacies* (1975).

Critics have also said Truman used the bomb because it cost $2 billion in development (see Chapter 8, pages 190–2) and there had to be some return on such high investment. Importantly, Truman was aware of the peace-feelers that the Japanese government had made towards the USSR. Another theory of the motive for using the bomb is that it avenged Pearl Harbor and the ill-treatment of US soldiers.

John Dower, *War Without Mercy: Race and Power in the Pacific War* (1986) and Ronald Takaki, *Hiroshima: Why America Dropped the Atomic Bomb* (1995) have even cited racism as a reason behind Truman's decision to use the atomic bombs.

How might a utilitarian ethical argument be applied to Truman's decision to drop the atomic bombs on Hiroshima and Nagasaki? (Logic, Ethics.)

T O K

The USA and the war against Hitler

▶ **Key question:** *Why was the role of the USA crucial in the war against Hitler?*

As soon as Germany declared war on the USA, Roosevelt and Churchill agreed that it was imperative to meet to determine a long-term strategy (see page 86). They decided that Hitler posed the greater world threat whereas Japan was only a regional threat. They had already signed the Atlantic Charter (see page 44) and decided to set up a **Combined Chiefs of Staff** committee whereby the military experts of the USA and the UK could co-ordinate plans for the defeat of the Axis powers.

🔑 **KEY TERM**

Combined Chiefs of Staff
The supreme military staff of each of the Western Allies working together in one group.

Assistance in any land campaign would be slow in forthcoming because the US Army was not fully prepared and existing theatres of war in Europe and Africa required careful planning for amphibious attacks. Roosevelt could, however, give immediate and extensive assistance in the naval and air war, including supplying *matériel* to the USSR to help their efforts, and did so immediately by means of Lend–Lease (see pages 41–2). For Roosevelt, granting assistance was a way of improving US–Soviet relations and also making Hitler's war more difficult. See Chapter 9 for more on US–Soviet relations.

The USA and the USSR

The German invasion of the USSR

On 22 June 1941, the Germans invaded the USSR in Operation Barbarossa. However, Stalin made sure that most of the Red Army retreated and as they did so, they carried out a 'scorched earth' policy of burning crops, homes and places of shelter. The German armies were left desperately short of supplies. The well-equipped Red Army was used to fighting in freezing temperatures; the German army was not.

← **How did the USSR contribute to the Allied war effort, and how did the USA help it?**

The Battle of Stalingrad

Early in September 1941, the Germans began to close in on Stalingrad. For the next four months, Germany and the USSR fought a ferocious battle for Stalingrad (now called Volgograd). On 19 November, Marshall Zhukov, the Soviet commander, mounted a counter-offensive and the Red Army surrounded Stalingrad, trapping 278,000 Germans. The Germans surrendered on 31 January 1943. The USSR had killed some 200,000 German troops since November and taken a further 91,000 as prisoners.

In many ways, Stalingrad represented the turning point in Allied fortunes.

Eastern Front 1943–5

The Eastern Front was the name given to the area of fighting between Germany and the USSR in the years 1941–5. By 1943, the Germans were outnumbered three to one in tanks and the USSR was manufacturing them at an astonishing rate. Germany faced an enemy that seemed to have limitless numbers of soldiers and, after the shock of the first months of the invasion, vast amounts of war *matériel*. What marked out the war on the Eastern Front was its intensity and savagery. The USSR and the Germans killed millions of civilians and soldiers.

The Germans were pushed out of the USSR by the end of 1944, and after a lull in the fighting, the USSR's advance began again in mid-January 1945. Its forces captured Berlin on 2 May following an assault by around 1.5 million soldiers.

The cost for the USSR

It is estimated that the army of the USSR lost about nine million killed with about 15 million wounded. No one knows the exact number of dead Soviet civilians, but the figure is between seven million and 20 million. The Germans considered the Soviet civilians as sub-humans (*Untermenschen*). By the end of the war, 25 million people were homeless in the USSR, and 1710 towns and 70,000 villages were classed as 'destroyed'.

The USA, the USSR and war *matériel*

The USSR had difficulties producing *matériel* for the war because Germany occupied much of its territory for part of the time. The table below gives some figures for production:

	1941	1943	1945
Coal (million tonnes)	151	93	149
Oil (million tonnes)	33	18	19
Tanks (approx.)	6,600	24,000	15,400
Aircraft (approx.)	16,000	35,000	20,000

Under the Lend–Lease agreement, the USSR received about 18,000 aircraft, 11,500 tanks, 7300 armoured vehicles, 435,000 trucks and jeeps and more than 500 naval vessels. Lend–Lease *matériel* assisted the USSR to overcome the initial shock of the German invasion and later supplemented USSR production.

Fighting on the Eastern Front bled Germany dry, not only in terms of labour but also in terms of military *matériel*. Germany's defeat on the Eastern Front contributed hugely to its overall defeat in the war. The USSR had taken on the main part of the German army and had eliminated more than 600 German divisions (a division was about 12,000 men). British and US forces had faced only 176 divisions on the Western Front. On the Eastern Front, about 3.5–4 million German soldiers died. At the end of the war, there were about three million German prisoners of war in the USSR.

The war at sea

What was the role of the USA in the naval war?

When the Second World War broke out in 1939, the Germans adopted a **'sink on sight' policy**. As a result, even though Roosevelt was not yet at war with Germany, he introduced an identical policy in September 1941, calling Germany 'the rattlesnakes of the Atlantic', and amended the Neutrality Act (see page 47). The aim of the Germans was to blockade the UK and starve the country into submission. Convoys of food and war *matériel* were sent from Canada and the USA on a regular basis to ensure that the British population did not starve. Once the USSR entered the war on the side of the Allies, the Allied leaders recognized that if control of the Atlantic was not secured, the war would be lost because it was imperative that the Lend–Lease convoys reached the UK and the USSR. The UK and the USSR would find it almost impossible to survive without US assistance and naval protection.

As we have seen in Chapter 2, US vessels had already been attacked prior to their entry into the war. Now, with the German declaration of war on the USA, Germany started to attack US shipping in earnest.

The U-boat war

Germany sent a pack of U-boats to attack US merchant shipping in mid-January 1942 and within three weeks they had sunk more than 150,000 tons (135,000 tonnes) of shipping without loss. By June 1942, the USA had lost more than 360 merchant ships and had not sunk one U-boat.

Although the USA tried to protect its ships, the Germans concentrated their U-boat packs in the areas that could not be protected by US anti-submarine planes or aircraft carriers. The success of the U-boats threatened the whole war effort.

The Germans destroyed a huge amount of shipping in their U-boat campaigns although these were quickly replaced thanks to the industrial might of the USA. Although the UK was unable to rebuild ships as quickly as the USA, their allies helped them. In 1942, the USA built four million tons (3.6 million tonnes) of merchant shipping and the following year 11 million tons (ten million tonnes). The UK needed immediate replacements to its fleet to ensure the country did not starve. Crucially, in May 1943, Roosevelt overruled his Chiefs of Staff, who wanted to use most of the merchant fleet to supply US forces, and ordered that 150–200 vessels to be assigned to the UK. This ensured that the UK remained fed and supplied.

The Allies gradually gained the upper hand in the Battle of the Atlantic because of such developments as radar and sonar (see pages 185–6). The Allies overcame German **surface raiders** by the end of 1942 and had blunted the threat of U-boats by mid-1943, although U-boats continued to inflict damage almost until the end of the war.

🔑 **KEY TERM**

'Sink on sight' policy Any ship that was seen was immediately attacked without warning, whether the country the ship belonged to was at war with Germany or not.

Surface raiders Ships of the German navy used against Allied merchant vessels.

Excerpt from *The Battle of the Atlantic*, Vol. 1, September–May 1943 by Admiral Morrison of the United States Navy, 1949. Quoted in *A Democracy at War*, by W. O'Neill, published by Harvard University Press, USA, 1993, page 149.

Progress was made against the submarine only by cooperation between the US, British, Canadian and Brazilian navies, among different branches of the American forces and merchant marine, between all bureaus of the Navy Department, between naval officers specially detailed for anti-submarine work and the Operations Research Group of civilian scientists, between foreign policy and military operations, and between the armed forces and the public.

What can you learn from Source Q about the war against the submarine?

Successes in the naval war pushed the Allies to consider land attacks on Germany. Roosevelt always stated that he would concentrate on the defeat of Hitler and there was much debate between the UK and the USA about where they could attack Hitler.

The land war in North Africa and Europe

How did the USA contribute to the North African and European campaigns?

The UK favoured North Africa and the USA wanted to attack through France. Churchill argued the Allied forces were not yet strong enough to move into France but would find success if North Africa was invaded through Morocco and Algeria. British forces had defeated the Italians but suffered several setbacks until the Battle of El Alamein in October 1942. At El Alamein, British forces defeated the German army, which was then forced to retreat westwards. The Germans lost several thousand men and more than 300 tanks, and were forced to abandon plans for offensive operations once and for all.

The invasion of North Africa

Roosevelt thought that Churchill was interested in protecting British interests in the Middle East, but he eventually accepted his plan for North Africa, Operation Torch.

Operation Torch was headed by US General Eisenhower and began in November 1942. Army troops were trained in **amphibious warfare**. There were no dedicated **landing craft** and so they modified existing small vessels. Eventually, the combined US and British forces numbered 100,000.

The British victory at El Alamein was the first major defeat experienced by Germany and led to the retreat of German forces. Operation Torch's quick successes in the west soon meant that the Axis forces found themselves squeezed in a pincer movement. Axis forces surrendered on 13 May 1943 and more than 250,000 troops became **prisoners of war**.

KEY TERM

Amphibious warfare Military operations launched from the sea against an enemy shore.

Landing craft A vessel used for landing troops and equipment on beaches.

Prisoners of war Members of the armed forces captured by an enemy in time of war.

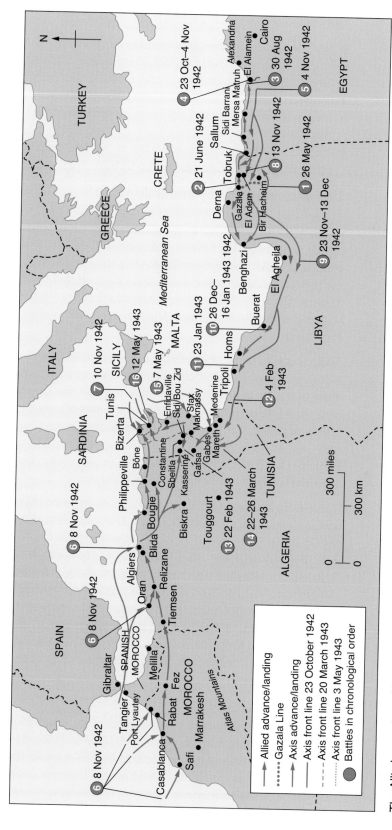

Legend (map key):

- Allied advance/landing
- Gazala Line
- Axis advance/landing
- Axis front line 23 October 1942
- Axis front line 20 March 1943
- Axis front line 3 May 1943
- Battles in chronological order

Map labels:

TURKEY

GREECE

CRETE

Mediterranean Sea

ITALY

SARDINIA

SICILY

MALTA

SPAIN

SPANISH MOROCCO

MOROCCO

Atlas Mountains

ALGERIA

TUNISIA

LIBYA

EGYPT

Gibraltar, Tangier, Port Lyautey, Melilla, Rabat, Fez, Casablanca, Safi, Marrakesh

Oran, Relizane, Tlemsen, Algiers, Blida, Bougie, Philippeville, Bône, Bizerta, Tunis, Biskra, Constantine, Sbeitla, Kasserine, Touggourt, Gafsa, Gabès, Mareth, Medenine, Maknassy, Sfax, Sidi/Bou Zid, Enfidaville

Tripoli, Homs, Buerat, El Agheila, Benghazi, Derna, Tobruk, El Adem, Bir Hacheim, Gazala, Benghazi

Sidi Barrani, Mersa Matruh, Sallum, El Alamein, Alexandria, Cairo

300 miles
300 km
0
0

N

Battle markers (chronological):

- 1 — 26 May 1942
- 2 — 21 June 1942
- 3 — 30 Aug 1942
- 4 — 23 Oct–4 Nov 1942
- 5 — 4 Nov 1942
- 6 — 8 Nov 1942
- 6 — 8 Nov 1942
- 6 — 8 Nov 1942
- 6 — 8 Nov 1942
- 7 — 10 Nov 1942
- 8 — 13 Nov 1942
- 9 — 23 Nov–13 Dec 1942
- 10 — 26 Dec–16 Jan 1943
- 11 — 23 Jan 1943
- 12 — 4 Feb 1943
- 13 — 22 Feb 1943
- 14 — 22–26 March 1943
- 15 — 7 May 1943
- 16 — 12 May 1943

The Allied campaign in North Africa 1941–3

The success of Operation Torch had many results. It:

- saw the capture of Rommel's forces in North Africa
- helped Allied shipping in the Mediterranean because Axis airbases in North Africa were captured
- relieved pressure on the crucial Allied base in Malta
- was an encouragement to resistance movements in Axis-occupied countries
- forced Hitler to commit essential forces that he would have preferred to be on the Eastern Front against the USSR.

The invasion of Sicily and Italy

At the Casablanca Conference in January 1943 (see page 87), the Combined Chiefs of Staff agreed that after the Axis surrender in North Africa, Sicily should be invaded. The bomber offensive on Germany would be increased and the **USAAF** would assist the **RAF** in this campaign. The USA accepted the plan (Operation Husky) because they agreed that it would force Hitler to disperse his forces and there would be additional protection for Allied shipping in the Mediterranean. A successful invasion of Sicily might push Italy to surrender.

Stalin was extremely angry when he was informed that the invasion of Sicily was to go ahead. He felt that Soviet forces were taking a disproportionate share of the casualties on the Eastern Front and that an attack on France across the English Channel would save millions of lives. Stalin was under immense pressure at this time. Fighting on the Eastern Front was relentless and German forces were still deep in Soviet territory. Military and civilian casualties were mounting at a rapid rate. To show his anger, Stalin recalled his ambassadors from London and Washington.

There were in excess of 200,000 Axis soldiers in Sicily: the majority were Italians, with around 30,000 Germans. The invasion began on the night of 9–10 July 1943, and over the next few days the Allies landed about 500,000 men. By 17 August, the Allies forced the Axis forces to surrender. During the fighting, the Allies lost about 6000 men and the Axis forces about 12,000. The Allies took about 140,000 Axis men as prisoners. However, what detracted from the success of Operation Husky was the inability of the Allies to prevent over 100,000 German and Italian troops and 10,000 vehicles from being evacuated to the Italian mainland. When the Allies did eventually attack the Italian mainland in September, these soldiers and weapons were used against them.

The fall of Mussolini

On 25 July, at the height of the fighting in Sicily, King Victor Emmanuel III removed Mussolini from his position as *Duce* and placed him under arrest. Marshall Pietro Badoglio, who declared that Italy would continue to fight alongside Germany, replaced him. However, Badoglio carried out secret talks with the Allies to arrange the surrender of Italy, which was formally signed

KEY TERM

USAAF United States Army Air Forces – the USA's air force during the Second World War.

RAF Royal Air Force – the British air force.

Duce 'Leader', the title assumed by Mussolini in 1922 as dictator of Italy.

on 8 September. The surrender created problems for Germany because it had to alter its plans. Hitler decided to secure control of Italy, send more troops there and make a robust defence of the peninsula.

The end of the Italian campaign

Allied forces landed on the Italian mainland on 9 September but encountered fierce German resistance at Salerno. Their progress through Italy was slow and, as a result, they launched a new strategy. On 22 January 1944, landings were made at Anzio behind German lines in the hope that a rapid assault on Rome could be made. However, Allied forces numbered only two divisions and they were slow moving inland. Any element of surprise was soon lost and **stalemate** followed. It took four offensives before the Germans were pushed back beyond Rome, which was liberated on 4 June 1944.

When Italy surrendered in 1943, the Germans rescued Mussolini and set up the Salò Republic, a puppet regime with the *Duce* as leader. Fighting in central and northern Italy continued until 1945 and the Salò Republic surrendered on 29 April. Some historians have questioned the value of the Italian campaign. The Allies suffered some 300,000 casualties and this theatre of war created more problems for them than it did for the Germans.

The decision to open a Second Front

In January 1943, Roosevelt and Churchill met in Casablanca. They invited Stalin but he declined to attend because of the German siege of Stalingrad. Here they decided that all the necessary conditions required for the invasion of Europe would be ready for action in 1944. In December 1943, Roosevelt, Stalin and Churchill met together for the first time at Tehran in Iran (see pages 91–3). The 'Big Three' now agreed that the **Second Front** would open in May or June of 1944. The USSR agreed to declare war on Japan as soon as Germany was defeated.

Operation Overlord

After the conference, US General Eisenhower became Supreme Commander of the Allied Expeditionary Forces (SHAEF). By the time he took over this post, initial plans for the invasion were under the codename of Operation Overlord.

Secrecy and deception

Secrecy was paramount. Moreover, it was imperative that the Germans were convinced that the invasion would take place in an area other than the site chosen, Normandy, France. The deception plan was named Operation Fortitude.

The British had broken the German codes using **Ultra** and were therefore aware of what Germany was thinking in terms of the Allied invasion. The UK used a double agent, Garbo, to convince them that the invasion would be a two-pronged thrust based on Calais and Normandy, with the more important attack coming at Calais. Operation Fortitude also convinced the

> 🔑 **KEY TERM**
>
> **Stalemate** Situations in which two opposing forces find that any further action is impossible or futile.
>
> **Second Front** Stalin's wish for the USA and the UK to open another theatre of war in France against the Germans in order to take the pressure off the Soviet forces on the Eastern Front.
>
> **Ultra** The British project which successfully decrypted German codes.

Germans that there was a First US Army Group stationed in south-east England at the closest point to France. There was no such group. There was also a fictitious Fourth Army Group in Scotland which was ready to invade Norway. Fake army camps, vehicles and landing craft in south-east England also helped to convince the Germans that the Allies were landing at Pas de Calais.

Preparations for D-Day

The Allies took countless aerial photographs of the Normandy area and the **French resistance** provided information on German defences and troop deployments. The BBC asked British civilians to submit holiday postcards and photographs of the whole of France, and the intelligence services then used the ones of Normandy.

As hundreds of thousands of US soldiers, and thousands of other soldiers from Allied nations, came over to Britain, training, feeding and keeping them occupied created logistical problems. There was more than a year of training for some of the troops and many were killed during **manoeuvres**.

Before the invasion, the Allies needed to have air superiority. In the six months before **D-Day** more than 2600 German fighter pilots were killed and this was an attrition rate that Germany could not sustain. There were specific bombing raids on the German aircraft industry and, by May, the *Luftwaffe* was virtually powerless. On D-Day it flew hardly any **sorties** to challenge the invasion. As D-Day approached, the air campaign began to focus on preventing the Germans' ability to move reserves. French and Belgian railways were crippled, bridges demolished in north-western France, and enemy airfields within a 130-mile (210-km) radius of the landing beaches put under heavy attack. The raids were also synchronized with increased attacks by the French resistance. However, an unfortunate result of the Allied bombing was the death of about 10,000 French civilians.

Perhaps the most important issue for the Allies was neither the invasion nor the deception plans, but the ability to supply thousands of troops once the landings had been made. Floating harbours, nicknamed Mulberries, were constructed because the Allies did not know how long it would be before they had control of any French harbour. An underwater pipeline carrying oil (nicknamed PLUTO – PipeLine Under The Ocean) was built to ensure rapid delivery of fuel for tanks, lorries, motorbikes and so on. Without the Mulberries and PLUTO, the invasion would have stalled.

D-Day, 6 June 1944

D-Day began on the night of 5–6 June when paratroopers and soldiers in gliders landed in Normandy. The USA landed 15,500 airborne troops and the British 7900 behind enemy lines using almost 1000 gliders. Almost 7000 naval vessels assembled in the English Channel off Normandy and the first landings at the designated beaches (Utah, Omaha, Gold, Juno and Sword) were at 6.30a.m. on 6 June. By the end of the day, the Allies had landed

KEY TERM

French resistance Anti-German groups that were based within France which organized fighting for liberty while under German occupation.

Manoeuvres Military exercises simulating actual wartime situations.

D-Day The selected day for the start of Operation Overlord, 6 June 1944.

Luftwaffe The German air force.

Sorties Operational flights of military aircraft.

156,000 troops with supporting mechanized vehicles. The Allied deception plans had worked. Even on D-Day, the Germans continued to believe that the main attack would come at Calais and Hitler would not allow reserves to move to Normandy.

Number of Allied troops landed at the beachheads on D-Day, 6 June 1944

Utah	Omaha	Gold	Juno	Sword
🇺🇸	🇺🇸	🇬🇧	🇨🇦	🇬🇧
23,250	34,250	24,970	21,400	28,845

What can we infer about US invasion forces from Source R?

SOURCE R

Troops of the US Army's First Division landing at Omaha Beach on 6 June 1944 (D-Day).

An estimated 10,000 Allies were injured and 2500 died on D-Day. The heaviest losses were sustained by the USA on Omaha Beach. By the end of July 1944, one million American, British, Canadian, French and Polish troops, hundreds of thousands of vehicles and supporting *matériel* had landed in Normandy.

The breakout from Normandy

Despite the successful establishment of **bridgeheads** around the four landing beaches, the Allies found it difficult to break out into Normandy and beyond because of the **bocage**. The Allies' position was improved on 25 June

KEY TERM

Bridgehead An advanced position seized in hostile territory.

Bocage Thick hedgerows 10–13 feet (3–4 m) high which tanks and infantry found almost impossible to negotiate.

77

Looking at Source S, why were Allied forces able to break out of Normandy?

SOURCE S

The deployment of Allied forces on D-Day and their movement inland during June–August.

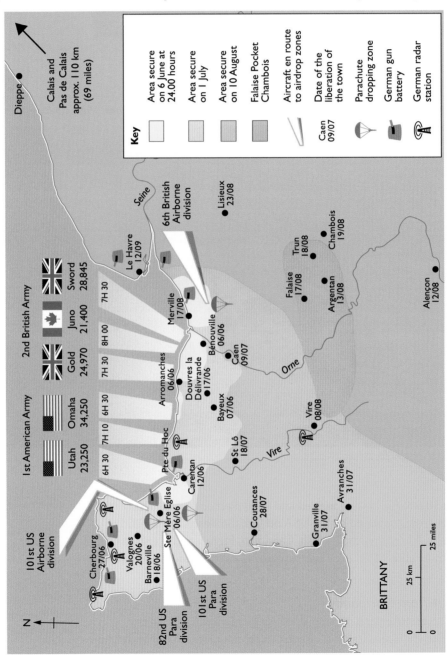

Key

Area secure on 6 June at 24.00 hours

Area secure on 1 July

Area secure on 10 August

Falaise Pocket Chambois

Aircraft en route to airdrop zones

Caen 09/07 — Date of the liberation of the town

Parachute dropping zone

German gun battery

German radar station

Dieppe

Calais and Pas de Calais approx. 110 km (69 miles)

1st American Army

Utah 23,250
Omaha 34,250

6H 30
7H 10
6H 30

2nd British Army

Gold 24,970
Juno 21,400
Sword 28,845

7H 30
8H 00
7H 30

82nd US Para division

101st US Para division

101st US Airborne division

Cherbourg 27/06
Valognes 20/06
Barneville 18/06
Ste Mère Eglise 06/06
Carentan 12/06
Pte du Hoc
St Lô 18/07
Coutances 28/07
Granville 31/07
Avranches 31/07

Arromanches 06/06
Douvres la Délivrande 17/06
Bayeux 07/06
Bénouville 06/06
Merville 17/08
Le Havre 12/09

6th British Airborne division

Caen 09/07
Vire 08/08
Lisieux 23/08

Seine

Orne

Vire

Falaise 17/08
Trun 18/08
Chambois 19/08
Argentan 13/08
Alençon 12/08

BRITTANY

N

0   25 km
0   25 miles

when the port of Cherbourg was taken. The Mulberries had suffered damage in violent storms which made it difficult to adequately supply the troops. However, a more easterly port was still needed to bring in the huge amount of supplies for the ever-growing forces. Further advances into Normandy were made in July when St Lô and Avranches were taken in the west and then Caen in the east.

The Allies advanced quickly after the breakout from Normandy and reached the suburbs of Paris on 24 August. On 25 August, **Free French** soldiers, led by General Charles de Gaulle, were allowed to liberate Paris. However, Cherbourg was still the main port for bringing in *matériel* and the Channel ports (Dieppe, Le Havre and Boulogne) were still in German hands. The Allies reasoned that if the war could be brought to a quick end, then their supply problems would be of little importance. With this desire, General Montgomery suggested an airborne attack behind the German lines. This was an attack on Arnhem, in the Netherlands – Operation Market Garden. It was estimated that success would mean that the Western Allies would be in Berlin by Christmas 1944.

More than 30,000 British and US airborne troops were flown behind enemy lines on 17 September to capture the eight bridges spanning the network of canals and rivers on the Dutch–German border. Logistical problems such as poor radio communication, bad weather and poor intelligence (which failed to detect the presence of the Second SS *Panzer* Corps) all contributed to the failure of the operation. More than 10,000 Allied soldiers were killed in the operation. The Germans lost only 2000.

KEY TERM

Free French The military units led by General Charles de Gaulle after the fall of France in 1940.

The Battle of the Bulge, December 1944 to January 1945

In December 1944, Hitler made his final attempt to defeat the Allies in the west. He wanted to split the Allied forces and prevent them from using the port of Antwerp, Belgium. The Allies were still experiencing supply problems (it was taking five gallons of fuel to deliver just one gallon to the front (5 litres for 1 litre)). If successful, Hitler hoped that the UK and the USA would make a separate peace, independent of the USSR.

The offensive was made through the Belgian Ardennes and achieved total surprise. The Germans made rapid advances into Belgium and Luxembourg, creating a 'bulge' in the US lines.

US casualties were about 19,000 killed and 60,000 injured. The Germans suffered about 100,000 casualties, which included about 20,000 killed. However, the results of the Battle of the Bulge were devastating for the Germans. Their final reserves had been used and they found themselves being pushed back in the west and the east; they could no longer hold back the Allies' juggernaut.

In March 1945, the Allies pushed across the River Rhine and, in April, Soviet forces captured Berlin (see page 70). Germany, unable to match the Allies in men and supplies and trapped in a vice with the USSR in the east and the

US, British and other Allied forces in the west, surrendered on 8 May 1945, eight days after Hitler had committed suicide.

The US contribution to the defeat of Hitler was decisive because, without its supplies, the UK and the USSR would have found it impossible to continue the war. The USA was fortunate not to have its mainland suffer attack and hence there was never any disruption to its manufacturing output. It had the raw materials, workforce and management skills to manufacture war *matériel* on a massive scale. The USA was, as Roosevelt said, 'the arsenal of democracy'.

SOURCE T

German advances at the Battle of the Bulge.

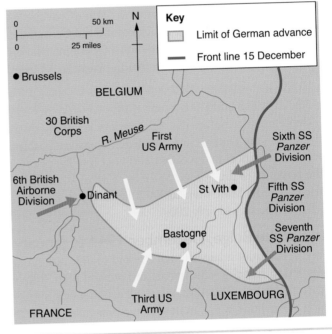

? Look at Source T. Why was the German attack dangerous for Allied forces?

Table showing US losses 1941–5

	Killed	Injured	Total
Military	416,000 (including the merchant marine and coast guard)	670,000	1,086,000
Civilian	1,700	120	1,820

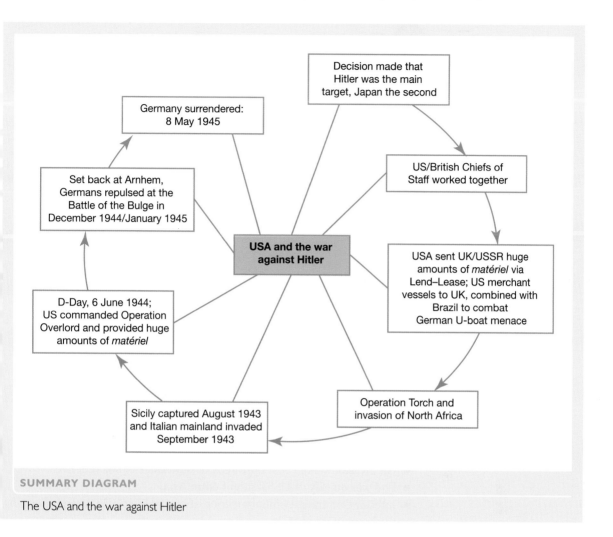

SUMMARY DIAGRAM

The USA and the war against Hitler

Chapter summary

The military role of the USA during the Second World War

Having spent the 1930s pursuing a policy of neutrality and then two years avoiding involvement in the European war, there was some irony that the USA found itself declaring war on an Asian nation in 1941. Yet, when involvement did come, the USA did not shun its responsibilities. The USA mobilized its people and industry with tremendous efficiency. Vast quantities of war *matériel* were supplied to its Allies, in particular the UK and the USSR, through the Lend–Lease agreement. The USA's own military forces were successful in the Battle of the Atlantic, the Pacific War against Japan, and in Africa and Europe against the forces of Germany.

Operation Overlord could not have taken place without the contribution of the USA. The construction of the amphibious fleet, the aircraft, men and logistical support were not within the capabilities of the UK. The success of the Second Front was a result of the US war machine.

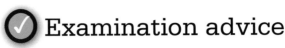

✓ Examination advice

How to answer 'to what extent' questions

The command term <u>to what extent</u> is a popular one in IB exams. You are asked to evaluate one argument or idea over another. Stronger essays will also address more than one interpretation. This is often a good question in which to discuss how different historians have viewed the issue, which does not mean dropping in as many historians' names as possible. It is better to identify different schools of thought and evaluate these. Finally, it is not very convincing to suggest that an event or an issue was 100 per cent this or 100 per cent that. It would be better to look for nuances in your argument.

Example

> <u>To what extent</u> was President Truman justified in ordering the atomic bomb attacks on Japan?

1 To fully answer this question, you should think of as many reasons as you can for and against Truman's decision. This will help hone your argument. Your essay should be based on supporting evidence, not generalized statements about whether or not you feel it was an immoral decision.

2 First take at least five minutes to write up a list of possible reasons and historians' major arguments.

For:
- Japan refused unconditional surrender.
- US invasion would cost hundreds of thousands of soldiers' lives.
- End war quickly or USSR might enter Asia.
- Interim Committee (initial meeting at end of May 1945) urged dropping the bomb immediately.
- In his memoirs, Truman said top military advisers favoured dropping the bomb, as did Churchill.
- High casualty rates on Iwo Jima and Okinawa suggested Japanese would fight to the death.
- Henry Stimson: least possible cost in US Army lives.
- Would avenge Pearl Harbor attack.
- The USA had spent tremendous amounts of money developing the atomic bomb and it would be foolhardy not to use it.

Against:
- Possible to invade Japan.
- It would have been possible to demonstrate the power of the atomic bomb by dropping one over the Bay of Tokyo.
- Better to negotiate on mutually agreeable surrender terms.
- Entry of the USSR into Pacific War would push Japan to surrender.
- Some thought dropping the bomb would precipitate an arms race.

- Some military advisers thought a naval bomb would force Japan's surrender.
- USA would lose high moral ground. Admiral William Leahy thought dropping bomb was unethical. Was the USA acting out of revenge?
- Was the USA motivated by racism?
- Orthodox view: these historians saw Truman's decision as one based solely on military grounds.
- Revisionist view: Truman dropped the bomb to demonstrate US power. The decision was more about keeping the USSR out of Asia. Some of the revisionists felt that the anticipated Soviet entry into the war brought about Japan's surrender.

3 In your introduction, you should define 'justified'. You need to explain this word because your essay should be based on this definition. What factors did Truman consider when making this decision? It is plausible that he wished to avoid further US casualties and end the war as quickly as possible. He may also have wished to prevent the USSR from making territorial and strategic gains in Asia in case the war continued much beyond August 1945. Remember that you are not judged by whichever side you take on the issue. It is more important to write a coherent and well-argued essay that is supported by historical evidence.

An example of a good introductory paragraph for this question is given below.

In early August, 1945, the USA dropped two atomic bombs on the Japanese cities of Hiroshima and Nagasaki. Within days, Japan agreed to surrender without conditions. President Truman, who had only been president for four months, took the decision to unleash this new technology on Japan. For a variety of reasons, Truman felt he had to employ this devastating weapon of mass destruction, chief among them the urgent need to end the war in the Pacific quickly and the fear of enormous casualties if the USA had to invade Japan. In this case, he felt that the reasons for dropping the atomic bomb far outweighed other options available to him at the time, including a demonstration of the power of the atomic bomb without actually destroying one or more cities. That said, justified means more than just his own personal opinions. The word also suggests that other factors played into his decision. Were these as important or more important when he gave the order to drop the bomb?

4 In the conclusion, you will want to summarize your findings. This is your opportunity to support your thesis. Remember not to bring up any evidence that you did not discuss in the body of your essay. An example of a good concluding paragraph is given below.

> In conclusion, President Truman was partially justified in his decision to level two Japanese cities. He desired as quick an end to the bloody war in the Pacific as possible. He felt his actions were necessary to avoid the projected tremendous loss of US lives if an invasion of Japan was undertaken. However, there were other factors beyond just this. Truman did not trust the USSR and he hoped his actions might forestall a rapid expansion of Soviet influence in Asia. In this sense, his actions were not justifiable because he had no way of knowing what Soviet intentions were. Furthermore, not all his military advisers were in agreement about the necessity of dropping the atomic bomb. Some felt there were moral aspects to consider and that the Japanese were in no position to resist a concentrated US invasion of Japan.

5 Now try writing a complete answer to the question following the advice above.

 # Examination practice

Below are two exam-style questions for you to practise on this topic.
1 Assess the military strategy of the USA in the European theatre of the Second World War.
   (For guidance on how to answer 'Assess' questions, see page 106.)

2 Analyse US–Japanese relations prior to December 1941 and how these contributed to the attack on Pearl Harbor.
   (For guidance on how to answer 'Analyse' questions, see page 49.)

CHAPTER 4

The diplomatic role of the USA in the Second World War 1941–5

When Japan attacked Pearl Harbor, the USA faced a single enemy. Four days after the attack, Germany and Italy declared war on the USA. This chapter looks at how the USA needed to be seen to act on Hitler's declaration of war and how it pursued a foreign policy to maintain and improve its position, not only during the war but also in the post-war world.

This chapter also discusses the series of conferences held throughout the war to establish policies and military strategies, although the USA, the UK and the USSR only met twice. There were plenty of disagreements because each country wanted to follow its own interests. The chapter ends with a discussion on US relations with Latin America.

You need to consider the following questions throughout this chapter:

✪ Why was there a series of conferences between the Allies?
✪ Why were the results of the Tehran Conference important for the Allies?
✪ Why was there tension between the Allies at Yalta?
✪ Why were there differences between the Allies at Potsdam?
✪ How did the Second World War change relations between the USA and its Latin American neighbours?

 ## The first Allied conferences: Washington 1941 to Quebec 1943

▶ **Key question:** Why was there a series of conferences between the Allies?

The Allies held a number of conferences during the war, some of which were led by senior political figures and military Chiefs of Staff. Roosevelt met Churchill on many occasions and kept in close contact by telephone and cable, although he only met Stalin twice. Roosevelt and Churchill developed a close relationship but had many disagreements as well, especially towards the end of the war. They tended to disagree about dealing with Stalin, the shape of Europe and the fate of European colonial empires after hostilities ceased.

Washington Conference, December 1941 to January 1942

Co-operation

After Japan's attack on Pearl Harbor and Hitler's declaration of war on the USA in 1941, Roosevelt and Churchill met in Washington to discuss a joint approach. They decided to concentrate on defeating Germany, rather than Japan, and pool Anglo-US military resources under one command. Significantly, the USSR was not included in this conference. Not only was it not at war with Japan, but it also could not be expected to send military staff to the USA at such a crucial period in the war on the Eastern Front.

General George C. Marshall, the chairman of the US Joint Chiefs of Staff, said that the Washington Conference provided '… the most complete unification of military effort ever achieved by two allied nations'.

On 1 January 1942, continuing the theme of co-operation and their vision of a post-war future, Roosevelt and Churchill issued the 'Declaration of the United Nations' which invited all of the countries fighting the Axis powers (Germany, Italy and Japan) to join and pledge to remain together until the Axis powers were defeated. It was hoped that such a pledge would ensure that no one would leave the alliance. (At this time, the term 'United Nations' simply meant those countries which were at war with the Axis powers.)

Disagreements

Among the many substantial agreements made at Washington were several differences of opinion. Roosevelt saw the maintenance of the British Empire after the hostilities as an anachronism and, additionally, wanted to ensure open trading across the world – Churchill disagreed.

The US staff proposed a second front but Churchill opposed this and wanted to defeat the Germans in North Africa first (see page 72). Roosevelt saw the dangers of a British defeat in North Africa and overruled his Chiefs of Staff, thus starting what became Operation Torch (see page 72). Roosevelt prevented a rift with the UK by approving Operation Torch with skilful diplomacy.

Some of the general war aims laid down by Roosevelt and Churchill when the Atlantic Charter was drawn up in August 1941 irked Stalin because some of the ideals it put forward, such as self-determination, were not a part of his own world outlook. In the end, he had to accept that the United Nations were fighting for ideals such as 'religious freedom'. Stalin did make it clear that although he accepted the Charter, he did not wish to be involved in a war with Japan. He needed to concentrate his forces and resources to confront Hitler. Nevertheless, Churchill stated that any differences at the conference concerned 'emphasis and priority' rather than 'principle'.

Casablanca Conference, 14–24 January 1943

← **Why were the decisions at Casablanca important for the Allies?**

Once the German and Italian forces had been forced to retreat in North Africa following the British victory at El Alamein, Roosevelt and Churchill met again, this time in Casablanca, French Morocco. Stalin had been invited to the conference but declined because the siege of Stalingrad (see page 69) was reaching a critical point. The aim of this conference was to decide future strategy. Attacking the Germans in France was the first thing to do. However, the Second Front was still a source of tension between the USA and the UK.

The Second Front

Roosevelt needed to employ all his diplomatic skills during the conference to ensure that Churchill was not disappointed (by any decisions about a second front) and Stalin was not alienated (by the lack of action against France). He had to ensure that Churchill's desire to concentrate action in the Mediterranean did not deflect the USA from starting the Second Front. He and Churchill compromised to make one of the most important decisions of the war, to invade Sicily. The issues of preparation for amphibious landings, support and supply led the Chiefs of Staff to accept that the invasion of France would have to take place in 1944.

To keep up good relations, Roosevelt mollified Stalin to a degree by confirming that the USA would continue to send military *matériel* under the Lend–Lease agreement to the USSR. Roosevelt and Churchill also agreed that a combined bomber offensive against Germany would be launched from Britain, codenamed Operation Pointblank, knowing that, for Stalin, this was a poor substitute for the long-awaited invasion of France.

The policy of unconditional surrender

Usually, wars were ended by negotiations, but it was decided at Casablanca that Germany, Italy and Japan should surrender unconditionally. Roosevelt announced the policy of unconditional surrender at a press conference; doing so without consulting Churchill. Roosevelt wanted it noted that he was driving policy in relations with both Churchill and Stalin.

SOURCE A

Excerpt from Roosevelt's press conference at the end of the Casablanca Conference, 24 January 1943. Quoted from *Traitor To His Class*, by H.W. Brands, published by Anchor, UK, 2009, page 705.

I think we have all had it in our hearts and heads before … that it is the determination that peace can come to the world only by the total elimination of German and Japanese war power. The elimination of German, Japanese and Italian war power means the unconditional surrender … That means a reasonable assurance of future world peace. It does not mean the destruction of the population of Germany, Japan or Italy, but it does mean the destruction of the philosophies in those countries which are based on conquest and the subjugation of other people.

What does Source A suggest as to why Roosevelt was seeking unconditional surrender of the Axis Powers? **?**

Tensions following Casablanca

At the end of the conference, there was a series of letters between Roosevelt and Stalin concerning the decisions taken at Casablanca. Stalin's message of 16 March to Roosevelt was rather threatening – see Source B.

? What does the tone of Source B convey?

SOURCE B

Excerpt from Stalin's message to Roosevelt, 16 March 1943. From *Traitor To His Class*, by H.W. Brands, published by Anchor, UK, 2009, page 708.

I must give a most emphatic warning, in the interest of our common cause, of the grave danger with which further delay in opening a second front in France is fraught. That is why the vagueness of both your reply and Mr Churchill's as to the opening of a second front in France causes me concern, which I cannot help expressing.

Why was the Washington Conference important for Churchill?

→ # Washington Conference, 12–27 May 1943

British Foreign Secretary Anthony Eden visited Roosevelt before this second Washington Conference. Their talks covered the borders of Poland and what should happen to Germany after the war.

When Roosevelt and Churchill met in May, they continued debating the thorny problem of the invasion of Italy and the Second Front. Roosevelt and his military advisers were concerned that any invasion of Italy would result in the diversion of many troops who could be better employed in preparing for the attack on France. His advisers also pointed out that the burden of supplying troops and the civilian population on the Italian peninsula would benefit Germany more than it would the Allies. This could jeopardize the success of the Second Front.

? How useful is Source C in helping you understand the problems of opening up the Second Front?

SOURCE C

German cartoon of 1943, entitled 'Little Winston's fear of water'.

However, when Churchill made a speech to Congress during the conference, Roosevelt was persuaded to side with Churchill and invade Italy. Churchill's powerful oratory won the day.

SOURCE D

An excerpt from Churchill's speech to a joint meeting of the US Congress, 19 May 1943. Quoted from *Churchill: A Life*, by Martin Gilbert, published by Heinemann, UK, 1991, page 746.

Any discord or lassitude [among the Allies] will give Germany and Japan the power to confront us with new and hideous facts. We have surmounted many serious dangers but there is one grave danger which will go along with us until the end; that danger is the undue prolongation of the war. No one can tell what new complications and perils might arise in four or five more years of war. And it is in the dragging out of the war at enormous expense, until the democracies are tired or bored or split, that the main hopes of Germany and Japan must now reside.

> What does Source D show about how Churchill was able to win over the US Congress? **?**

Once Italy was defeated, the Allies decided to invade France on 1 May 1944. The two leaders agreed to discuss details of the operation at future meetings.

Quebec Conference, 17–24 August 1943

← **Why was Quebec significant for US–British relations?**

During the Sicily campaign, Mussolini resigned from office, completely unforeseen by the Allies. As fighting continued, Roosevelt demanded the unconditional surrender of Italy (see page 87). General Eisenhower wanted to offer the Italians some inducements to surrender, hoping that a quick victory would reduce casualties. There was also hope that Italian forces might be used against Germany. However, the demand for unconditional surrender gave Germany time to send additional forces to the peninsula. The reinforcements meant that hopes for a quick victory were dashed and fighting was, as Eisenhower expected, prolonged. Indeed, the campaign in Italy tied down Allied forces unnecessarily and did not hasten the end of the war.

Before the conference, the USA and the UK each considered how best to deal with Italy and the strategy beyond its invasion. The USSR was not included in this meeting because the USA and the UK were to discuss their joint military operations to be carried out during 1943 and 1944.

At Quebec, meetings between the combined Chiefs of Staff soured and discussions about the forthcoming campaign in Italy were rancorous. Later, in his memoirs, Field Marshall Brooke (Chief of the British General Staff) described them as poisonous. Quebec also covered discussions about US strategy in the Pacific War and assistance to the **partisans** in the Balkans. Partisan groups had grown up in countries occupied by the Nazis and one of the strongest groups was in Yugoslavia.

🔑 KEY TERM

Partisans Members of armed resistance groups within occupied territory.

The Balkans and the Far East

Churchill continued his Mediterranean theme and Roosevelt and his advisers ensured that he did not win the debate over the Balkans. It was decided that operations in the Balkans should be restricted to supplying the partisans. General Marshall was concerned that the Pacific War was becoming too much of a subsidiary front and insisted that the war against Japan should be intensified to exhaust Japanese resources. He proposed plans to secure islands close to Japan from which the Japanese mainland could be attacked. In addition, Roosevelt ensured that the South-east Asia Command in the China–Burma–India theatre was established to maintain the supplying of Nationalist China. Roosevelt did not wish to see the Chinese Nationalists, led by Chiang Kai Shek, defeated by Japan.

Operation Overlord

Churchill saw that a force of over two million troops, with a US majority, had to have a US commander. The decision was a clear reminder that the balance of power had shifted to the USA. It was expected that General Marshall would command the operation.

As well as the decision concerning Operation Overlord, the Allies decided to increase the bombing offensive against Germany. There were also discussions about improving the co-ordination of efforts by the USA and the UK in the field of nuclear technology.

The discussions at Quebec raised issues about the end of the war. Peace seemed to be on the horizon, albeit a distant one. The Atlantic Charter and the future of Germany and Poland had already proved to be sensitive issues at the Washington Conference in May. Roosevelt began to see that he had to prepare plans on how to deal with Stalin. He thought that Stalin would remain dependent on the USA for goods for some years after the war, but he was aware that the issues of Germany and Poland would need careful discussion.

Washington Conference, December 1941–January 1942
- USA/UK confirm decision to defeat Germany first
- Issued declaration of United Nations
- Agreed on Operation Torch

Casablanca Conference, January 1943
- Decision made to open Second Front in 1944
- Unconditional surrender of Germany demanded
- Stalin sought an earlier date for the Second Front

First Allied conferences, Washington 1941 to Quebec 1943

Washington Conference, May 1943
- Decision to confirm Italian invasion
- Date set for Second Front as 1 May 1944

Quebec Conference, August 1943
- Tension between USA/UK over Italian campaign
- Continued assistance to China
- Eisenhower chosen to head Operation Overlord
- Bombing campaign against Germany was to be intensified

SUMMARY DIAGRAM

The first Allied conferences, Washington 1941 to Quebec 1943

2 The Tehran Conference and its aftermath

▶ *Key question: Why were the results of the Tehran Conference important for the Allies?*

The Tehran Conference was the first of two conferences held during the war between Roosevelt, Churchill and Stalin (the scond was at Yalta – see page 95). Roosevelt was keen to improve relations between the three Allies and agreed to hold the meeting in Tehran, Iran, during 28 November to 1 December 1943. The venue was convenient for Stalin but not for Roosevelt, whose health was beginning to fail. Roosevelt sought to win the trust of Stalin following the series of conferences in which Churchill had successfully delayed the opening of the Second Front. Roosevelt was now looking to the end of the war and wanted to establish good relations with Stalin.

Roosevelt accepted Stalin's invitation to stay in the Soviet embassy in Tehran during the conference because it was feared that there might still be German agents in the city.

> **The Cairo Declaration**
> *En route* to the Tehran Conference, Roosevelt and his staff met his British counterparts and Chiang Kai Shek. Following discussions, the Cairo Declaration was published. This stated that the USA, the UK and China would strip Japan of all its pre-war and wartime conquests. Roosevelt was keen to ensure that China remained an ally and a counter-point to the USSR.

What decisions were made at Tehran?

The Tehran Conference 1943

At the first meeting, the main areas of discussion dealt with possible future Allied advances, the future of Germany and Poland and the date for Operation Overlord. One suggestion which Stalin immediately rejected was an Allied push through Italy and then a move north-east to the river Danube. Stalin did not like the idea of US and British forces moving towards eastern Europe.

The conference also discussed the outlines of a proposed new world organization to be called the United Nations Organization (see page 97).

Germany

When discussing Germany, the three leaders each agreed that Germany should be broken up into a number of smaller states. Roosevelt wanted the 'Nazi experience' to be removed from German minds and Stalin sought a permanent Allied occupation of German territory.

? What does Source E suggest about Stalin's attitude to Germany?

SOURCE E

A compilation of parts of Stalin's conversation with Churchill and Roosevelt on the first day of the Tehran Conference from TeachingAmericanHistory.org (www.teachingamericanhistory.org/library/index.asp?document=906).

[The] Reich itself must be rendered impotent ever again to plunge the world into war … Unless the victorious Allies retain in their hands the strategic positions necessary to prevent a recrudescence of German militarism, they would have failed in their duty … At least 50,000 and perhaps 100,000 of the German Commanding Staff must be physically liquidated.

🔑 KEY TERM

Buffer state A small and usually neutral state between two rival powers.

Poland

There were major discussions about the future of Poland. Stalin sought to create a **buffer state** but Churchill could not agree. Stalin pointed out that his country had been attacked by Germany in 1914 and 1941. He wanted

Poland's borders to move to the west to provide security for his western borders. He desired a government in Poland that would be friendly to the USSR, as the then exiled Polish government in London was the opposite.

Roosevelt informed Stalin that he could not make a decision about Poland because of the approaching presidential election. It was the wrong time to upset the seven million Polish Americans.

Decisions made at Tehran

The conference was mainly a success for Stalin, who achieved most of what he wanted. The main agreements covered two main areas: the war and the post-war situation.

War aims

- The UK and the USA agreed to open up a second front by invading France, with 1 May 1944 fixed as the date. Stalin promised to attack in the east simultaneously to the cross-Channel invasion.
- Yugoslav partisans were to be given assistance such as supplies and tactical air support. The Yugoslav partisans were very successful in their activities and the Germans had to have large numbers of troops based here to combat them.
- The USA would continue its offensives in the war in the Pacific, including seizure of the Marianas as a base for B-29 raids on Japan.
- Neutral Turkey would be encouraged to enter the war on the side of the Allies before the end of the year. There were to be high-level talks between the Allies and Turkish leaders.
- The USSR was to wage war against Japan once Germany was defeated.

Post-war aims

- The USSR was to have a free hand with Finland. The two countries had been at war in 1939–40 and the USSR had taken ten per cent of Finland's territory and about 30 per cent of its assets.
- Königsberg, part of East Prussia, was to be given to the USSR as an enclave giving access to the Baltic Sea.
- Part of the Italian navy was to be given to the USSR.
- An area of eastern Poland was to be added to the USSR. At the insistence of Stalin, the borders of post-war Poland were to be along the Oder and Neisse rivers.

The conference also pushed Roosevelt into making a decision about the overall commander of Operation Overlord as Stalin expressed his concern yet again about the willingness to open the front when no overall commander had been chosen. It was thought that Roosevelt would choose General Marshall but he selected Dwight D. Eisenhower, seeking to keep Marshall as his closest adviser.

Why were there
disagreements at
Quebec?

Quebec Conference, 12–16 September 1944

Following the successful D-Day landings and eventual breakout in Normandy, Allied forces liberated Paris in August 1944 and the vital port of Antwerp on 4 September 1944. Roosevelt and Marshall decided that with the end of the war seemingly almost in sight, the time was ripe for another meeting with Churchill. Quebec was again chosen as the venue.

The US and British military chiefs had heated debates about the use of the British navy in the Pacific. The US did not want the Royal Navy to participate in the main Japanese theatre. It is thought that the commanders of the US Navy did not want the UK to win credit for the approaching victory. The differences of opinion were the most acrimonious of the almost 200 meetings between the Joint Chiefs of Staff during the war. However, Roosevelt overruled his commanders and the British naval Task Force 57 was set up and served in the Pacific from March to August 1945.

Roosevelt and Churchill initialled the Morgenthau Plan for post-war German deindustrialization which would return Germany to an agricultural nation.

Nevertheless, there were agreements about continued US aid to the UK, British and US **zones of occupation** in Germany and the US invasion of Leyte.

🔑 KEY TERM

Zone of occupation
An area of a defeated country occupied by the victors' armed forces.

Why was the 'percentages agreement' important for the post-war world?

Second Moscow Conference, 9–19 October 1944

A further conference was called to discuss the developing military situation in eastern Europe. Churchill was keen to meet Stalin once again but Roosevelt decided not to attend the Moscow Conference because of the presidential elections. The US was represented by Averell Harriman, US ambassador to Moscow, and John Deane, the head of the US military mission to the USSR. Harriman and Deane were essentially observers and the absence of Roosevelt meant that key issues could not be resolved. Issues such as the future of Poland, the Soviet entry to the Pacific War and the return of Soviet citizens who had been liberated from the Germans in France were discussed and some groundwork was prepared for what was eventually covered at Yalta (see pages 95–6).

The 'percentages agreement'

It was at Moscow that Churchill and Stalin came to the 'percentages agreement'. Churchill suggested that the UK should have 90 per cent influence in Greece and 50 per cent in Hungary and Yugoslavia, while the USSR should have 90 per cent influence in Romania and 75 per cent in Bulgaria. Roosevelt did not ratify Churchill's deal. However, this agreement seemed to anticipate what would eventually happen after the end of the war.

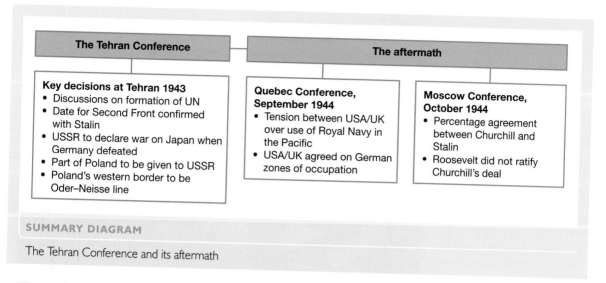

SUMMARY DIAGRAM

The Tehran Conference and its aftermath

The Yalta Conference, 4–11 February 1945

▶ **Key question:** *Why was there tension between the Allies at Yalta?*

By early 1945, Germany was near to defeat, with Allied armies closing in on Berlin. The three allied leaders met at Yalta, a Soviet resort on the Black Sea, in early 1945 to consider what to do with Germany and Europe once victory was achieved. They were still fearful of Hitler despite continued victories against him.

It was clear by Yalta that the two main powers of the world were the USA and the USSR. The UK was almost bankrupt and in some of the discussions, Roosevelt deliberately excluded Churchill. Roosevelt and Churchill had many areas of disagreement such as the future of the monarchy in Italy, Middle Eastern oil, supervision over the election in Poland, and involvement in the Balkans and Greece.

The negotiations at Yalta

The conference dealt primarily with the future of Germany, but also looked at the Pacific War. Roosevelt wanted to settle unresolved issues related to the United Nations with Stalin and to ensure that the USSR would enter the war against Japan. There was also the broader US aim of establishing democracy in Europe. Roosevelt was aware that it would be difficult persuade Stalin to remove his forces from occupied areas when fighting ceased. Stalin wanted to secure control of eastern Europe and create a large buffer zone on the USSR's western borders. Churchill sought to restrict the growth of the USSR

> **What were the aims of the conference?**

What does the clothing of
each leader in Source F
suggest?

SOURCE F

Churchill, Roosevelt and Stalin at the Yalta Conference, February 1945.

but at the same time he realized that he was now very much the junior
member of the 'Big Three'.

**How did tensions
between the Allies
grow at Yalta?**

→ # Agreements made at Yalta

The Big Three agreed the following:

- The USSR would enter the war against Japan three months after Germany
  had surrendered, but this was not made public. The USSR was to be given
  land lost to Japan in their 1904–5 war.
- Germany would be divided into four zones: US, British, Soviet and French.
  Stalin had objected to Churchill's request that France be given a part of
  Germany, so it was decided to create it from the US and British zones.
  Roosevelt was happy to give up part of the US zone because he did not
  want US forces to remain in Europe for too long after the war. (He stated
  that the US people and Congress would put up with about a period of two
  years. Moreover, Roosevelt was keen to secure a definite date for Soviet
  intervention against Japan and surrendering part of the US zone did not
  antagonize Stalin.)
- Berlin, Germany's capital, would be divided into four zones in the
  same way.
- An Allied Control Council would be set up to administer national policies
  for Germany as a whole, and it would consider issues such as reparations
  and war crimes.

- Nazi war criminals would be tried in an international court of justice.
- Countries that had been liberated from German occupation were to have free elections to choose the government they wanted (this was known as the Declaration on Liberated Europe – see page 98).
- The new United Nations Organization would be a global organization (China, France, the UK, the USA and the USSR would be permanent members of the Security Council).

> **The United Nations Organization**
> President Roosevelt first used the term 'united nations' in 1942, to describe the Allied countries which were fighting against the Axis powers. The Tehran Conference (see pages 92–3) discussed the outlines of a proposed new world organization to be called the United Nations Organization (UNO). However, the need for an international organization to replace the League of Nations was first stated officially on 30 October 1943, in the Moscow Declaration, issued by China, the UK, the USA and the USSR.

The UNO's aims

The founding conference of the United Nations (UN) was held in San Francisco, USA, in April 1945. The principles of the UN, as listed in its Charter (which laid down its aims and constitution and was signed by all participating members), were to save future generations from war, reaffirm human rights and establish equal rights for all persons. In addition, it aimed to promote justice, freedom and social progress for the peoples of all of its member states. The UN Charter was officially ratified on 24 October 1945 by the five permanent members of the Security Council. The first meetings of the General Assembly and the Security Council took place in London in January 1946.

The structure of the UNO

The structure of the UNO was confirmed at the Dumbarton Oaks Conference Washington, DC, August to October 1944. China, the UK, the USA and the USSR were involved in negotiations and it was decided that there would be a General Assembly and a Security Council.

The organization of the General Assembly

All member nations were to have equal representation in the General Assembly. It was designed as the forum for the discussion of issues related to the maintenance of international peace and security, the promotion of international co-operation and the advancement of international human rights. It could make peaceful recommendations (resolutions), to member countries or to other UN organizations. The General Assembly was not authorized to pass any resolutions calling for the use of force except in extreme circumstances.

Stalin wanted the Ukraine, Byelorussia and possibly Lithuania to be allowed to sit in the assembly. He felt that otherwise there would be an in-built majority of the Americas and the British Commonwealth. Roosevelt was happy to concede because he knew that power in the UN would be with the Security Council.

The Security Council

The Security Council consisted of the five permanent members (China, France, the UK, the USA and the USSR) and six additional members. The additional members were elected by the General Assembly for a period of two years. Each member was to have one vote. No decision could be made without the approval of seven members of the Council, including all five permanent members. Thus the five permanent members had the power of veto.

Disagreement at Yalta

Although there were many agreements at Yalta, there were some major areas of disagreement about the amount of reparations Germany was to pay and the borders and government of Poland. Roosevelt was aware that the Allies would have to continue to act closely together in a post-Hitler Europe and knew that rifts were beginning to open. However, he thought that his personality would be able to overcome any problems with other leaders. He also hoped that the Declaration on Liberated Europe would establish democracy in eastern Europe.

? Why did Roosevelt consider point (c) of Source G to be vitally important?

SOURCE G

An excerpt from the Declaration on Liberated Europe, February 1945. Quoted from Temple University, USA (isc.temple.edu/hist249/ declaration_of_liberated_europe_.htm).

The establishment of order in Europe and the rebuilding of national economic life must be achieved by processes which will enable the liberated peoples to destroy the last vestiges of Nazism and fascism and to create democratic institutions of their own choice. This is a principle of the Atlantic Charter [see pages 44–5] – the right of all people to choose the form of government under which they will live – the restoration of sovereign rights and self-government to those peoples who have been forcibly deprived to them by the aggressor nations.

To foster the conditions in which the liberated people may exercise these rights, the three governments will jointly assist the people in any European liberated state or former Axis state in Europe where, in their judgment conditions require,

(a) to establish conditions of internal peace;

(b) to carry out emergency relief measures for the relief of distressed peoples;

(c) to form interim governmental authorities broadly representative of all democratic elements in the population and pledged to the earliest possible establishment through free elections of Governments responsive to the will of the people;

(d) to facilitate where necessary the holding of such elections.

However, there was a degree of irony in the publication of the declaration. Despite Roosevelt's hopes, he knew that Stalin would not give up any conquered territory in eastern Europe. He also knew that elections were not free in the southern states of his own country and that the UK would not allow free elections in India.

SOURCE H

Excerpt from *A History of the United States*, by Hugh Brogan, published by Pelican, UK, 1987, page 597.

Roosevelt said repeatedly that the USA would never fight the Soviet Union just for the liberties of Eastern Europeans … He hoped that by exhibiting frank, warm and honest collaboration to the Soviet Union, to induce it to modify the full rigour of its foreign policy and to persuade the Poles, Lithuanians and others to accept the fact of Soviet hegemony.

Can you suggest reasons from Source H why Roosevelt was criticized by some US politicians for his attitude towards eastern Europe?

For Roosevelt, US foreign policy needed to ensure that Stalin was not antagonized, because co-operation between the USA and the USSR was the key to a peaceful world. Yalta seemed to offer the hope of a just settlement but the death of Roosevelt in April 1945 disturbed the international equilibrium and, for the next year, caused US foreign policy to become inconsistent and unpredictable and as a result any hope of a permanent understanding with the USSR gradually evaporated.

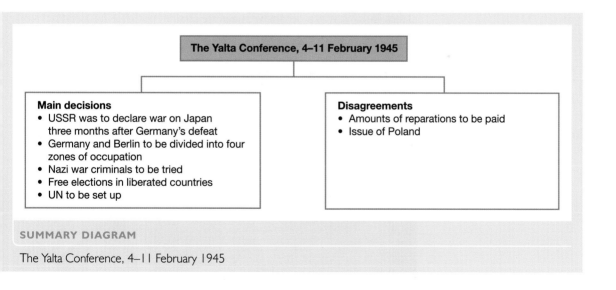

The Yalta Conference, 4–11 February 1945

Main decisions
- USSR was to declare war on Japan three months after Germany's defeat
- Germany and Berlin to be divided into four zones of occupation
- Nazi war criminals to be tried
- Free elections in liberated countries
- UN to be set up

Disagreements
- Amounts of reparations to be paid
- Issue of Poland

SUMMARY DIAGRAM

The Yalta Conference, 4–11 February 1945

The Potsdam Conference, 17 July to 2 August 1945

> ▶ **Key question:** *Why were there differences between the Allies at Potsdam?*

Why did the Allies experience problems at Potsdam?

→ The negotiations at Potsdam

Potsdam Conference

In April 1945, Roosevelt died. Vice-President Harry Truman replaced him. Truman had no experience of foreign affairs but he determined from the beginning to display toughness with Allied diplomats. Truman was different from Roosevelt and distrusted Stalin. He was convinced that the USSR would break its promises and intended to take over the whole of Europe. Truman was determined to stand up to the Soviet leader. By the end of the war, the USSR had occupied Latvia, Lithuania, Estonia, Finland, Poland Czechoslovakia, Hungary, Bulgaria and Romania. The Soviet troops had 'liberated' these countries in eastern Europe but did not remove their military presence. Stalin had set up a communist government in Poland, ignoring the wishes of the majority of Poles and the agreements made at Yalta. Stalin ignored protests from the UK and the USA. He insisted that his control of eastern Europe was a defensive measure against possible future attacks on the USSR.

? What can you infer from the body language of the three leaders in Source I?

SOURCE I

Attlee, Truman and Stalin at the Potsdam Conference, July 1945.

When Germany surrendered in early May 1945, the Allies decided to hold a final conference in Potsdam, Germany. The war in Asia and the future of Germany were the key issues to be discussed. The UK still sought a free Poland and the USA wanted unconditional surrender from Japan and above all some assistance from the USSR in the conflict.

A significant development came on 16 July 1945 when the US successfully tested an atomic bomb at a desert site in the USA. This new weapon encouraged Truman to see the USA as invincible and he knew he could be more robust in his dealings with Stalin. During the conference, Churchill was replaced by Clement Attlee, who had become prime minister following the British general election.

Agreements made at Potsdam

The Allied leaders agreed to the following:

How did the Allies deal with Germany?

- To divide Germany and Berlin as previously agreed at Yalta (see pages 95–7). Each of the four zones of Germany and four sectors of Berlin was occupied and administered by one of the Allies.
- To demilitarize Germany, which meant that it would not be allowed any armed forces.
- The re-establishment of democracy in Germany including free elections, a free press and freedom of speech.
- Germany to pay reparations to the Allies in equipment and materials. Most of this would go to the USSR, which had suffered most. The USSR would be given a quarter of the industrial goods made in the Western zones in return for food and coal from the Soviet zone.
- To ban the Nazi Party. Nazis were removed from important positions in central and local government and leading Nazis were put on trial for war crimes at Nuremberg in 1946.
- To participate fully in the UNO.
- To move Poland's frontier westwards to the rivers Oder and Neisse.

The Potsdam Declaration

The USA, the UK and China issued the Potsdam Declaration on 26 July, which addressed the issue of the war against Japan. It called for:

- Japan's unconditional surrender and warned that the alternative was Japan's 'prompt and utter destruction'
- Japan's sovereignty being limited to four main islands
- Japanese disarmament
- the prosecution of Japanese war criminals
- Japan to promote democratic principles
- the occupation of Japan until these terms were met.

Stalin confirmed that the USSR would declare war on Japan as promised.

Post-war Europe

Key

☐	Land taken by the USSR in 1945
▨	Land taken by Poland in 1945
—	Poland 1921–38
━	Polish frontier after 1945
●	Divided cities occupied by Allied forces

Why were there disagreements at Potsdam?

Disagreement at Potsdam

However, there were disagreements about the amount of reparations to be taken from Germany. Twenty million Russians had died during the war and Stalin wanted compensation that would have permanently crippled Germany. Truman refused. He saw a revived Germany as a possible barrier to future Soviet expansion. Stalin wanted to disable Germany completely to protect the USSR against future threats. Truman did not want Germany to be punished the way it had been by the Treaty of Versailles in 1919.

There were also continued disagreements about free elections. Truman wanted free elections in the countries of eastern Europe occupied by Soviet troops. Stalin refused to submit to US pressure, believing it was unwelcome interference. Truman was furious and began a 'get tough' policy against the USSR. He did not want Stalin to take advantage of his lack of experience in international affairs and wanted to show that he could be robust. Truman also wanted Stalin to keep to the agreements he had already made and felt that displays of overt toughness would bring results.

SOURCE J

Clement Attlee recalling the Potsdam Conference in 1960, from *A Prime Minister Remembers*, by Francis Williams, published by Heinemann, UK, 1961.

The Russians had shown themselves even more difficult than anyone expected. After Potsdam, one couldn't be very hopeful any longer. It was quite obvious they were going to be troublesome. The war had left them holding positions far into Europe, much too far. I had no doubt they intended to use them.

> What are the values and limitations of Source J? ?

The end of the war with Japan

← How was the war brought to an end?

After the USA used atomic bombs on 6 and 9 August 1945 (see pages 61–4), the Japanese announced that it had accepted the USA's demand of unconditional surrender. The surrender document was finally signed on 2 September. Truman and Secretary of State Byrnes wrongly assumed that possession of the atomic bomb was the guarantee of success in any diplomatic negotiations.

The Potsdam Conference, 17 July–2 August 1945

Tension at Potsdam
- President Truman disliked communism
- USSR continued to occupy eastern European countries
- Truman knew that the atomic bomb worked

Main decisions
- Confirmed decision at Yalta to divide Germany and Berlin
- Germany to be demilitarized and democracy re-established
- Nazi Party to be banned
- Reparations to be paid, mainly to USSR
- Potsdam Declaration – agreed policy about the defeat of Japan

Disagreements
- Amount of reparations not decided
- Free elections were not being held by USSR
- Stalin keen to establish buffer zone in eastern Europe

SUMMARY DIAGRAM

The Potsdam Conference, 17 July to 2 August 1945

US–Latin American relations during the Second World War

▶ **Key question:** *How did the Second World War change relations between the USA and its Latin American neighbours?*

When war broke out in Europe in 1939, the USA was keen to ensure that it could develop allies in Latin America. Roosevelt sought to secure, at the very least, the neutrality of his neighbours to prevent any fascist expansion in the area. The USA also wanted to establish military bases and guarantee uninterrupted trade so that vital raw materials could be imported. During the early 1940s, several US missions went to Latin America and signed trade agreements. Roosevelt was able to offer protection, economic and military aid and was largely successful in achieving his aims with Latin America.

By 1945, US influence in Latin America was at an all-time high.

> **How did the USA assist Brazil?**

The USA and Brazil

Before the outbreak of war, Germany had been one of Brazil's major trade partners but as soon as the British blockade of Germany began, trade became difficult. Brazil had been in trade negotiations with Germany in the early part of the European war and had been offered various beneficial trade inducements which would help Brazil during and after the conflict. However, the USA also sought to ensure Brazil's assistance and wanted to develop closer trading and diplomatic relationships. It was clear to Vargas, the leader of Brazil, that the USA could offer loans, technical assistance and a larger market for Brazilian goods.

One of the most important factors behind closer US–Brazilian ties was the US promise to help finance the construction of Brazil's first large-scale steel mill at Volta Redonda. Once the agreements had been reached in September 1940, Brazil ended talks with Germany and allowed the USA to develop military bases on its territory.

> **?** What does Source K suggest about President Vargas' attitude to the USA?

SOURCE K

Excerpt from a speech by President Vargas to Brazilian workers, 1 May 1942. It was published in the *New York Times* on 2 May 1942.

Our solidarity with the USA is ... an obligation based on continental solidarity and the Americas' political unity. So defining ourselves, we declared our desires to maintain peace unless attacked. Notwithstanding Brazil's declaration, Brazil's ships have been torpedoed and lives lost in violation of international law ... To preserve America against the designs of conquerors, we must make it independent, raising a wall of economic resistance ...

Brazil remained neutral until August 1942. There were several German submarine attacks against Brazilian ships between February and August that year and there were more than 1000 casualties. In response, the Brazilian government declared war on Germany and Italy on 22 August 1942.

Brazilian naval forces helped to patrol the south and central Atlantic Ocean, combating German U-boats. The naval base at Recife was used by the US Fourth Fleet.

The USA built several airfields on Brazilian soil with the understanding that shortly after the war ended, they would be handed over to Brazil. The US air base at Parnamirim, in north-east Brazil, became the largest single US air base outside its own territory. The Parnamirim airfield at Natal became the focal point in the Allied air transport system that went east over the Atlantic via Ascension Island to Dakar in French West Africa. Supplies were then sent to either North Africa or the China–Burma–India theatre. Parnamirim was eventually given the nickname 'Trampoline to Victory' because of its major contribution to the war.

Chapter 5 has more detail about Brazil's role in the Second World War.

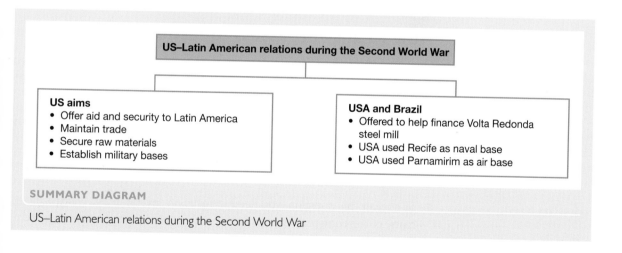

SUMMARY DIAGRAM

US–Latin American relations during the Second World War

The diplomatic role of the USA in the Second World War 1941–5

The USA became involved in the war following Japan's attack on Pearl Harbor and Germany's declaration of war. The USA then found itself at the head of an alliance with the UK and the USSR. It was an alliance whose members did not always see eye to eye. In order to ensure co-ordination of goals and effort, there was a series of conferences which began with setting grand overall ideals in the Atlantic Charter, 1941, and ended with the dismemberment of Germany at the Potsdam Conference in 1945. Roosevelt had to ensure that he maintained US interests as well as satisfying the wishes of Churchill and Stalin. This was not easy and Churchill was sometimes rebuffed. By the time of the Potsdam Conference, Truman, who had become president on Roosevelt's death in April 1945, was antagonistic towards the USSR because Stalin was breaking promises.

Importantly, the USA willingly became involved in the United Nations Organization in 1945 to try to keep peace in the world. The USA ensured that its position as a great power was not diluted by the new organization and the introduction of the veto in the Security Council affirmed this. In addition, the USA tried to keep Latin America on its side by means of offering aid and security.

 # Examination advice

How to answer 'assess' questions

Questions that ask you to assess want you to make judgements you can support with evidence, reasons and explanations. It is important to demonstrate your analytical skills.

Example

> Assess the effectiveness of the various wartime conferences in maintaining Allied unity.

1 To answer this question, you need to focus on several items. Discuss as many of the conferences as you can, while explaining the extent to which these were successful or not in keeping the major powers unified in their strategy to win the Second World War. You will also need to explain the different goals of the USA, the UK and the USSR, and how they may have changed during the war.

2 First, take five minutes to jot down as many of the conferences as you can and how each contributed to allied unity. Your list might look something like this:

Washington Conference (Dec. 1941–Jan. 1942)

- FDR+Churchill agreed to defeat Hitler first in North Africa – Operation Torch.
- Stalin kept out.

Casablanca Conf. (14–24 Jan. 1943)
- FDR+Churchill decided to attack Sicily first.
- Second front in France postponed.
- Stalin declined attendance but was upset at result.
- FDR declared Axis would have to surrender unconditionally.

Washington Conf. (12–27 May 1943)
- FDR+Churchill.
- US still skeptical about Italy campaign but Churchill convinced FDR.

Quebec Conf. (17–24 Aug. 1943)
- FDR+Churchill. Operation Overlord and end of war.
- Stalin absent because conference was about joint US/UK military operations.

Tehran Conf. (28 Nov.–1 Dec 1943)
- FDR+Stalin+Churchill.
- Future of Germany + Poland (Germany divided into three, disagreements over Poland).

Quebec Conf. (12–16 Sept. 1944)
- FDR+Churchill.
- Disagreement over role of British navy in Pacific War. FDR agreed to British role.
- UK/US zones of occupation in Germany.

Second Moscow Conf. (1–9 Oct. 1944)
- Churchill+Stalin+US ambassador.
- Percentages agreement.
- East Europe discussions.
- FDR's absence = unresolved issues.

Yalta Conf. (4–11 Feb. 1945)
- FDR+Stalin+Churchill.
- Achieved: Germany and Berlin divided into four. War criminal trials. UNO = global. USSR to enter Pacific War.
- FDR knew USA and USSR would be two main post-war powers.
- Major disagreements: German reparations, Poland borders.

Potsdam Conf. (7 July–2 Aug. 1945)
- Truman+Stalin+Churchill.
- War in Asia and future of Germany. Truman distrusted Stalin but felt secure (successful A-bomb test).
- Disagreements over German reparations, Eastern Europe.
- Stalin agreed to declare war on Japan.

3 Because of the great amount of information here, you need to choose which issues to focus on. One approach would be to write this essay thematically instead of chronologically. You could choose to concentrate on areas of agreement and disagreement among the three main nations involved. In your introduction you should explain how you will use 'effectiveness' and 'maintaining unity'. An example of a good introduction is given overleaf:

The three main allied powers in the Second World War II, the USA, the USSR and the UK, were able to maintain an effective alliance from 1941 to 1945. It is somewhat remarkable that they could achieve this since each represented different ideologies and aims. The USA hoped to reshape the world so that military action would not be necessary while the UK desired to stop the spread of first fascism and then communism and still be able to keep control of its enormous empire. The USSR was focused on setting up buffer zones and sympathetic allies in eastern Europe to ensure that it was never invaded again from the west. However, all three countries did share one over-arching goal, that of defeating the Axis powers. How they were able to realize this was not without serious disagreements. Conflicts over military strategy, the makeup of a post-war Europe and even the personalities of leaders occurred over the course of the war once the USA joined in December 1941.

4 In the body of the essay, you need to discuss each of the points you raised in the introduction. Devote at least a paragraph to each one. It is a good idea to order these in terms of importance. Be sure to connect the points you raise with the major thrust of your argument, which could be that, overall, the conferences succeeded in keeping the alliance together but there were serious disagreements. An example of how one of the points could be addressed is given below.

At the Casablanca Conference held in January 1942, Roosevelt and Churchill met. Stalin declined to attend as the ferocious battle at Stalingrad was still taking place. The primary goal of the meeting was to plan military strategy in Europe. Roosevelt and Churchill were not of one mind when it came to what would be the next target for US and British forces, the former wanting to attack German forces in France and the latter arguing for an attack in Sicily. Stalin was upset that opening a second front in mainland Europe was delayed because until then, Soviet troops would face the bulk of Germany's forces. Roosevelt hoped to assuage Stalin by informing him that US-produced war materials would continue to flow to the USSR as part of the Lend–Lease programme and that there would be a combined US and British bomber offensive against Germany. These measures did not fully satisfy Stalin. Further strains in the alliance were caused by Roosevelt's surprise announcement that the Allied forces would fight until the Axis powers unconditionally surrendered. Churchill, ever suspicious of Stalin's plans for eastern Europe after the war, understood this to mean that there would be no possibility of a separate peace with Hitler. However, he was in no position to protest as the USA comprised the bulk of the fighting forces in the west. These strains on the alliance would become more serious as the war turned definitively in favour of the Allies and when it was time to restructure post-war Europe. For the time being, though, the alliance held.

5 Now try writing a complete answer to the question following the advice above.

 # Examination practice

Below are two exam-style questions for you to practise on this topic.

1 Compare and contrast the different visions for post-war Europe as discussed at the Yalta and Potsdam conferences.
(For guidance on how to answer 'Compare and contrast' questions, see page 224.)

2 Roosevelt's foreign policy led to a successful outcome for the USA by the end of the Second World War. To what extent do you agree with this statement?
(For guidance on how to answer 'To what extent' questions, see page 82.)

The military and diplomatic role of Canada and Brazil in the Second World War

This chapter begins by examining Canada's military and diplomatic role in the war. Canada declared war on Germany in September 1939. When Japan attacked Pearl Harbor on 7 December 1941, Canada declared war on Japan the day after. The country gave great help to the UK in terms of *matériel* and troops. Canada was a firm ally and played a key role on D-Day (6 June 1944), with Canadian troops on their own landing beach alongside the USA and the UK.

The chapter then goes on to discuss the military roles of Brazil and Argentina during the war. Most Latin American countries broke relations with the Axis Powers of Germany, Italy and Japan, but only Brazil and Mexico sent members of their armed forces into combat. The chapter looks at the reasons for Brazil's contribution and why Argentina actively pursued neutrality only to eventually join the Allies in March 1945.

You need to consider the following questions throughout this chapter:

✪ Why was Canada's role in the Second World War important for the Allies?

✪ How important was Canada's diplomatic role during the war?

✪ Why did Brazil play an active role and Argentina remain neutral for so long?

① Canada's military role in the Second World War

▶ *Key question: Why was Canada's role in the Second World War important for the Allies?*

Canada was an independent country and part of the British Empire and Commonwealth. However, its official head of state was the British monarch and its relationship with the UK was very close. When the UK declared war on Germany on 3 September 1939, there was a two-day debate in the Canadian parliament to determine Canada's reaction. Both houses agreed on a bill to declare war on Germany and it was signed by the British Governor-General on 10 September.

The contribution of Canada's armed forces

← **How did Canada's military role develop?**

This section will consider Canada's military contribution, including its air force and navy, and will look at the army's role in the Dieppe raid and D-Day.

Air force

In September 1939, the Royal Canadian Air Force (RCAF) had about 4000 servicemen, of whom only 235 were pilots. It had 275 aircraft but only 19 were considered modern.

Shortly after the beginning of the war, the British Commonwealth Air Training Plan was established. It was based in Canada and comprised the UK, Canada and other Commonwealth Dominions which offered training programmes for aircrew. It successfully trained about 50,000 pilots, half of whom were Canadian, and a further 80,000 aircrew such as navigators, aerial gunners, bombardiers and flight engineers, from 1940 to 1945.

By 1945, the RCAF had 86 squadrons and 249,000 personnel (of which 17,000 women) in the war. They played a considerable part in the Allied advance across western Europe, among other successful campaigns. In addition, thousands of Canadians fought in the British Royal Air Force. This was a significant contribution to the war effort.

The Canadian air force retained its own identity in the UK and its aircrews saw active service in almost every theatre of war. Its Number 6 group in bomber command suffered more than 4200 aircrew deaths in the bombing campaign over Germany in 1943–5. Some Canadian pilots and naval personnel did serve in Asia but it was only after the war in Europe ended that large numbers were transferred there.

On the civilian front, Canada produced more than 16,000 aircraft of various types. President Franklin Roosevelt praised Canada as the 'aerodrome of democracy'.

During the war 232,632 men and 17,030 women served in the RCAF and 17,101 lost their lives.

Navy

At the beginning of the war, the Royal Canadian Navy had only 1800 servicemen and 15 ships. Although small, it was efficient and well trained. Later, this increased to more than 400 ships comprised mainly of destroyers and corvettes. These vessels were used primarily for anti-submarine warfare and convoy duty during the Battle of the Atlantic (see page 71). Some ships did serve in the Pacific but were used as a defensive force. By the end of the war, the Royal Canadian Navy had almost 100,000 personnel and was the third largest navy among the Allies with 471 ships. Canadian industries also built more than 400 merchant ships between 1939 and 1945. These merchant ships completed more than 25,000 trips across the Atlantic.

Army

Canada only had a small army of about 5000 well-trained soldiers at the start of the war. Its artillery consisted of only 16 light tanks, four anti-aircraft guns and two anti-tank guns. It was supported by a militia of 50,000 but these were also ill-equipped.

By the end of the war in 1945, more than 700,000 men had enlisted in the Canadian army. Around 15,000 women served in the Canadian Women's Army Corps in the European and Pacific theatres of war.

The first part of the Canadian Active Service Force (numbering 7400 of all ranks) sailed for Britain in late December 1939. By 21 February 1940 its strength had grown to 1066 officers and 22,238 other ranks. It was ready for service in France by the spring of 1940. Although some senior officers were sent to France, they returned to Britain following the Dunkirk evacuation. Some Canadian forces did land at the French port of Brest, but spent only a week there and were evacuated from St Malo on 16 June 1940.

Helping the Allies

After the surrender of France, the Canadian army spent 1940 and 1941 training, helping to build defences and guarding beaches ready for the anticipated German invasion.

Additional Canadian forces were also despatched to Iceland to assist the British occupation and stayed six months before being sent on to Britain in October 1940. By the end of 1940 there were 57,000 members of the Canadian army in Britain and 125,000 by the end of the following year.

Two battalions of Canadian troops (approximately 2000) were sent to help the British defend Hong Kong in 1941. Few Canadian soldiers had much experience of military action before arriving in Hong Kong. When the colony was captured by the Japanese at the end of that year, the Canadian soldiers remained prisoners of war (POW) until 1945. Two hundred and sixty-seven died in Japanese POW camps.

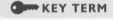
KEY TERM

Mediterranean campaign
The Allied attacks on Sicily and mainland Italy.

As the war progressed, the Canadian government and senior Canadian army officers pressed Allied commanders for their army to be involved in the **Mediterranean campaign**. They did so because it was felt that their forces had not been used sufficiently.

Following Canadian requests to be more actively involved in military actions, it was decided to use Canadian forces in the assault on Dieppe (see below). This was because Canada's military commanders felt that their fully trained troops had seen too little action.

The Dieppe Raid, 19 August 1942

What was Canada's role in the Dieppe raid?

In the early summer of 1942, the Allies decided to mount a major commando raid on the French Channel coast. It was designed to increase the German fears of an attack in the west and force them to divert resources away from other theatres of war. Such an attack would enable the Allies to test new equipment, gain experience of amphibious assaults and, above all, gain valuable experience for the eventual Second Front. Eventually, the port of Dieppe was selected as the target; the codename was Operation Jubilee.

It was decided that some of the Canadian troops (4963) would be used with some British commandos (approximately 1000) and some US Rangers (approximately 50). Dieppe was the first major engagement of the enemy by Canadian forces based in England. The attack on Dieppe took place on 19 August 1942. The raid was supported by eight Allied destroyers, and RAF and RCAF fighter planes.

The attack

The Allies planned to attack and capture the port of Dieppe, hold it for several hours and then withdraw. The troops were taken across the Channel in 250 ships and then transferred to the landing craft ready for a landing in the dark.

The assault was unsuccessful because:

- The element of surprise was lost when some landing craft shot at some German ships, alerting the German shore defences earlier than expected.
- There was a poor choice of landing – there were cliffs which gave defenders the advantage and the beach was unsatisfactory for landing tanks.
- The information on the German defences was out of date.
- The bombing force was withdrawn because smokescreens hampered visibility.
- Heavier naval bombardment was needed because the accompanying destroyers were outgunned by the German land guns.
- The poor communications meant that the force commanders did not receive intelligence from the beaches as a result of the deaths of so many officers.

Within hours of landing, it was decided to evacuate the force. Of the 4963 Canadians who embarked for the operation only 2210 returned to bases in Britain. Nine hundred and seven Canadians lost their lives and 1856 were taken prisoner. (More Canadian prisoners were taken at Dieppe than in the 11 months after D-Day.) The RCAF lost 13 aircraft and the RAF lost 106 aircraft – the highest single-day total of the war.

Despite this failure, the Canadian army did not suffer a loss of morale, but rather it sought to prove itself in future actions. During 1943, the army fought in the campaigns in Sicily and Italy where many casualties were suffered, especially in the Battle of Ortona, where 1372 soldiers died – almost 25 per cent of all Canadians killed in the Mediterranean campaign. The remaining soldiers in Britain began training for D-Day.

Captured Canadian soldiers being marched through Dieppe after the failed raid in 1942.

?

Why was the photograph in Source A widely published in Nazi-occupied territories?

Canada and D-Day

By 1944, Canada's forces were sufficiently large to be given their own section (Codename Juno) in the Normandy landings on 6 June (see pages 76–7). Their first objective was to establish a **beachhead** and advance ten miles (16 km) inland. They were then to capture the strategic airport at Caen and link up with the British beachheads Sword and Gold.

As well as the Canadian infantry, there were some 109 vessels and 10,000 sailors of the Royal Canadian Navy in the massive Allied **armada**. The RCAF also played an important part by bombing key targets before and during D-Day.

Juno Beach

The Canadian forces encountered immediate problems when approaching Juno Beach. The plan was to land at low tide so that German defences would be exposed.

> **How did Canada's military contribute to D-Day?**

> 🔑 **KEY TERM**
>
> **Beachhead** An area on a beach that has been captured from the enemy and on which troops and equipment are landed.
>
> **Armada** A large naval force.

German beach defences
The beaches were covered with mines and tetrahedral obstacles (three iron bars intersecting at right angles) to stop any vehicle from landing.

However, they landed early and consequently the defences were partially hidden by the sea. In addition, many landing craft hit mines and when the infantry began to advance across the beach, the Germans retaliated with sustained machine-gun fire. Despite this, by the end of D-Day, some 14,000 troops of the 3rd Canadian Infantry Division had landed on Juno Beach.

SOURCE B

Quoted from *Six Armies in Normandy*, by John Keegan, published by Pimlico, UK, 2004 and *Citizen Soldiers*, by Stephen Ambrose, published by Touchstone, USA, 1997.

At the end of D-Day, Canadian forward elements stood deeper into France than those of any other division. The opposition the Canadians faced was stronger than that of any other beach save Omaha. That was an accomplishment in which the whole nation could take considerable pride.

What does Source B suggest about the Canadian army? **?**

Look at Source C. What does it show about German resistance at Juno Beach by the afternoon of 6 June 1944? **?**

SOURCE C

Canadian forces landing on Juno Beach on 6 June 1944.

Map of 3rd Canadian Infantry Division landings on Juno Beach showing D-Day objectives and front line at midnight, 6 June 1944.

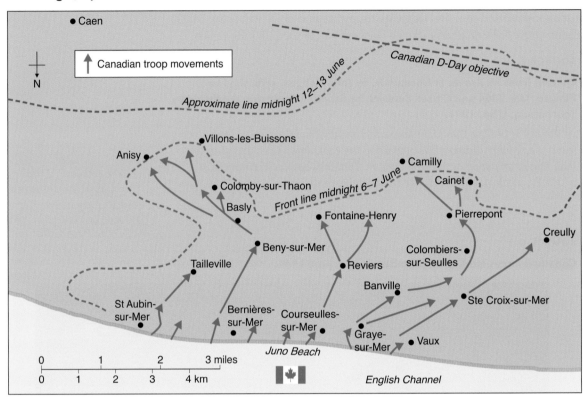

Canadian troops in the Netherlands

Canadian forces were also involved in the Battle of the Scheldt in Belgium and the Netherlands, resulting in the opening of the port of Antwerp, which was crucial for supplying the Allies in the push into Germany.

On 28 April 1945, the Canadians negotiated a truce with German forces in order to permit relief supplies to enter the western Netherlands and end the '**hunger winter**'. By the time supplies were sent, some 22,000 Dutch people had died from malnutrition. To show their appreciation to the pilots who dropped food from the air, many Dutch people painted 'Thank you, Canadians!' on their rooftops.

German forces in the Netherlands surrendered to the Canadian army on 5 May 1945. This was fitting because the Dutch royal family had been in exile in Canada during the war.

?
What does Source D suggest about the Canadian landings on D-Day?

KEY TERM

Hunger winter The famine in the Netherlands during the winter of 1944–5.

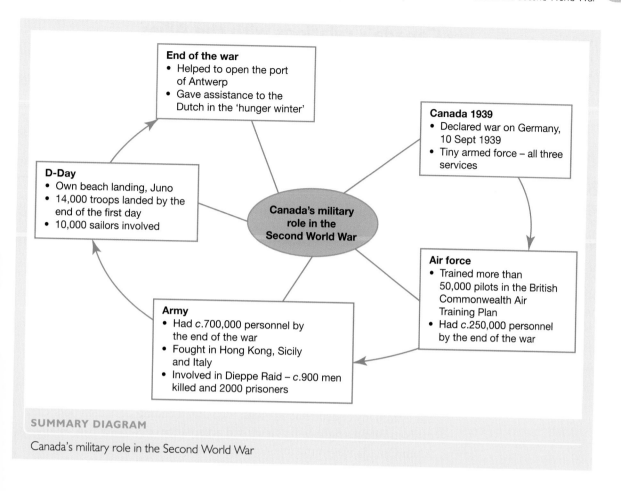

SUMMARY DIAGRAM

Canada's military role in the Second World War

② Canada's diplomatic role in the Second World War

▶ **Key question:** *How important was Canada's diplomatic role during the war?*

Canada's relations with its allies were good throughout the war, developing closer relations with the USA, strengthening those with the UK and balancing the issues relating to France. Canada introduced the Mutual Aid programme in 1943 whereby it assisted its allies with food, raw materials and munitions.

Canada's diplomatic status increased when it hosted the Quebec Conferences (see pages 89–90 and 94), although Prime Minister Mackenzie King was always aware that Roosevelt and Churchill were the leading players and he remained in the background.

Why were Canada's relations different with each of the Allies?

Canada's relations with the Allies

Relations with France

Canada's relations with France were not easy during the war because of the large number of French Canadians in the province of Quebec. French was their first language and they viewed themselves differently to the English-speaking Canadians. Some of these people still looked to France because of the linguistic connection. Many were anti-British and did not wish to be involved in a war which they believed had been caused by the UK. Nor did the *Québecois* wish to support the UK financially and materially.

When the French government surrendered to Germany in 1940, Germany set up the **Vichy government** based in central and southern France. (The French Channel and Atlantic coast were controlled by Germany.) The leader of the Vichy government was Marshal Pétain, whose beliefs – work, family and country – strongly appealed to the right-wing French Canadians in Quebec.

However, the French forces who had escaped to Britain set up their own government in London. The Free French movement was led by General Charles de Gaulle and he vowed to liberate France from the German yoke which caused many French Canadians to support de Gaulle.

For part of the war, Mackenzie King dealt with both de Gaulle and Pétain but eventually ended relations with the latter. Leading Canadian politicians disliked Pétain's right-wing views and acceptance of Nazi control. Moreover, when Canada was in the midst of the conscription crisis (see box on page 119), the Vichy government recommended that French Canadians retain **voluntarism**. This exacerbated an already poor situation because some French-language newspapers in Quebec were openly anti-war, anti-British and **anti-Semitic**.

When de Gaulle visited Ottawa in June 1944, he met Mackenzie King and secured promises of aid from Canada for the future rebuilding of France. This seemed to cement the idea that there would be no dealings with Vichy France in the future.

Relations with the UK

Canada's links with the UK were close and remained so for the duration of the war. Canada supplied the UK with food and war *matériel* worth $2.5 billion. More than half the material that Canada produced went to the UK. The UK was unable to pay for all of the goods, so Canada financed a high proportion, in the interest of helping to win the war and keeping its factories working. At the beginning of 1942, Canada gave an interest-free loan of $700 million to the UK, although many people in Quebec opposed this because they felt it should be spent on Canada itself. Another reason Canada's close relationship with the UK did not sit well with some Canadians was because of Canada's relationship with France.

KEY TERM

Québecois A French-speaking native or inhabitant of Quebec.

Vichy government The puppet government of France after Germany defeated and occupied it in 1940.

Voluntarism The principle of depending on volunteers to join the armed forces.

Anti-Semitic Prejudiced against Jews.

Canada's conscription crisis

Background

There had been a crisis in Canada during the First World War about conscription and politicians were unwilling to resurrect the issue again in the new conflict. At the beginning of September 1939, Prime Minister Mackenzie King promised that there would be no overseas conscription. In June 1940, the Canadian parliament passed the National Resources Mobilization Act (NRMA). The Act meant that the government could requisition property and conscript Canadians for home defence. King's promise of 1939 was upheld by the NRMA but the act was a compromise.

Volunteers

Large numbers of Canadians volunteered for the armed forces as soon as the war broke out in September 1939. Many French Canadians volunteered but wanted to join the traditional French regiments of the army. However, the army chiefs were unwilling to create new regiments or expand existing ones. Thus a pool of volunteers was turned away.

Conscription

However, as the Allies suffered several defeats in the years 1940–2, many in Canada began to suggest that there should be conscription for overseas service. King held a plebiscite in 1942 asking the nation whether the government should introduce conscription, thereby breaking its promise of 1939. The problem of conscription was aptly summed up by King during the many debates, when he said 'conscription if necessary, but not necessarily conscription'. The plebiscite showed English-speaking Canadians in favour of conscription (80 per cent) but 73 per cent of French Canadians in Quebec were largely against it. In Quebec, there was an antipathy towards conscription which went back to the First World War. With a majority of the country supporting conscription, King was able to introduce the bill.

D-Day

However, there was no real need for Canadian reinforcements until after the D-Day landings, when advances were made into Belgium. The Canadian Defence Minister, Colonel J. Ralston, visited Canada's forces and informed King that conscripted troops should be sent immediately. King was unsure what to do and he dismissed Ralston. McNaughton, Ralston's successor, suggested that those serving under the NRMA could volunteer for overseas service but insufficient numbers came forward. Some of the ministers favouring conscription in King's cabinet threatened to resign, forcing the prime minister's hand. King then agreed to send conscripts and about 13,000 men, mostly NRMA, were sent to Europe. However, only about 2500 of the conscripts saw front-line action and about 75 were killed.

There was a brief mutiny of some troops at Terrace, Vancouver, who refused to be sent to Europe but this lasted only a few days and news of it was censored. Those involved were moved to other military bases in Canada.

Relations with the USA

Deteriorating global diplomacy pushed Canada and the USA to consider joint defence matters. President Roosevelt and Prime Minister Mackenzie King met in August 1940 in New York to issue the Ogdensburg Agreement which established the Permanent Joint Board on Defence. The two leaders said that the board (comprising both Canadian and American military and civilian representatives) would consider the defence of the northern half of the Western Hemisphere.

When the USA entered the war, the US Navy took the main responsibility for the defence of the Canadian–US coast but Canada built and controlled its own coastal defence system.

When King visited Roosevelt at his home, Hyde Park, in New York in April 1941, they issued the Hyde Park Declaration which stated that US-produced components of war *matériel* assembled in Canada for the UK were to be included in the Lend–Lease programme (see pages 41–2). It was agreed that Canada would supply the USA with between $200 million and $300 million worth of *matériel*. This deal helped Canada's economy and alleviated Canada's trade deficit.

In the continuing spirit of co-operation, the Canadian government allowed the construction of the Alaska Highway in 1942, which would connect Alaska to the USA through Canada, on the proviso that the USA would pay for the project. Canada would also be allowed to own the Canadian section of the highway when the war ended. However, the USA stationed its own troops along the highway during and after its construction, although they agreed to remove the troops at the end of the war. Canada's relations with the USA were much better than those with the USSR.

Relations with the USSR

As with many countries, Canada had been frightened by the Bolshevik revolution and the spread of Bolshevism. There had been concerns that Bolsheviks had been involved in some Canadian strikes after 1919 and thus Canada kept its dealings with the USSR to a minimum. However, just as with the other Western Allies, there was a change of mind when Germany invaded in 1941. Allying with the USSR against Germany now seemed a favourable option and once relations were established, an embassy opened in 1941 in Ottawa. The USA then used Canada as a conduit to the USSR for US Lend–Lease *matériel* such as aircraft and armoured vehicles.

SOURCE E

? Is Source E an accurate verdict on Canada in the Second World War?

Extract from *The Penguin History of Canada*, by R. Bothwell, published by Penguin, Canada, 2006.

Canada's wartime diplomacy was modest, proportionate and effective. Canada was not a great power and did not attempt to become one, but its government was able to act effectively in the Canadian interest by not overstretching its reach and not abusing its credibility.

When the war ended, almost 45,000 Canadians had been killed and there were about 54,000 casualties, roughly ten per cent of those who had enlisted. There were also some 9000 Canadians who became prisoners of war. Despite all these losses, Canada's foreign relations were solid and it remained a firm ally of the USA and the UK after the war. Financially, the war had cost more than $20 billion but Canada's economy was strong and the post-war outlook was favourable.

Canada's diplomatic role in the Second World War			
Canada and France • Tension with Vichy France and Free French because of Canada's French-speaking population	**Canada and UK** • Agreed to supply UK with food and war *matériel* • Gave monetary loan to UK	**Canada and USA** • Aimed to secure good relations • Ogdensburg Agreement – Canada/USA Permanent Joint Board on Defence established • Canada agreed to supply USA with war *matériel* • Canada agreed to assemble Lend–Lease materials for USA • Canada allowed the USA to construct Alaska–US highway	**Canada and USSR** • Diplomatic relations started when USSR entered the war • Canada allowed USA to send USSR Lend–Lease materials across its territory

SUMMARY DIAGRAM

Canada's diplomatic role in the Second World War

Brazil, Mexico and Argentina's role in the Second World War

> ▶ *Key question: Why did Brazil play an active role and Argentina remain neutral for so long?*

President Roosevelt hoped that he could secure the co-operation of Latin America during the war. His 'Good Neighbor' policy (see pages 18–22) had improved relations but it was not guaranteed that any Latin American country would join the USA in its fight against Germany and Japan.

Brazil's military and diplomatic role in the Second World War

After Pearl Harbor, Roosevelt tried to persuade the Brazilian President Getúlio Vargas to commit troops to the war, indicating that this would give Brazil a superior position when peacemaking eventually happened.

Vargas initially did not wish to become involved in a war that might leave Brazil defenceless against Argentina. Each country vied with the other for the position of the most powerful nation in South America. Roosevelt wanted

> **How did Brazil contribute to the war?**

closer links with Brazil and sought its participation in the fight against Nazism. However, during the 1930s, Brazil grew rather close to Nazi Germany.

Brazilian–German relations

Trade between these two countries increased fourfold during the 1930s. Germany became Brazil's most important trading partner after the USA. When the war in Europe began, Brazil was neutral and remained so after the involvement of the USA. President Vargas followed the 'pendulum policy', that is, he took what he could from both sides of the conflict. However, the naval war in the Atlantic meant that Brazil's exports to Germany fell in value by 400 per cent. Exports to the UK almost doubled in value and exports to the USA rose by ten per cent. The friendship with Germany began to diminish when Germany introduced the Atlantic blockade on the UK and announced that it would sink any ship from the Americas wanting to trade with the UK. This challenged Brazil's neutrality and consequently Brazil broke off diplomatic relations with Germany in January 1942. The USA approved and the Roosevelt administration decided to double the amount of the Lend–Lease aid to Brazil that had been previously allocated in October 1941.

Brazil and the USA moved even closer in May 1942 when they signed an agreement whereby the USA would help to equip the Brazilian army and Brazil would provide materials such as iron ore, chrome, manganese, nickel, bauxite and rubber for the US war effort.

Brazilian entry into the war

In May 1942 the German navy increased its submarine campaign against Brazil and more ships were sunk. During the following month, Hitler ordered further U-boat attacks against Brazil because he felt that Brazil was co-operating too readily with the USA and, in his eyes, this put Brazil in a state of war with Germany. He was aware of the USA using Brazilian air bases and knew of the close trade and commercial links. As more and more ships were sunk, public opinion in favour of the Allies grew, as did antipathy towards Germany. Almost 40 Brazilian merchant ships were sunk, resulting in approximately 1700 dead and 1100 wounded during 1941–2. There were demonstrations in major cities where people burned Axis flags and chanted 'We want war!'

Vargas saw that Brazil could secure a better position in world politics and establish itself as the foremost power in South America if they helped to defeat Germany. He recognized that US military aid would strengthen all sections of Brazil's armed forces and that additional aid would help greatly in the development of its industries.

The Brazilian government declared war on Germany and Italy on 22 August 1942. Within days of the declaration of war, President Vargas gave complete responsibility for the defence of Brazil's coastline to the USA. In addition, its air and naval bases were given over to help in the war effort. These bases became invaluable in the North African campaign (see page 105).

SOURCE F

An excerpt from President Roosevelt's message of 25 August 1942 to President Vargas, following Brazil's declaration of war on Germany and Italy.

I have been informed that a state of war exists between Brazil, on one hand, and Germany and Italy on the other hand. On behalf of the Government and people of the United States I express to Your Excellency the profound emotion with which this courageous action has been received in this country. This solemn decision more firmly aligns the people of Brazil with the free peoples of the world in a relentless struggle against the lawless and predatory Axis powers. It adds power and strength, moral and material, to the armies of liberty. As brothers in arms, our soldiers and sailors will write a new page in the history of friendship, confidence, and cooperation which has marked since the earliest days of independence relations between your country and mine. The action taken today by your Government has hastened the coming of the inevitable victory of freedom over oppression, of Christian religion over the forces of evil and darkness.

> What does Source F show about Roosevelt's attitude to Brazil and its president?

The Brazilian Expeditionary Force

Brazil was the only Latin American country to send its army into combat overseas during the Second World War. In 1944, the Brazilian Expeditionary Force (BEF) and the air force's First Fighter Group were sent to Italy. The BEF comprised just over 25,000 soldiers. It joined the US Fifth Army and fought in the Italian campaign (see pages 74–5) until the end of hostilities. Altogether, over 15,000 Germans soldiers were captured or surrendered to the BEF during the Italian campaign. Five hundred and nine men of the BEF were killed and 1577 were wounded.

Brazil's military contribution became more significant when Germany's relationship with Brazil deteriorated over trade issues in 1942. The strengthening of US–Brazil relations accrued benefits on both sides, as the USA sent Lend–Lease goods and Brazil exported coffee and cacao. However, US–Argentinian relations took longer to establish because of Argentina's determination to remain neutral.

Mexico's military and diplomatic role in the Second World War

> How did Mexico contribute to the war?

Mexico and the war

At the beginning of the conflict, Mexico looked to enhance trade with Japan and Germany. However, Mexico was unable to make favourable agreements with them and the attractive offers of aid from the USA were taken up. In addition, German U-boat attacks on Mexican shipping in 1942 and a public which feared German and Japanese invasions pushed the Mexican government into declaring war on the Axis powers in June 1942.

The USA offered Lend–Lease aid to Mexico, as a result of which the Mexican armed forces were built up with weapons and training. Furthermore, US capital was used to develop industry and build new factories. In return, Mexico supplied the USA with much needed oil and other raw materials such as mercury, zinc and copper. These crucial goods were readily transported by land and thus their supply was not jeopardized by the naval war.

In terms of its military contribution to the war, the Mexican army had no involvement. However, many thousands of Mexicans joined the US armed forces and served in all theatres of war.

The Mexican air force sent the 201st Fighter Squadron (*Escuadrón Aéreo de Pelea* 201) to serve with the US Fifth Air Force in the Philippines in 1945. The squadron was made up of 300 volunteers and it was commonly known by the nickname *Aguilas Aztecas* (Aztec Eagles). It fought in the liberation of the main Philippine island of Luzon and had little opportunity for aerial combat. The squadron's main tasks were to destroy strategic ground objectives including oil depots, bridges, ground forces, ships and ports. During its fighting in the Philippines, five squadron pilots died and three others died in accidents during training.

Why did Argentina remain neutral for so long?

Argentina's neutrality

Argentina's links with Europe

The government of Argentina wished to remain neutral when war broke out in Europe in 1939 and saw no reason to change when the USA became involved in the war.

Initially, Argentina wanted to stay neutral because it could see a chance of removing the British grip on its economy. The UK controlled transport and had huge investments in the country. It was also Argentina's biggest trading partner; one-third of Argentina's exports went to the UK and more than a fifth of its imports came from the UK.

There were about 250,000 people of German origin in Argentina and many supported Nazi Germany. Some did so because they objected to what they perceived as the heavy influence of the UK and the USA.

There was a general feeling that the conflict could be a means by which Argentina's economy could grow. Indeed, it was felt that neutrality could enable trade with both sides. In 1941, the USA said it would supply arms to Latin American countries but declined to send any to Argentina because of its refusal to renounce its neutrality and join the anti-Axis alliance. Argentina's decision to remain neutral meant that it received no aid from the Lend–Lease programme.

Even when the Argentine government was overthrown after an army coup in 1943, there was no desire to go to war because some of the army leaders had fascist leanings and looked favourably on the regimes in Germany and Italy. However, the USA now started to pressure Argentina into joining its side.

US pressure

There were talks between the USA and Argentina in 1943 about ending neutrality but they failed to produce a settlement. The USA pointed out that Argentina was the only country in Latin America not to have broken off diplomatic relations with the Axis powers. Following this, the USA took action to persuade Argentina to join the Allies' side. Economic sanctions were used such as halting loans, seizing Argentine companies' assets and stopping exports (for example, electronic goods and newsprint).

On top of this, in March 1944, the USA refused to recognize the new government of Edelmiro Farrell and officially broke off diplomatic relations. The USA then announced that it would cease trade with Argentina and that US ships would not dock in Argentine ports. Secretary of State Hull openly talked of Argentina as the Nazi headquarters in the Western Hemisphere. There were even talks between the USA and Brazil about supporting a possible attack on Argentina.

Under such pressure and with the war nearing its end, some of the military leaders of Argentina such as Perón saw that the situation had to be rectified. The USA could not be ignored and a potentially hostile neighbour (Brazil) had to be placated. Argentina declared war on Germany and Japan on 27 March 1945.

Despite the antipathy of some Argentines towards the UK, many Argentines volunteered to fight for Allied forces during the war. Some 750 fought in the British, South African and Canadian air forces and almost 4000 others volunteered for other services.

Argentina's contribution to the war was negligible whereas Brazil's was extensive and crucial (see Chapter 9). As a result of the Lend–Lease aid from the USA and the construction of air and naval bases, Brazil emerged the strongest country in South America. After the war, many Nazis fled Europe and were allowed to settle in Argentina with permission of the Argentinian government. Indeed, many escaped Europe with assistance from Argentina. Some Nazis also settled in Paraguay and Brazil.

Brazil
- President Vargas tried to keep in with USA and Germany
- Vargas sought best trading deal with USA and Germany
- USA offered Brazil Lend–Lease, October 1941
- 1941–2: Brazil's relations with Germany deteriorated
- German U-boats sank c.40 Brazilian merchant ships
- August 1942: Brazil declared war on Germany and Japan
- Brazil sent 25,000 soldiers to fight in Italy

Mexico
- Initial attempts to increase trade with Japan and Germany
- US offers were attractive
- Fear of Japanese and German invasion
- German U-boat attacks and public opinion pushed Mexico to join USA
- Supplier of oil and minerals to USA, US Lend–Lease aid
- Mexican air force fought in the Philippines
- Many Mexicans volunteered for service in US forces

Argentina
- Strong trading partner with UK
- c.250,00 German immigrants in Argentina
- Not given Lend–Lease by USA
- 1943–4: pressured by USA to join Allies – Argentina refused
- March 1945: declared war on Germany and Japan

SUMMARY DIAGRAM

Brazil, Mexico and Argentina's role in the Second World War

Chapter summary

The military role of Canada and Brazil in the Second World War

Canada played an impressive part in the Second World War. Its air training plan was crucial in the provision of well-trained pilots throughout the war and its army also made significant contributions. Despite the failure at Dieppe, the lessons learnt were valuable for D-Day, where Canada had its own landing beach. The army's contribution was particularly memorable in the Netherlands. In addition, Canada's diplomatic role was important during the war. It was situated away from hostilities and hosted several wartime conferences between the USA and the UK. Furthermore, Canada's economic assistance to the UK and the USSR with the provision of war *matériel* was critical to their ability to wage war against Germany.

Brazil and Mexico played far more active roles than Argentina during the war, with the latter remaining neutral until the final stages in March 1945. As a trading and military partner with the USA and the UK, Brazil gave invaluable help to the war in North Africa and helped to secure Allied victory there. Brazil sent part of its army to fight in Europe and its navy was of great value in the efforts to defeat the German U-boat threat. Mexico was a crucial supplier of oil and metals to the USA and had the added advantage of sharing a land border.

 Examination practice

Below are two exam-style questions for you to practise on this topic.

1 Examine the military and diplomatic role of **one** country in the region during the Second World War.
   (For guidance on how to answer 'Examine' questions, see page 155.)

2 Assess the military and diplomatic activities of **one** Latin American country during the Second World War.
   (For guidance on how to answer 'Assess' questions, see page 106.)

CHAPTER 6

The social impact of the Second World War on the USA

Once the war had started, it became clear that the whole of the USA had to become involved, whether at home or abroad. What could not be anticipated was the impact of the war on US citizens and how they would react to events. The chapter first looks at the treatment of Japanese Americans and Japanese Canadians, the descendants of Japanese immigrants in the Americas and ethnic minorities in the USA during the war. It then considers the changing role of women and analyses the impact of the war on African Americans. Finally, it considers the impact of the war on civil rights and how the war changed life in general for the US people.

You need to consider the following questions throughout this chapter:

✪ How did the war affect Japanese Americans and Japanese Canadians?
✪ How did the war affect other minority groups?
✪ How did the position of women change during the war?
✪ How did the war change the position of African Americans?
✪ What were the effects of the war on civil rights?
✪ How did the war change the lives of US people?

1 The impact of the war on Japanese Americans and Japanese Canadians

▶ *Key question:* How did the war affect Japanese Americans and Japanese Canadians?

This section will consider how the Japanese immigrants and their descendants in the Americas were treated during the war. Generally, treatment was harsh and in countries where there was a significant number of Japanese, little regard was given to their civil rights.

Japanese Americans

The Japanese attack on Pearl Harbor in December 1941 brought a wave of anti-Japanese feeling from most, but not all, Americans.

What was the initial attitude of the US government and public to Japanese Americans?

The USA had a large Japanese immigrant population. About 110,000 lived along the Pacific coast and about 150,000 lived in Hawaii. There were about 15,000 Japanese Americans living elsewhere on the mainland. The deteriorating US–Japanese relations in the 1930s had concerned the US intelligence agencies. Americans of Japanese descent had been under surveillance after 1935. By 1940, the intelligence agencies had the names of potential Japanese activists and within weeks of the outbreak of war, some 3000 Japanese Americans had been arrested.

When the war began, the danger of a Japanese attack on the west coast led to growing pressure to remove people of Japanese descent from the coastal region. This pressure grew due to fears of espionage, sabotage or general acts of disruption. At the beginning of 1942, some of the Californian press claimed that there were around 20,000 Japanese in the San Francisco area ready to take action against the USA. Some people on the west coast who knew the Japanese immigrants well were sympathetic to their neighbours but the majority believed the anti-Japanese propaganda which portrayed Japanese residents as potential spies and a possible threat to internal security. This fear and pressure led to presidential action.

The internment of Japanese Americans

On 19 February 1942, President Roosevelt signed Executive Order 9066. This allowed the US government to relocate the *Issei* and *Nisei*. Some high-ranking officials' opinions about the Japanese reflected the racism inherent in the policy.

Following the Pearl Harbor attack, General de Witt, head of Western Defence Command, openly said that the Japanese race was an enemy race. However, there was also an economic motive behind the policy of relocation. Some Californian farmers saw a way to end Japanese American competition (Japanese American farmers grew 40 per cent of the state's produce). Most of the farms were sold at a loss. Total estimated losses amounted to $500 million in 1942 values. The Japanese Americans were allowed to take only a few possessions with them when they were relocated.

KEY TERM

Issei First generation of Japanese immigrants to the USA.

Nisei The children of first generation Japanese immigrants (*Issei*).

? What does Source A suggest about attitudes to security in the USA?

SOURCE A

Extract from President Roosevelt's Executive Order 9066, issued 19 February 1942, from US National Archives and Records Administration (www.ourdocuments.gov/doc.php?flash=old&doc=74&page=transcript).

I hereby authorize and direct the Secretary of War, and the Military Commanders whom he may from time to time designate, whenever he or any designated Commander deems such action necessary or desirable, to prescribe military areas in such places and of such extent as he or the appropriate Military Commander may determine, from which any or all persons may be excluded, and with respect to which, the right of any person to enter, remain in, or leave shall be subject to whatever restrictions the Secretary of War or the appropriate Military Commander may impose in his discretion. The Secretary of War is hereby authorized to provide for residents of any such area who are excluded therefrom, such transportation, food, shelter, and other accommodations as may be necessary, in the judgment of the Secretary of War or the said Military Commander, and until other arrangements are made, to accomplish the purpose of this order.

The internment camps

More than 100,000 Japanese Americans were moved from their homes on the west coast to ten main relocation camps in bleak parts of the USA in the spring of 1942. Once identified, they were moved to **internment camps**. One such camp was at Topaz in Utah. The camp was 4600 feet (1400 m) above sea level and had a temperature range of 106 °F (41 °C) in the summer to −30 °F (−34 °C) in the winter.

In the internment camps the Japanese Americans acted with great dignity and patriotism. They raised the **Stars and Stripes flag** each morning.

SOURCE B

Excerpt from an interview with Mary Tsukamoto, a Japanese American internee. Here she is describing being taken to an assembly point before being sent to an internment camp. From Smithsonian National Museum of American History (www.americanhistory.si.edu/perfectunion).

And I never will forget, the train stopped and we got off and they put us on a big truck. It looked like one of those cattle cars. Anyway, we stood up because there were no chairs for us to sit on this pickup and crowded into this truck. They drove us to the Fresno Assembly Center. And then we got off there and they told us to get in and there was the barbed wire gate, and the MPs [military police] around there and … we had to go in through that gate and after we got in there we knew that the gate was shut. And so, we saw all these people behind the fence, looking out, hanging onto the wire, and looking out because they were anxious to know who was coming in. But I will never forget the shocking feeling that human beings were behind this fence like animals [crying]. And we were going to also lose our freedom and walk inside of that gate and find ourselves … cooped up there. And the police, the MPs with their guns and some of them had bayonets. But anyway, when the gates were shut, we knew that we had lost something that was very precious; that we were no longer free.

Reactions to internment

At the time, only a few people criticized Executive Order 9066. Some US citizens called the policy 'government racism'. Some disliked the policy because it did not differentiate between *Issei* and *Nisei*. In some US states, Japanese people faced vandalism and even attempts on their lives. Chinese Americans were often subjected to attacks because people thought they looked Japanese. Not all Japanese Americans were interned. Japanese Americans in Hawaii were not interned because martial law was imposed and it was felt that this would reduce the risk of espionage and sabotage.

🔑 **KEY TERM**

Internment camps Places where people were imprisoned or confined without trial.

Stars and Stripes flag The national flag of the USA.

What does Source B tell you about the treatment of Japanese Americans? **?**

Japanese American soldiers

More than 30,000 Japanese Americans served in the US armed forces. The 442nd Regimental Combat Team, almost entirely made up of Japanese Americans, was the most decorated combat force in the US army. It fought in Italy and across southern France and its soldiers were at the liberation of **Dachau concentration camp**. It became known as the 'Purple Heart Battalion', with more than 700 men killed and 9500 **Purple Hearts**, having the highest casualty rate in US Army history.

Other Japanese Americans in the armed forces interrogated Japanese prisoners and translated Japanese documents in the Army's Military Intelligence Section and also assisted the UK in the intelligence war against the Japanese in the Burma conflict. The Women's Army Corps (WAC) recruited 50 Japanese American and Chinese American women and sent them to the Military Intelligence Service Language School at Fort Snelling.

Some Americans pointed out that the USA was at war with Italy and Germany but no Germans or Italians were interned. (About 600,000 Italian aliens (emigrants from Italy who did not have US citizenship) were subjected to strict travel restrictions but these were lifted in October 1942.) Gradually, opposition to the policy grew and in December 1944, the Justice Department, on Roosevelt's approval, allowed internees to return to California.

Nevertheless, many were not released until May 1945. On release, some of those who had not sold their property found that it had been destroyed and possessions ruined. For most internees, it was difficult to begin life again. In 1948, the US Congress passed the American Japanese Claims Act which granted $37 million in compensation to surviving internees. During the 1960s, young Japanese Americans began the Redress Movement which sought compensation and an apology for the internment. The movement continued to stress the point that many had made since 1942, that it had been a gross violation of civil rights. Most of those interned were US citizens and as such the policy was unconstitutional. (In 1988, Congress at last offered an apology for the policy of internment and gave $20,000 compensation to each surviving internee.)

It is worth noting that in the entire war only ten people in the USA were convicted of spying for Japan and these were all Caucasian.

The treatment of Japanese Canadians

At the beginning of Canada's involvement in the war in 1939, there were about 23,000 Canadians of Japanese ancestry in **British Columbia**. Of this total, about 13,000 were born in Canada. Actions against the Japanese Canadian (**Nikkei Kanadajin**) population were taken after the attack on Pearl Harbor. Many Canadians began to show prejudices which, to some extent, had been latent before 1941. Japanese Canadians had experienced

SOURCE C

Shigeo Nagaishi and his family returning to their home in Seattle, 10 May 1945. They had been in the relocation centre at Hunt, Idaho.

discrimination and occasional violence before, but after Pearl Harbor, there were more incidents such as vandalism of Buddhist temples and the Canadian–Pacific Railway Company sacking Japanese Canadian workers. Just as in the USA, there were fears of espionage and sabotage.

More internment camps

On 24 February 1942, a 100-mile (160-km) wide strip inland from the Pacific coast was created. All Japanese men between 18 and 45 years old were removed from that area and sent to camps within the interior of Canada. In the following nine months, all those of Japanese origin were forced to leave the containment strip and were placed in internment camps. Ten camps were set up to house the internees. If internees wished to leave a camp they could do so, but they could not seek work or go to school. With no means to exist, remaining in the camps was the only realistic option. They could not own land and if they were able to lease land they would have to pay high rents. They had to apply for special licences if they wished to grow crops.

Initially, some of the male Japanese Canadians were sent to work on road construction projects in the interior of British Columbia. Some worked on

How useful is Source C as evidence of the treatment of Japanese Americans during the war?

farms on the prairies because of the labour shortage. If they worked on the sugar-beet farms, the males were allowed to have their families with them. Those who did not work were sent to internment camps in Ontario.

An excerpt from an interview with a Japanese Canadian internee called Hideo Kukubo (from http://canadianjapaneseinternmentcamps. wordpress.com/).

I was in that camp for four years. When it got cold the temperature went down as much as 60 below [–60 °C]. We lived in huts with no insulation. Even if we had the stove burning the inside of the windows would all be frosted up and white, really white. I had to lie in bed with everything on that I had … at one time there were 720 people there, all men, and a lot of them were old men.

Women and children were moved to six inland camps set up to house the relocated populace. The living conditions were so poor that when Japanese citizens heard about them, they sent food shipments through the Red Cross. During the period of detention, the Canadian government spent one-third of the per capita amount on Japanese Canadian internees expended by the USA on Japanese American internees.

Japanese Canadian property

The government stated that those in the camps could leave if they had permission but were not allowed to take up work or go to school. In 1943, the Canadian government introduced the Custodian of Aliens measure whereby all the Japanese property which had been under 'protective custody' during the previous year was to be sold off. The Japanese Canadians had been led to believe that their property would be held in trust until they had resettled elsewhere in Canada. However, their property, land and even clothes were sold off. They also lost any money in their bank accounts and stocks and shares were confiscated. As in the USA, prices for their goods were extremely low.

The government used some of the money that was raised from the sale of Japanese Canadians' property for running the internment camps. All of this was completed without permission or consultation. Many Japanese Canadians pointed out that Austrians, Italians and Germans were not interned and could move around Canada freely.

Extract from a statement to the press in December 1941, by Ian King, a leading British Columbia politician and government minister (from www.cbc.ca/history/EPISCONTENTSE1EP14CH3PA3LE.html).

It is my personal intention, as long as I remain in public life, to see they never come back here. Let our slogan be for British Columbia: 'No Japs from the Rockies to the seas.'

? What does this Source D tell you about the treatment of the interned Japanese Canadians?

? What does Source E tell you about attitudes to Japanese Canadians?

The end of the war

Of the 22,000 Japanese Canadians placed in the internment camps, 4000 were stripped of their Canadian citizenship and deported to Japan. After the war, 6000 people were 'repatriated' to Japan by this policy, which many considered racist. There was a public protest which argued that Canadian policy was 'a crime against humanity and that a citizen could not be deported from their own country'. The policy was stopped in 1947.

On 1 April 1949, the Canadian government announced that Japanese Canadians could live anywhere in Canada. However, most of the surviving internees decided not to return to British Columbia. In the following year, compensation of $1.3 million was awarded to 1434 Japanese Canadians for damages to property, but the government refused to award any compensation for civil rights violations. In 1988, 46 years after the first Japanese internment camps, Japanese Canadians were compensated for all that they had experienced during the war. A compensation package was put forward which amounted to $12 million and each surviving internee received $21,000.

The harsh treatment of Japanese immigrants and their Canadian or US-born descendants clearly displayed the racist attitudes of the Canadian and US governments. Initial xenophobia, then a fear of espionage and even sabotage led to governmental policies. For some people, the harsh treatment was a means of restricting the economic power of both Japanese Americans and Japanese Canadians and acquiring their possessions at a very low cost. In Canada, Prime Minister King was also politically motivated. He sought to win votes in British Columbia, where there was an open anti-Japanese feeling.

There was no real debate about the withdrawal of basic human and civil rights at the time. When the war finished, apologies, recompense and redress were given grudgingly and over a period of years.

Both Japanese Americans and Japanese Canadians suffered the same types of government restriction and unlawful policies. Internment, and especially that the majority of internees were American or Canadian citizens by birth, is the most well-known example, yet there are other lesser known aspects, such as enforced repatriation to Japan (by Canada) or the expulsion of Japanese Peruvians to the USA (see pages 134–5) which are equally important to consider.

The impact of the war on Japanese Americans and Japanese Canadians

Japanese Americans
- USA concerned about Japanese espionage, arrested 3000 shortly after Pearl Harbor attack
- February 1942: Executive Order 9066 – Japanese Americans interned
- About 100,000 interned; lost property and most of belongings
- Yet, 30,000 Japanese served in the US Army
- December 1944: slow release of internees began

Japanese Canadians
- Japanese Canadians moved from the west coast areas
- Interned – had to work to pay for their upkeep
- Property sold; bank accounts appropriated
- 6000 deported after the war

SUMMARY DIAGRAM

The impact of the war on Japanese Americans and Japanese Canadians

2 The impact of the war on other minority groups

▶ *Key question: How did the war affect other minority groups?*

Such was the power of the USA that it was able to determine how South American countries dealt with their own Japanese immigrants, especially in Peru.

→ Japanese citizens in South America

The treatment of Japanese Peruvians

At the time of Pearl Harbor, there were about 26,000 people of Japanese descent living in Peru. The USA had been concerned about the possibility of Japanese spies in Latin America before 1941 and moved quickly after Pearl Harbor to ask neighbouring governments to help prevent possible espionage and sabotage.

The US State Department made an agreement with Peru about potential troublemakers and 1800 Japanese Peruvians were arrested and sent to internment camps in the USA. The camps were run by the Immigration and Naturalization Service. On internment, the Japanese Peruvians had their passports confiscated and became stateless people.

The USA also asked Peru to prevent Japanese officials from leaving the country.

What was the situation like for those of Japanese ancestry in South America?

As in the USA and Canada, Japanese Peruvians lost their property and other belongings. Only 79 internees returned to Peru at the end of the war.

The treatment of Japanese Brazilians

Brazil entered the Second World War in August 1942. At the time there were about 200,000 Japanese Brazilians. As soon as war was declared, there were a number of punitive restrictions placed on the Japanese community. Japanese Brazilians could not travel the country without permission and were not allowed to drive cars, and drivers employed by Japanese Brazilians had to have permission from the police.

In July 1943, in a move similar to that of the Canadian government, large numbers of Japanese (and German) immigrants were removed from the Brazilian coast.

Both Japanese Peruvians and Japanese Brazilians suffered restrictions in their movement and lives during the war, and their civil rights were severely infringed.

Native Americans

The position of Native Americans in society

The war had a significant impact on **Native American** people in the USA. They played their part in the war by joining in combat and the general war effort. This involvement began to lead to a greater demand for equal rights.

There were about 350,000 Native Americans living in the USA at the beginning of the Second World War. Most lived on **tribal reservations**. It was as late as 1924 that most Native Americans had finally been granted US citizenship. Life on the reservations had been difficult. Native Americans were marginalized and suffered poverty, poor education and poor health provision. Nevertheless, when war was declared in 1941, they volunteered for military service on a large scale.

The participation of Native Americans in the war

At the beginning of the conflict, there were some 5000 Native Americans serving in the US military and by the end a further 40,000 had enlisted. The number involved was more than ten per cent of the Native American population. However, some who tried to enlist were rejected because they were unfit due to years of poverty, illiteracy and ill health.

One important contribution to the military was the use of 400 members of the Navajo tribe as code talkers, serving in all six Marine divisions, Marine Raider battalions and Marine parachute units. They transmitted coded messages by telephone and radio in their native language, a code that the Japanese never broke.

> **How did the war affect the Native Americans?**

 **KEY TERM**

Native Americans The indigenous people of the USA.

Tribal reservations Areas of land managed by Native American tribes.

In addition, several hundred Native American women served as WACS, WAVES, and in the Army Nurse Corps (see page 141).

The impact of the war

For many Native Americans, the income from a permanent post in the military and work in the war industries meant that their standard of living dramatically improved. By 1944, the annual income of the average Native American was two and a half times greater than that of 1940. During the war, leaders of various tribes came together and formed the National Congress of American Indians, which sought to establish equal rights in areas such as education and health.

At the end of the war, many Native Americans who had served in the war moved to live in urban America; on their return to the reservations, some began to campaign for improved rights.

Hispanic Americans

Hispanic migrants on the west coast of America

There was racial tension during the war between whites and **Hispanic Americans**, the descendants of Mexican migrants and who had settled in the USA, mainly in California, in the late nineteenth and early twentieth centuries. There were also issues with those who came to work in the USA during the war under the Bracero Agreement (see below).

Southern California became a place of conflict in 1942 and 1943. In 1942, there were clashes between members of the armed forces and members of Mexican youth gangs. The area between San Diego and Los Angeles had several military bases and at weekends, as many as 50,000 servicemen could be found in Los Angeles. The servicemen saw the Hispanic Americans as delinquents who spoke and dressed differently, and challenged US values and customs.

The young Hispanics had their own fashion uniform called the **zoot suit**, although many young whites also wore these clothes. The intermittent clashes between the zoot suiters and members of the armed services broke out into continued rioting in June 1943. Police only arrested zoot suiters even though sailors had been known to start the trouble. The mayor of Los Angeles declared the city off limits to US sailors and gradually the rioting subsided.

KEY TERM

Hispanic American A person of Spanish ancestry, particularly Latin American, living in the USA.

Zoot suit A suit with a long jacket that reached to the fingertips, heavily padded shoulders, pleated trousers tapered at the turn-ups and long key chains, occasionally with a wide-brimmed hat.

? Look at Source F, why was there concern about the treatment of those of Spanish American ancestry?

SOURCE F

Excerpt from 'Strong measures must be taken against rioting' in the Los Angeles Times, 9 June 1943, page 4 (from http://invention.smithsonian.org/centerpieces/whole_cloth/u7sf/u7materials/cosgrove.html).

To preserve the peace and good name of the Los Angeles area, the strongest measures must be taken jointly by the police, the Sheriff's office and Army and Navy authorities, to prevent any further outbreaks of 'zoot suit' rioting. While members of the armed forces received considerable provocation at the hands of the unidentified miscreants, such a situation cannot be cured by indiscriminate assault on every youth wearing a particular type of costume. It would not do, for a large number of reasons, to let the impression circulate in South America that persons of Spanish-American ancestry were being singled out for mistreatment in Southern California. And the incidents here were capable of being exaggerated to give that impression.

The Governor of California ordered the creation of a citizens' committee to investigate the cause of the riots. In 1943, the committee issued its report; it determined racism to be a central cause of the riots. At the same time, the mayor of Los Angeles said that the riots were caused by juvenile delinquents and by white southerners, and that racial prejudice was not a factor.

Rioting was just one of the ways in which the war made an impact on Hispanic Americans. Employment was also affected.

Mexican migrant workers

There had been substantial emigration from Mexico to the USA in the early twentieth century as people came to look for work in the border states of California and Texas. They had sought work mainly in agriculture and despite low wages, life in the USA was an improvement on that in Mexico. However, because of the lack of work during the Depression of the 1930s, immigration had stopped and almost 500,000 returned to Mexico. Nevertheless, a 1940 census indicated that there were almost 400,000 people who had been born in Mexico living in the USA. They were called *chicanos* in a derogatory manner by white Americans.

When the USA became involved in the war, farmers soon began to complain that there was a shortage of labour as a result of workers joining the armed forces. In June 1942, the USA and Mexico signed the Bracero Agreement (which stood until 1964) by which Mexican citizens were allowed to work temporarily in the USA. The agreement meant that Mexican workers could be employed in agriculture and on the railroads. It was hoped that this emergency measure would stem the labour shortage. One key point of the agreement stated that Mexicans working in the USA would not experience discriminatory acts of any kind (Executive Order 8802).

Despite this, the Bracero workers did experience discrimination. Many had to long work hours and received poor pay, and lived in run-down, unsanitary housing. Mexican workers went on strike in California because of the low pay and farmers eventually agreed to increase wages.

The Bracero Agreement had an unintended consequence. Prospective workers brought their families with them and this increased pressure on local areas for housing, education and hospitals. By the end of the war, more than 100,000 Braceros were working in the USA and many more had worked temporarily during 1942–5 and returned to Mexico.

Conclusion

The war had an impact on several ethnic groups, including Japanese Peruvians, Japanese Brazilians, Hispanic Americans and Mexicans. Other groups, such as women and African Americans, were also severely affected by the war.

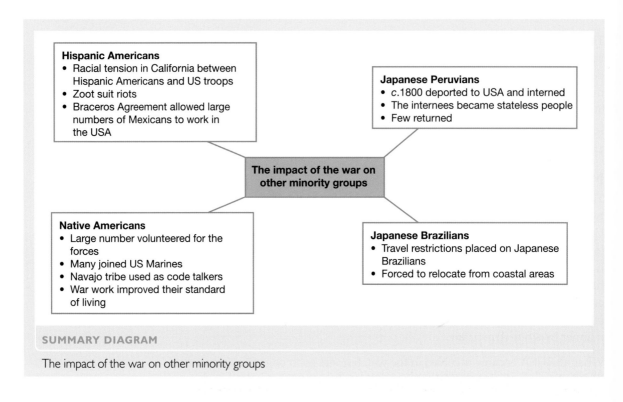

Hispanic Americans
- Racial tension in California between Hispanic Americans and US troops
- Zoot suit riots
- Braceros Agreement allowed large numbers of Mexicans to work in the USA

Japanese Peruvians
- *c.*1800 deported to USA and interned
- The internees became stateless people
- Few returned

The impact of the war on other minority groups

Native Americans
- Large number volunteered for the forces
- Many joined US Marines
- Navajo tribe used as code talkers
- War work improved their standard of living

Japanese Brazilians
- Travel restrictions placed on Japanese Brazilians
- Forced to relocate from coastal areas

SUMMARY DIAGRAM

The impact of the war on other minority groups

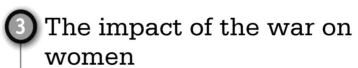

③ The impact of the war on women

▶ *Key question: How did the position of women change during the war?*

This section will look at the changing employment patterns of women during the war and how they were able to work in the armed services.

How did the role of women in work change?

→ The impact of the war on female employment

During the 1940s, the traditional role of a woman was still seen as a wife and mother. Nevertheless, at the beginning of the Second World War, there were about 13 million female workers and at the height of the war in 1944, this figure had increased to 19 million. Many did take on the jobs of men but many employers and male workers considered them inferior colleagues.

Eleanor Roosevelt, the First Lady, was a powerful spokeswoman for female workers during the war.

SOURCE G

An excerpt from an article by Eleanor Roosevelt published in the *Reader's Digest* in January 1944.

Some of the married women workers are not doing their best because we haven't taken into consideration their personal problems. Their homes must still go on. Their children must be cared for. Day nurseries are now being established, but they are not always properly organized. Sometimes they are not located conveniently for the mothers – I was told of one nursery which was five blocks from a bus stop, which meant that a woman had to walk 20 blocks every day. To a tired woman carrying a child, those blocks seem very long.

> What does Source G suggest about the treatment of women during the war? ?

It is clear that women did make a tremendous contribution to the war but there were constant attempts to trivialize their role by the press, male soldiers and those who thought that a woman's place was in the home.

SOURCE H

US servicewomen photographed in 1944, who were in a contest to find the most attractive woman in the US armed forces.

> How useful is Source H as evidence of attitudes towards women during the war? ?

Women and the war effort

Many new jobs during the war were in traditionally 'male' occupations such as the shipyards, aircraft factories and munitions. One in three aircraft workers and half of those working in electronics and munitions were women. Indeed, the pay in munitions work could be double that normally paid to women in 'female' occupations.

In 1942, a poll showed that 60 per cent of Americans were in favour of women helping with the war industries, yet there was a degree of ambivalence to the employment of women throughout the war.

SOURCE I

Excerpt from an interview with a female worker at the Douglas Aircraft factory in Los Angeles. Quoted from *Rosie the Riveter Revisited*, by Sherna Gluck, published by Twayne, USA, 1987, page unknown.

The men really resented the women very much, and in the beginning it was a little bit rough … The men that you worked with, after a while, they realized that it was essential that the women worked there. Because there wasn't enough men and the women were doing a pretty good job, the resentment eased. However, I always felt that they thought it wasn't your place to be there.

Wartime changes

Some US states made equal pay between men and women (for the same role) compulsory, while others tried to protect women from workplace discrimination. However, racial discrimination continued, for instance African American women were, by and large, almost always the last to be hired. There were also many 'hate strikes' such as the ones at the Packard car factory in Detroit as a result of the employment of African American women.

At the end of the war, the majority of women willingly gave up their wartime jobs and returned to their traditional pre-1941 'female' roles. In 1945, despite some progress in the position of women, there were still problems:

- They were generally excluded from the top, well-paid jobs.
- On average, women earned 50–60 per cent of the wage that men earned for doing the same job. In 1944, the average weekly wage for working women was $31.21 and for men it was $56.65.
- A woman could still be dismissed from her job when she married.

How did women serve the USA in the armed forces?

→ # The role of women in the US military during the war

By 1945, the numbers of women serving in the various forces were as follows:

- army: 140,000
- navy: 100,000
- marines: 23,000
- coastguard: 13,000
- air force: 1000
- army and navy nurse corps: 74,000.

The army

The Women's Army Auxiliary Corps (WAAC) was set up in 1941, but there was antipathy from senior members of the army who did not want to accept women directly into its ranks. The WAAC allowed women to contribute to the US war effort directly by carrying out non-combatant military jobs for which they were already trained, such as clerical work. Thus, to some degree, his perpetuated the female employment stereotype and did not create a situation for barriers to be removed or broken.

The Women's Army Corps (WAC) was formed in 1943 and most WAACS transferred across. The creation of the corps was a clear recognition of the work that women had carried out. From a position of being in groups which assisted the army when and where necessary, soldiers of the WACs were now an integral part of the army.

However, there was no improvement in the poor esteem in which the women were held, not only by their male counterparts, but also by much of US society in general. WACs were regularly accused of being promiscuous, something which deterred many women from joining up.

The navy

In 1942, Women Accepted for Volunteer Emergency Service (or WAVES) became a female-only division of the US Navy. The WAVES could not serve aboard ships that went into combat and did not serve in any theatres of war. They were instead involved in clerical, medical, communications, intelligence and technical work. African American women were not accepted into the WAVES until 1944.

The air force

The US Army Air Force (USAAF) established the Women's Flying Training Detachment (WFTD) to teach women to fly. At the same time, the Women's Auxiliary Ferrying Squadron (WAFS) was set up in September 1942 to fly aircraft within the USA. Both of these merged to become the Women Airforce Service Pilots (WASPs).

More than 25,000 women applied to join the WASPs in 1943. Almost 2000 were accepted into WASP training and more than 1000 graduated. The WASP was never a full part of the USAAF, and those who served as WASPs were considered civil service employees. The WASPs were disbanded in December 1944.

Army nurse corps

Army nurses received little training, except in general military matters. Members of the army nurse corps served in theatres all over the world. The importance of nurses can be seen in the changing status of the profession. In June 1944, the army granted its nurses **officers' commissions** and full retirement privileges, dependants' allowances, and significantly, equal pay.

The army nurse corps accepted only a small number of African American nurses during the Second World War – there were only 479 African American nurses serving when the war ended. The army authorities argued that the appointment of African American nurses was limited because they were only allowed to care for black troops in black wards or hospitals.

 **KEY TERM**

Officers' commission
Being granted the position of an officer.

SUMMARY DIAGRAM

The impact of the war on women

4 The impact of the war on African Americans

▶ *Key question:* How did the war change the position of African Americans?

This section will consider the changing position of African Americans and their contribution to the war both at home and abroad. Before the Second World War, African Americans experienced segregation and discrimination in all walks of life. When war broke out, there was increased optimism that things would change. After all, if the USA was fighting fascism and racism, how could it continue to discriminate and deny civil rights to large sections of its own population?

How did the war change employment for African Americans?

Employment and African Americans

In 1940, there were 12.9 million African Americans in the USA. The census of that year showed that there were almost 5.4 million employed, of whom 3.5 million were male. The vast majority of those employed had menial jobs which were low paid. The average annual wage was $537 for men in 1939 and $331 for women. Both earned less than half that of their white counterparts. When the war broke out in Europe, unemployment among whites was 14 per cent and as war-related industries began to seek workers, whites were taken on immediately. Unemployed African Americans did not benefit from this initial boom.

A survey conducted by the US Employment Office in 1940 among the defence industries indicated that more than half would not employ African Americans. In some cases, it was not simply the companies' owners who were propounding discrimination, it was their workers. The owners did not wish to fall foul of their employees.

SOURCE J

Excerpt quoting the president of the North American Aviation Company in 1942 from *Mr. Black Labor*, by D. Davis, published by E.P. Dutton, USA, 1972, page unknown.

While we are in complete sympathy with the Negro, it is against company policy to employ them as aircraft workers or mechanics, regardless of their training, but there will be some jobs as janitors for Negroes.

> What does Source J tell you about attitudes to African American workers at the beginning of the war?

The March on Washington Movement

A. Philip Randolph, one of the most prominent leading African American activists and trade unionists, was appalled at the discrimination not only in the war industries but also in the US armed forces. Randolph called for immediate action and sought to shame the government into action and bring an end to the inequality. He was unwilling to follow the legal and political route that the National Association for the Advancement of Colored People (NAACP) followed (see page 149); he wanted **direct action** and organized the March on Washington Movement. He used the slogan 'We loyal Americans demand the right to work and fight for our country' and proposed a demonstration, a mass march on Washington, DC, together with a possible strike to try to make the government bring an end to discrimination in the workplace.

It was expected that the march would include up to 100,000 demonstrators and, if this were publicized across the world, then it could do little to sustain the USA's image of the upholder of liberty and democracy.

Roosevelt was concerned that the march would discredit and embarrass not only the government, but the USA as a whole. Senior government members and Eleanor Roosevelt were sent to meet Randolph in an attempt to persuade him to call off the march. Even though President Roosevelt openly condemned job discrimination, Randolph refused. Eventually they came to a compromise. Randolph called off the march and Roosevelt issued Executive Order 8802 and set up the Fair Employment Practices Commission (FEPC) to prevent discrimination at work.

However, Randolph did not completely disband the March on Washington Movement. He continued to encourage African Americans to go on protest rallies to ensure that the issue of discrimination remained firmly in the public view. He also encouraged acts of **civil disobedience** to show opposition to laws which permitted unfair and unequal treatment.

🔑 KEY TERM

Direct action The use of acts, such as strikes, marches and demonstrations, to achieve a political or social end.

Civil disobedience A non-violent way of protesting in order to achieve political goals.

? Why were Roosevelt's instructions in Source K important for African Americans?

SOURCE K

President Roosevelt's Executive Order 8802, 25 June 1941.

1. *All departments and agencies of the Government of the United States concerned with vocational and training programs for defense production shall take special measures appropriate to assure that such programs are administered without discrimination because of race, creed, color, or national origin.*

2. *All contracting agencies of the Government of the United States shall include in all defense contracts hereafter negotiated by them a provision obligating the contractor not to discriminate against any worker because of race, creed, color, or national origin.*

Fair Employment Practices Commission

As a result of Executive Order 8802, the FEPC was set up. Paragraph 3 of order 8802 permitted the FEPC to investigate complaints and take action against alleged employment discrimination. As jobs in the defence industries increased, many African Americans migrated from the south in search of employment. They were joined by those in the north who sought better paid jobs. However, when African Americans were hired for jobs most were still given menial posts.

A standard argument in the defence industry was that if African Americans were hired as caretakers or similar, employers would be forced to integrate their workforce. This would not only be expensive but would also be opposed by large numbers of white workers.

By 1943, the FEPC had become aware of widespread discrimination within a number of companies. Roosevelt then issued Executive Order 9346 which gave the commission greater powers, and increased its budget to nearly half a million dollars.

The work of the commission

The FEPC investigated about 8000 instances of discrimination and was successful with 66 per cent of its cases in the north-east, 62 per cent in the mid-west and 55 per cent in the west. There was general failure in the south because of a lack of co-operation from employers and local organizations and only 20 per cent of cases were upheld. During the war, the committee never asked President Roosevelt to revoke any employer's contract because of employment discrimination.

By the end of the war, as a result of the FEPC's work, the number of jobs held by African Americans was at an all-time high. They accounted for eight per cent of defence-industry jobs, whereas before the war they had held only three per cent, and 200,000 were employed by the government, more than three times the number before the war. However, despite this progress, the majority of those employed in all industries still held menial jobs and their average wages was just above half that of white workers.

Trade union involvement increased and African American membership rose from 15,000 in 1935 to 1.25 million in 1945. Members were able to fight for improved working conditions and wages.

The war also meant a broadening of opportunities for African American women. The number who worked in domestic service fell from 75 per cent to less than 45 per cent by 1945. As aviation worker Fanny Christina Hill said, 'The war made me live better. Hitler was the one that got us out of the white folks' kitchen.' Many became nurses but were only permitted to help African American soldiers (see page 141).

However, gains made in the war were small. Increased wages and improved opportunities had to be measured against similar and greater ones made by whites. Opportunities in education and employment prospects were still poor and segregation and discrimination continued. It was only when legislation was passed in the 1950s and 1960s that significant strides were made in achieving civil rights.

SOURCE L

Female workers in the arms industry during the war. This photograph, which is undated but thought to be from about 1940, shows Luedell Mitchell and Lavada Cherry at the El Segundo Plant of the Douglas Aircraft Company, USA.

Why was this photograph shown in Source L published in many US newspapers?

How did the role of
African Americans in
the armed forces
change during the
war?

African Americans and the armed forces

The army

In order to win the African American vote in the 1940 presidential election, Roosevelt promised that the army would comprise the same ethnic mix of society, that is, 90 per cent white and ten per cent African American. Nevertheless, African Americans were still underrepresented by early 1942 and at the end of the war accounted for less than three per cent of all men assigned to combat duty.

 **KEY TERM**

Jim Crow army Segregated
African American army units.
'Jim Crow' referred to US
laws that permitted
segregation.

The war highlighted the racism and discrimination in the armed forces. Many African Americans enlisted in what became known as the **Jim Crow army**. On occasions, African American soldiers were given inferior training, had few recreational facilities, and endured racial slurs and even serious physical mistreatment. Moreover, many white officers thought that African American soldiers were undisciplined, morally wanting, mentally deficient and even cowardly in battle.

They performed the menial non-combat tasks such as cooking, guarding prisoners, delivering supplies, and building camps and roads. They found promotion difficult and the highest rank most reached was first lieutenant. As late as the spring of 1943, only 79,000 out of a total of 504,000 black soldiers were overseas, simply because white army commanders did not want them.

General Eisenhower supported integrated combat units in the Battle of the Bulge but only because he was short of replacements for white soldiers. The 761st Tank Battalion won acclaim in the Battle of the Bulge (see pages 79–80) and received praise from General Patton, a leading US army general. The battalion's nickname was the 'Black Panthers'.

By the end of 1944, there were almost three-quarters of a million African Americans in the US Army and hundreds of officers. Many now fought in integrated combat units. However, the number of African Americans in the army never reached the planned ten per cent of 1940.

Similar to their experience in the army, African American recruits faced discrimination in the air force and navy.

The air force

African Americans had not been allowed to enlist in the developing air force. However, in 1940, President Roosevelt ordered the air corps to recruit an all-African American flying unit. By the end of 1945 more than 600 pilots had been trained, although they were not allowed to fly in the same groups as whites. The all-African American squadron was based in Tuskegee, Alabama. It became known as the Tuskegee Airmen (332nd Fighter Group) and won great acclaim acting as fighter escorts for US bombers.

The navy

Discrimination was worst in the navy with African American sailors given the most dangerous job of loading ammunition on ships bound for war zones. For example, in July 1944 a horrific accident occurred at Port Chicago in California when ammunition that was being loaded on to two vessels detonated, killing 323 people – most of them African American sailors. Hundreds of African American sailors went on strike the following month in protest at the dangerous working conditions. This was called the Port Chicago Mutiny and 50 sailors were arrested and imprisoned. The navy examined its treatment of African Americans in the light of events at Port Chicago and began to effect changes which would help lead to desegregation in the force in 1946.

Marine corps

The US Marine Corps started enlisting African Americans on 1 June 1942 but before 1944 did not allow them into combat. Initially, as in the army, African American **marines** were employed as cooks, labourers and guards.

Racial tension and the African American armed forces

There were many instances of race-related acts of violence within the USA and in the various theatres of war. There were riots at nine African American army-training camps during 1943–4, where the soldiers resented their unequal treatment, and sometimes people were killed:

- An African American soldier was shot by the Little Rock police in 1942.
- An African American soldier was killed in a race riot in Centreville, Mississippi, in 1943.
- Two African American soldiers were killed in riots in El Paso, Texas, in 1943.
- A firefight at Camp Stewart, Georgia, left five injured and one dead in 1943.

The treatment of African Americans abroad, by host nations, was often far better than that given by their own country.

> **KEY TERM**
>
> **Marines** Originally a branch of the US armed forces using the navy to deliver combined forces.

SOURCE M

This 'prayer' appeared in the *Baltimore Afro-American*, 16 January 1943, a weekly newspaper founded in 1842 and published in Baltimore, Maryland, USA.

Draftee's prayer

*Dear Lord, today
I go to war:
To fight, to die
Tell me what for
Dear Lord, I'll fight,
I do not fear
Germans or Japs,
My fears are here.
America!*

> Study Source M. What is the message of this 'prayer'?

? Why might the publication of this letter in Source N have been embarrassing for the USA?

SOURCE N

Excerpt from a letter written in April 1944 by Corporal Rupert Timmingham to the magazine *Yank* about travelling in Texas with other black soldiers. Quoted in *Citizen Soldiers*, by Stephen Ambrose, published by Simon & Schuster, UK, 1997, pages 345–6.

We could not purchase a cup of coffee at a Texas railroad depot but the lunchroom manager said we black GIs could go on around the back to the kitchen for a sandwich and coffee. As we did, about two dozen German prisoners of war, with two American guards, came to the station. They entered the lunchroom, sat at the tables, had their meals served, talked and smoked. I stood on the outside looking on, and I could not help but ask myself why are they treated better than we are? Why are we pushed round like cattle? If we are fighting for the same thing, if we are to die for our country, then why does the Government allow such things to go on?

On 26 July 1948, President Harry Truman signed Executive Order 9981 ending segregation in the US armed forces. This order was a clear indication to the people of the USA that the government was challenging segregation. It had come about because of the fight against fascism in Europe and the contribution of African Americans to the war effort. The fact that President Truman established a Committee on Civil Rights just after the war was another indication that the war had raised awareness of inequalities in US life

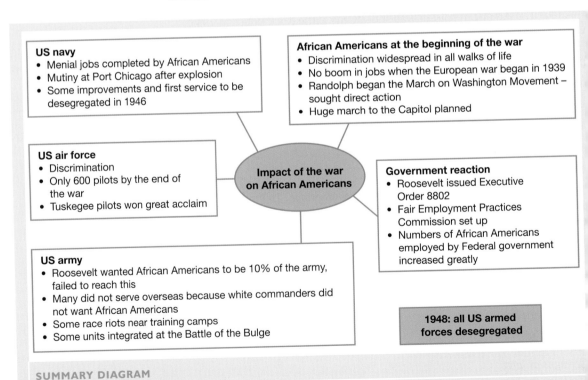

US navy
- Menial jobs completed by African Americans
- Mutiny at Port Chicago after explosion
- Some improvements and first service to be desegregated in 1946

African Americans at the beginning of the war
- Discrimination widespread in all walks of life
- No boom in jobs when the European war began in 1939
- Randolph began the March on Washington Movement – sought direct action
- Huge march to the Capitol planned

US air force
- Discrimination
- Only 600 pilots by the end of the war
- Tuskegee pilots won great acclaim

Impact of the war on African Americans

Government reaction
- Roosevelt issued Executive Order 8802
- Fair Employment Practices Commission set up
- Numbers of African Americans employed by Federal government increased greatly

US army
- Roosevelt wanted African Americans to be 10% of the army, failed to reach this
- Many did not serve overseas because white commanders did not want African Americans
- Some race riots near training camps
- Some units integrated at the Battle of the Bulge

1948: all US armed forces desegregated

SUMMARY DIAGRAM

The impact of the war on African Americans

The impact of the war on civil rights

▶ *Key question: What were the effects of the war on civil rights?*

During the war many African Americans became more active in campaigning for civil rights. New employment opportunities did not always bring improvements in the quality of life, and many pointed out the paradox of fighting fascist nations yet at the same time living in a country which denied equality to many of its own citizens.

African Americans and activism

Increasing activism
Some African Americans cited the Atlantic Charter (see pages 44–5) in their demands for better treatment, although many did not wish to challenge the *status quo* too much, for fear of a white backlash. In addition, they did not wish to be seen as unpatriotic or troublemakers. Yet there was some gradual change. It was noticeable that the number of registered African American voters increased during the war, showing a greater political awareness. In the south, among African Americans the numbers of registered voters rose from three to 12 per cent in the years 1940–7. In the north, activists such as Adam Clayton Powell Jr led the way. He was the first African American elected from New York state and, in 1944, the first elected to the House of Representatives in post-Reconstruction USA from any northern state except for Illinois.

Activism was also more clearly seen through the work of key organizations such as the NAACP and the Congress of Racial Equality (CORE).

The National Association for the Advancement of Colored People
The NAACP had been founded in 1909 by a group of leading African American intellectuals. The main aim of the NAACP was 'to ensure the political, educational, social, and economic equality of rights of all persons and to eliminate racial hatred and racial discrimination'. The NAACP sought to use all legal means to achieve equality. One case was *Smith v. Allwright* in 1944, where the Supreme Court stated that it was unconstitutional for states to prevent African Americans from voting in the Democratic **primaries**.

Throughout the war, growing awareness of discrimination, its injustice and a willingness to challenge it led to a growth in NAACP membership, from 50,000 in 1940 to 450,000 by 1945. Many of these were professionals, although there were also many new urban workers (whose wages now enabled them to afford subscriptions). The NAACP began to play an important part in the **civil rights movement** after the war because it raised

> **How and why did the status of African Americans change because of the war?**

🔑 **KEY TERM**

Status quo A Latin term meaning the existing state of affairs.

Primaries Preliminary elections in which the voters of a state choose a political party's nominee for president.

Civil rights movement A movement that attempts to secure equality in social, economic and political rights.

the profile of issues not only within the African American community but also within the white community, and encouraged activism.

The Congress of Racial Equality

CORE was founded by James Farmer, a civil rights activist, in 1942. CORE was inspired by the non-violent tactics of Mohandas Gandhi in India. Gandhi had confronted British authorities without reverting to violence and had mobilized mass support for his campaign of independence. CORE members felt that putting pressure on the government in wartime might bring about change because it would not wish to be seen to be too harsh on its own citizens. They used non-violent protest to achieve civil rights for African American and started to organize **sit-ins** against segregated restaurants and theatres, which led to the end of segregation in some northern cities in the years 1943–5. CORE continued to grow in importance and was crucial in the civil rights movement in the 1950s and 1960s.

As activism against racial discrimination increased, so did racial tension, especially regarding employment, housing and education.

KEY TERM

Sit-in A form of civil disobedience in which demonstrators occupy a public place and refuse to move as a protest.

The Double V campaign

Despite the valuable contribution that African Americans made to the war effort, they continued to be treated poorly. An African American newspaper, *Pittsburgh Courier*, created the Double V Campaign after readers began commenting on the second-class status of African American workers during wartime. Double V meant victory at home in terms of improved civil rights as well as victory abroad against fascism and dictatorship. The newspaper promoted the campaign by publishing numerous articles, letters and photographs. The effect was immediate and black newspapers across the USA began to support the campaign, thereby raising the profile of civil rights.

Increasing racial tension

There was increased racial tension as a result of the war. With thousands of African Americans migrating from the south to the north, pressure was placed on existing infrastructure. In urban areas such as Chicago, there was a shortage of housing and insufficient schools. Many whites felt that not only jobs but also houses were being taken away from them. The National Housing Agency estimated that the internal migration of US workers amounted to nine million workers who had to be housed. An example of this was Detroit, where 60,000 African Americans had migrated to in order to find work in the car industries in the years 1940–3. The Detroit housing commission indicated that most African American workers' houses were sub-standard.

The rapid growth and overcrowding of African American districts, discrimination in the armed forces and employment, demands for economic and social equality, and African American activists raising public awareness are all factors which contributed to riots during the war.

In Detroit, a riot broke out on 21 June 1943. The army had to be called in to end the disorder. By the time peace had been restored, 34 people had been killed, more than 600 injured and more than 1800 arrested. Damage to property was estimated at $2 million. German and Japanese propaganda broadcasts used the riots to criticize the US government's hypocrisy and encouraged African Americans not to fight for the white, racist 'democracy'. Troops occupied Detroit for six months until President Roosevelt felt it was safe to pull them out in January 1944.

Riots also erupted in Harlem, New York, in August 1943. The immediate cause was the intervention of a black soldier in the arrest of a black woman. In the ensuing fracas, the soldier was shot. Rumours quickly spread that he had been killed and this began the riot. Violence continued for two days during which six African Americans were killed, 300 people were injured and about 500 were arrested. It took 6000 police officers, 8000 state guardsmen and 1500 civilian volunteers to bring the rioting to an end.

There was also rioting in Philadelphia in 1944 when white streetcar workers refused to work with African Americans. Roosevelt had to deploy several thousand federal troops to restore order.

The impact of the war was to make visible many issues and tensions which had previously simmered under the surface. By the end of the war, many things had changed for African Americans.

The situation at the end of the war

By 1945, there had been some progress in employment and the armed forces, and many African Americans had become more active in campaigning for civil rights. On the other hand, discrimination and segregation remained a way of life in the southern states, while the migration of many African Americans to the industrial cities of the north had created greater racial tension. Yet, the work of NAACP, CORE and individuals such as Randolph had ensured that the position of African Americans would be under constant scrutiny and that efforts would continue to bring about further and far-reaching changes.

> **How had the status of African Americans changed by 1945?**

```
┌─────────────────────────────────────────────────────────────────────┐
│                  ┌──────────────────────────────────────┐            │
│                  │   Impact of the war on civil rights   │            │
│                  └──────────────────────────────────────┘            │
│                                                                        │
│  ┌──────────────────┐   ┌──────────────────┐   ┌──────────────────┐  │
│  │ Changes          │   │ Pressure groups  │   │ Reactions of      │  │
│  │ • Greater        │   │ • NAACP grew in  │   │ African          │  │
│  │   political      │   │   membership     │   │ Americans        │  │
│  │   awareness      │   │   from 50,000 to │   │ • Complained     │  │
│  │ • More African   │   │   450,000        │   │   about poor     │  │
│  │   Americans      │   │ • CORE set up in │   │   housing,       │  │
│  │   registered to  │   │   1942           │   │   overcrowding,  │  │
│  │   vote           │   │ • Impact of      │   │   discrimination │  │
│  │ • Greater        │   │   Gandhi         │   │   in the armed   │  │
│  │   employment     │   │ • Double V       │   │   forces         │  │
│  │   opportunities  │   │   Campaign       │   │ • 1943: riots in │  │
│  │                  │   │                  │   │   Detroit and    │  │
│  │                  │   │                  │   │   New York       │  │
│  │                  │   │                  │   │ • 1944: riots in │  │
│  │                  │   │                  │   │   Philadelphia   │  │
│  └──────────────────┘   └──────────────────┘   └──────────────────┘  │
└─────────────────────────────────────────────────────────────────────┘
```

SUMMARY DIAGRAM

The impact of the war on civil rights

6 The impact of the war on everyday life

▶ **Key question:** *How did the war change the lives of US people?*

All sections of US society became involved in the country's quest for victory. President Roosevelt urged Americans to join the war effort by 'out-producing and overwhelming the enemy'. To prosecute the war expeditiously, the government had to introduce measures which had a dramatic impact on the everyday life of all its citizens. The introduction of conscription (see page 38) resulted in more than 12 million men joining the armed forces, which meant that most families had someone serving. Employment opportunities saw large numbers people move to where there were jobs – the industrial north and California, where more than 1.4 million moved. Women become involved in industry and also joined the armed forces (see pages 140–1); however, for those who remained at home life also changed through the implementation of government programmes.

> In what ways did the war affect everyday life?

Government programmes and the war

Rationing

The Food Rationing Program was introduced in the spring of 1942 and did not end until 1947. Coupons were needed to buy goods such as meat, cheese, butter, sugar, milk, eggs, coffee and canned goods. This came as quite a shock for a country used to a plentiful supply of such items. Shopping became difficult as goods became scarce. Housewives grew used to queuing.

The Office of Price Administration (OPA) set up local rationing boards which issued a family's coupons based on the number of people in a household and also their needs. The ration books limited purchases of certain goods by assigning points to goods and allowing each person a certain number of points per year. The number of ration points required for certain items fluctuated each week, which made the task of shopping even more difficult. The OPA was able to control food distribution and prevent shortages. Non-foods such as clothing, car tyres, petrol and oil were also rationed. A speed limit of 35 mph (56 km/hour) (the 'victory speed') was imposed to ensure that petrol was used sparingly and that tyres were preserved.

The government asked people to restrict their consumption of red meat and fats and this resulted in healthier eating. There were even training sessions to teach women how to conserve food and shop wisely. The government also printed recipe books describing how to prepare home-grown vegetables from the 'victory gardens' (see below) to make nutritional and tasty meals. Advertisers encouraged Americans to use less – a popular slogan was 'use it up, wear it out, make it do or do without'.

Rationing also had a serious side effect, the introduction of the black market, where people could secretly buy rationed items but at higher prices in violation of the specified controls.

Victory gardens

In 1941, the Secretary for Agriculture asked the American people to plant 'victory gardens' and to begin growing their own vegetables. This was to permit farmers to concentrate on producing food for the armed forces. The food would also supplement the foods they could buy with their ration stamps. Almost 20 million victory gardens were planted and it was estimated that they produced about 10 million tons of vegetables, which was about 40 per cent of all the vegetables grown in the USA during the war. For many ordinary people planting a victory garden became the most patriotic thing they could do.

Victory gardens were planted in any available space. If people lived in apartment buildings, then the rooftops were used, and if people had no outdoor space, then window boxes were used. People came together and worked co-operatively, pooling their resources and planting a wide range of foods.

There were victory gardens in some unusual places: the prison at Alcatraz, **Ellis Island** and the lawn of the White House. Many schools planted victory gardens on their grounds and used their produce in school lunches. This ensured that the children received nutritious food but the gardens also involved them in doing something positive to help win the war.

 **KEY TERM**

Ellis Island The immigration processing centre in New York from 1892 to 1954.

Other government organizations

It was difficult for US citizens to avoid the requests and demands of the government during the war. The Office of Civilian Defence and people were asked to give 'an hour a day for the USA' to ensure the **blackout** was being obeyed or spend time 'spotting' for enemy aeroplanes.

The Office of War Information co-ordinated war news and Hollywood produced many films to keep up morale, with leading stars such as John Wayne. Even comic book characters such as Superman and Little Orphan Annie were used to maintain morale.

The government also exhorted people to recycle material and asked people to save metal and paper. About 50 per cent of the paper required by the government was provided in this way and thousands of tons of steel and tin were collected by volunteers.

Impact of the war on everyday life
- 12 million men conscripted
- People moved to where jobs were located
- Food rationing began in 1942 and lasted five years
- Office of Price Administration issued ration books
- Black market developed
- Victory gardens encouraged: some 20 million, which grew *c.*10 million tons of vegetables in the war
- Recycling encouraged
- Blackout introduced

SUMMARY DIAGRAM

The impact of the war on everyday life

Chapter summary

The social impact of the Second World War on the USA

The war affected all sections of society and had a profound impact on the daily lives of ordinary Americans. Japanese Americans, Japanese Canadians and those of Japanese descent in the Americas were treated appallingly and found themselves living a life with many restrictions. In Canada, they were deprived of their citizenship, interned, lost property and some were even 'repatriated' to Japan at the end of the war. In the USA, Japanese Americans were interned and lost property.

For women, the war offered many opportunities either working in industry or moving into the armed forces. However, they generally experienced discrimination in both these areas and most were expected to return to their pre-war position when hostilities ceased.

African Americans experienced continued segregation and discrimination yet, by 1945, there were some improvements. Wages had improved (to an extent), there had been grudging acceptance in the forces and the navy had begun to desegregate, giving hope for the future.

The Second World War also influenced and effected change at home. Few families were unaffected by the war. If relatives were not conscripted, then people found themselves working long hours in armaments and armament-related industries, enduring privations as a result of rationing, saving to buy 'War Bonds', and being exhorted to recycle or grow their own food – everyone was to do their duty for their country.

Examination advice

How to answer 'examine' questions

Questions that ask you to <u>examine</u> a particular topic want you to take a very close look at a particular topic while considering both positive and negative results.

Example

> <u>Examine</u> the social and economic impact of the Second World War on minorities in the USA.

1 For this question, you must understand what is meant by minorities. Appropriate groups could be Japanese Americans, African Americans, Hispanic Americans and Native Americans. Women do not constitute a minority. Your focus here should be on social and economic impact, not political impact. It is also worth noting that the question states minorities and not minority – in other words, you should examine more than one minority group although you do not have to use all of the above. Do use the groups for which you think you have the most supporting evidence. Finally, avoid writing a narrative and answer the question. Explain why the social impact on African Americans was what you think it was.
2 Take five minutes to make an outline for each of the groups you plan to use. Delineate between social and economic impact. Do not worry if there are some crossovers for both social and economic impact. You could describe these as socioeconomic impacts.

Japanese Americans
Social impact:

- Japanese Americans living on West Coast were forced into detention centres as a result of Roosevelt's Executive Order 9066 (9 February 1942).
- Even though they were overwhelmingly US citizens, they were subject to abuse and discrimination. Rampant racism.
- Forced to live in close quarters in one of ten desolate military bases.
- Some joined US military to demonstrate their loyalty and patriotism.

Economic impact:

- Forced to sell their properties for low prices.
- Once vibrant economic entity devastated.
- White farmers pushed for internment because Japanese American farmers were rivals.
- Most released in May 1945. Had to begin economic activity again without many resources.
- Partial restitution in 1948 and 1988.

African Americans

Social impact:

- Many joined armed forces.
- Discrimination in housing.
- Overcrowding in urban areas.
- Increased organization among African Americans as a result of unfair treatment.
- War was supposed to be a fight for democracy but in USA there was not much democracy for blacks, especially in southern states.

Economic impact:

- Some factories refused to hire blacks, others kept them in menial jobs.
- Because of Executive Order 8802, overt racism in workplace decreased.
- In government and defence-related industries, large advances in the number of African American workers.
- Union membership also increased greatly.
- Both men and women found greater opportunities than had existed before the war.

Hispanic Americans

Social impact:

- Both native born and immigrants from Mexico faced racism. Riots in California.
- Immigrants brought families with them.
- Often forced to live in substandard housing, poor conditions.

Economic impact:

- Greater employment opportunities offered by need for workers, particularly agricultural ones.
- Bracero Agreement: in order to meet needs, hundreds of thousands of Mexicans allowed to work in USA.
- Poor working conditions led to workers organizing strikes, resulting in higher wages in some cases.

3 In your introduction, state the groups you will be examining and your basic thesis. An example of this is given below:

> During the Second World War most Americans experienced great economic and social changes. This was due to the millions of young men who enlisted in the military and a total reorganization of the industrial direction of the country, one in which millions of formerly unemployed found work. Minority groups including Japanese Americans, African Americans and Hispanic Americans were also

socially and economically impacted by the war. In some cases the impact was very negative while in others the impact was mixed. For the Japanese Americans, the impact of the war was disastrous, while one might argue that African and Hispanic Americans did experience some benefits from a changing social and economic climate. These three groups did experience racism as they tried to assist their country while it was at war. The wartime economy meant there were more job opportunities for many and some betterment in living standards. Paradoxically, employment and higher wages could, sometimes, result in more crowded living conditions and uncertain futures, as well as increased racist attacks.

In your essay, you should devote at least a paragraph to each of the three minority groups you have chosen to examine. While it is sometimes impossible to bring an equal amount of analysis to both social and economic impact, try to balance the analysis so that it is about a 60/40 split (60 per cent on one type of impact, 40 per cent on the other).

In your conclusion, avoid bringing up new information or ideas not discussed in your essay. An example of a concluding paragraph is given below.

In conclusion, the social and economic impact for minorities in the USA was mixed. Japanese Americans on the west coast of the country paid the heaviest price and suffered both socially and economically. African, Hispanic Americans and Mexican immigrants found some economic gains but socially these groups were kept on the margins of mainstream USA. All suffered racism from some groups in the majority but the Second World War did provide these groups with the desire and experience to call for greater and more equitable participation in both the social and economic spheres in the USA.

Now try writing a complete essay for the question.

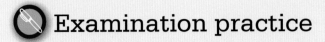

Examination practice

Below are two exam-style questions for you to practise on this topic.

1 Compare and contrast how Japanese Americans and Japanese Canadians were treated by their respective governments during the Second World War.
(For guidance on how to answer 'Compare and contrast' questions, see page 224.)

2. Assess the impact of the Second World War on women in the USA.
(For guidance on how to answer 'Assess' questions, see page 106.)

CHAPTER 7

Reaction to the Holocaust in the Americas

This chapter examines the reaction of the Americas to the treatment of the Jews in Nazi-controlled Europe in the 1930s and 1940s. First, it looks at the USA and considers the changing attitudes towards immigration before moving on to look at how it reacted to Nazi racial policies within Germany. It then considers US action during the Second World War and its policies with regard to the Holocaust. It debates whether President Roosevelt did sufficient to help the victims of the Holocaust, looking at his positive policies, and scrutinizes the State Department and discusses the hindering of admission of refugees into the USA during the Second World War. It concludes by looking at the treatment of Jews and reaction to the Holocaust in Latin America and Canada.

You need to consider the following questions throughout this chapter:

✪ What was the US reaction to Nazi anti-Jewish policies during the 1930s?

✪ What was the impact of the SS *St Louis* case?

✪ How did the US react to Nazi policies during the war?

✪ To what extent did Roosevelt attempt to save European Jews during the Second World War?

✪ How did Latin America and Canada react to the Holocaust?

① The US reaction to Nazi anti-Jewish policies during the 1930s

▶ **Key question:** *What was the US reaction to Nazi anti-Jewish policies during the 1930s?*

During the years 1881–1924, the USA received more than 26 million immigrants. People made the journey to the USA for many different reasons. Land was available for farming, although by 1900, good cheap agricultural land was becoming scarce. The USA was booming industrially, there were many employment opportunities and those with any business acumen could start new ventures quite easily. The USA was the land of opportunity for all. Other immigrants saw the USA as the land of the free and a country which guaranteed basic human rights.

Pogrom An organized massacre of an ethnic group.

Nuremberg Laws A series of measures aimed against the Jews in Germany in 1935. They included the Reich Law on Citizenship, which stated that only those of German blood could be German citizens. Jews lost their citizenship, and the right to vote and hold government office. The Law for the Protection of German Blood and Honour forbade marriage or sexual relations between Jews and German citizens.

Anschluss The union of Germany with Austria, March 1938.

Problems of immigration

Immigration to the USA

Jews from eastern Europe were seeking religious freedom and an escape from the **pogroms** of Russia, where many thousands had been massacred. However, by 1900, there were many in the USA who began to oppose the mass immigration. Intolerance towards immigrants began to grow and there was a feeling that the 'new' immigrants would take jobs and work for very low wages. It was also thought that the immigrants were responsible for increases in crime, drunkenness and prostitution. Above all, many Americans feared that immigrants would bring with them dangerous political beliefs, especially communism.

Restrictions on immigration

As a result of growing intolerance and fear of immigrants, the USA placed tougher immigration restrictions by means of legislation in 1917, 1921, 1924 and 1929. The Immigration Act of 1921 introduced a quota system. New immigrants were allowed in as a proportion of the number of people of the same nationality who had been living in the USA in 1910. The figure was set at three per cent and this figure was reduced to two per cent by the act of 1924. The 1929 act restricted immigration to 150,000 per year. There were to be no Asians at all. Northern and western Europeans were allocated 85 per cent of places. By 1930, immigration from Japan, China and eastern Europe had virtually ceased.

As a result of restrictions there was an anti-immigration climate in the USA by the early 1930s, and the legislation of the 1920s militated against European Jews. Despite the known persecution of Jews in Germany in the 1930s, opinion polls in the USA showed that the public was against increasing immigration quotas. Yet, in 1935, the **Nuremberg Laws** were condemned by many in the USA and *Newsweek* magazine stated that the laws 'relegated the Jews to the Dark Ages'.

Nazi and US policies

This section looks at reactions in the USA to Nazi anti-Jewish policies and the international attempts to assist the growing number of European refugees.

After Germany's *Anschluss* with Austria in March 1938, the situation for Jews in those two countries deteriorated sharply because Hitler felt that he would not be challenged by the international community. Austria's 185,000 Jews were now threatened with the restrictions and attacks on freedom under the Nuremberg Laws. By the end of 1938, Jews were officially excluded from economic life with decrees banning them from shops and businesses, from gaining public contracts and excluding them from schools, universities and cinemas. The number of Jews who left Europe (mainly Germany and

Austria) for the USA, Palestine, China and central and southern America began to rise. On 25 March 1938, Roosevelt called an international conference on the refugee crisis in order 'to facilitate the emigration from Germany and Austria of political refugees'. No other major political leader in any country matched his concern and involvement.

Evian Conference 1938

The conference met in Evian-les-Bains, France, where delegates from 32 countries and representatives from 24 organizations such as the League of Nations Union, World Jewish Congress and the Central Bureau for the Settlement of German Jews convened in July. Roosevelt hoped that the participating countries would pledge to take in some refugees, but he was also hoping to create an organization that would assist German and Austrian Jews to settle in large numbers in areas such as Africa and South America.

Roosevelt's representative was Myron Taylor, Chairman of the Board of US Steel, a businessman who had little knowledge or experience of refugee issues. Consequently, Roosevelt was criticized by Jewish organizations for this appointment. The conference lasted nine days and delegates expressed great sympathy for the refugees; however, most countries, including the USA and the UK, offered excuses for not letting in more refugees. The USA had set immigration quotas in 1924 and did not wish to amend them. It only reached the permitted maximum for Austria and Germany for the first time in 1939.

The Dominican Republic offered to accept about 100,000 refugees following Evian but only about 700 settled there and some who did go there then moved to the USA. There were suggestions that some Jewish families be allowed to settle in the Philippines and eventually some 1200 European Jews did settle there. Other plans to settle Jewish refugees in Alaska and the US Virgin Islands came to nothing. Some countries made excuses about not wishing to take in Jewish refugees. The Australian representative was rather blunt and said 'as we have no real racial problem we are not desirous of importing one'.

Following Evian, the Intergovernmental Committee on Refugees (IGCR) was established in August 1938 to pressure the Germans to allow the Jews to leave with enough resources to begin new lives. The IGCR attempted to negotiate the release of Jews by partially financing their emigration with confiscated Jewish assets, but the Nazi regime's plan to exploit the Jews economically before expelling them from Germany and Austria was against most countries' immigration regulations (which prevented the entry of massive influxes of impoverished refugees). The ICGR and Nazi Germany never came to an agreement.

?

How helpful is Source A as evidence of German actions against the Jews?

SOURCE A

Excerpt from a letter written 4 April 1939 by Raymond H. Geist, US Consul in Berlin, to George S. Messersmith, Assistant Secretary of State of the USA, about the failure of the IGCR to help Jewish people in Germany. Source: George S. Messersmith Papers, item 1187, University of Delaware Library, Newark, Delaware (http://germanhistorydocs.ghi-dc. org/pdf/eng/English36.pdf).

I am afraid that in the end the Germans will consider that the efforts of the Inter-Governmental Committee have produced so few results that they … will proceed to handle the Jewish problem entirely in their own way. There can, of course, be only an internal solution of the Jewish problem in Germany … It will, of course, consist in placing all the able-bodied Jews in work camps, confiscating the wealth of the entire Jewish population, isolating them, and putting additional pressure on the whole community, and getting rid of as many as they can by force.

🔑 KEY TERM

Kristallnacht 'Night of Broken Glass', the name given to the violent anti-Jewish riots that began on the night of 9 November 1938 and continued through the day of 10 November.

Concentration camp A camp where civilians, enemy aliens, political prisoners and sometimes prisoners of war are detained and confined under harsh conditions.

The impact of *Kristallnacht*, November 1938

Kristallnacht took place on 9 November 1938 following the murder in Paris of Ernst vom Rath, a German diplomat. Vom Rath was murdered by Herschel Grynszpan, a young Jew, and the Nazis used this as the excuse they needed to begin a night of violence against the whole of the German Jewish community. The Nazis claimed that the murder of vom Rath was part of a Jewish anti-Nazi conspiracy. In one night, more than 1000 synagogues were burnt to the ground or destroyed, 91 Jews were killed and about 30,000 Jews were placed in **concentration camps**. Seven thousand Jewish businesses were destroyed and thousands of Jewish homes were attacked. Finally, the Jews had to pay the Nazi government one billion marks as compensation for the damage.

There was huge condemnation of Germany in the USA following the events of *Kristallnacht*. In a statement read at a press conference a few days later, Roosevelt said that the tourist visas of 15,000 Germans and Austrians would be extended so that visiting Jews could stay in the USA longer and that the US ambassador would be recalled from Germany. This was the first time that the USA had withdrawn an ambassador in peacetime. In addition, Roosevelt announced that the German and Austrian immigration quotas would be combined to permit continued Austrian Jewish immigration following the absorption of Austria into the German Reich.

SOURCE B

Excerpt from President Roosevelt's press conference about *Kristallnacht* quoted from *Roosevelt and the Holocaust*, by R. Beir and B. Josepher, published by Barricade Books, USA, 2006, page 127.

The news of the past few days from Germany has shocked public opinion in the United States. Such news from any part of the world would inevitably produce a similar profound reaction among American people in every part of the nation. I myself could scarcely believe that such things could occur in a twentieth-century civilization …

Why did Roosevelt wish to make the comments in Source B during a press conference?

Despite the outrage of many senior US politicians and some people, a public opinion poll by Hadley Cantril, taken after *Kristallnacht* and asking 'should the USA take a large number of Jewish exiles from Germany to come here to live permanently?' showed 75 per cent of the respondents saying 'no'. It is difficult to say whether this was because of anti-Semitic or anti-immigration feelings.

Wagner–Rogers Bill 1939

The plight of Jewish refugees continued to be an issue in the USA and some politicians sought to alleviate their suffering. In February 1939, the Wagner–Rogers Bill (also known as the Child Refugee Bill) was introduced in Congress by Senator Robert Wagner, a Democrat from New York, and Representative Edith Rogers, a Republican from Massachusetts. The bill proposed admitting 20,000 Jewish refugee children into the USA above the specified quota. They would be allowed in over two years and all costs would be paid for privately. There was a good response from US citizens and many people offered to take the children, yet an opinion poll which asked if the children should be allowed into the USA still saw 61 per cent of respondents against the bill. These people thought that the USA should help its own poor children and should not be responding to external pressure to increase immigration.

There was also much opposition in Congress to the bill and a possibility that Roosevelt's opponents might introduce legislation to reduce, rather than increase, the current immigration quota. There were fears that such large numbers of children would mean parents would follow and become a burden at a time of high unemployment. Eleanor Roosevelt once more put pressure on the president to support the bill but, once he saw the scale of opposition, he took the pragmatic route and decided not to alienate too many members of Congress. The bill was defeated in February 1939.

Although the USA did not offer additional help to German Jews, Jewish immigrants comprised more than half of all immigrants admitted to the USA after *Kristallnacht*. However, even when the war in Europe began in September 1939, and the US economy began to boom and brought full employment, there was still general public antipathy to Jewish immigration.

US reaction to Nazi anti-Jewish policies during the 1930s

German anti-Jewish actions	US reaction to German policies
• 1935: Nuremberg Laws – Jews lost their citizenship, and the right to vote and hold government office • 1938: *Anschluss* drove Jews to leave Austria • November: *Kristallnacht* led to imprisonment of many Jews	• 1938: Roosevelt called the Evian Conference on political refugees • Evian resulted in the setting up of the Intergovernmental Committee (IGCR) on Refugees • IGCR failed to agree with Germany • *Kristallnacht* condemned by US government • Wagner–Rogers Bill to help Jewish children emigrate to USA defeated in Congress • 1939: half of emigrants to USA that year were Jewish; still US public opinion antipathetic to Jewish immigration

SUMMARY DIAGRAM

The US reaction to Nazi anti-Jewish policies during the 1930s

 # The SS *St Louis* case

▶ *Key question: What was the impact of the SS* St Louis *case?*

It was the decisions of the authorities and President Roosevelt about the SS *St Louis* which showed the world the attitudes of the USA towards Jewish refugees and the policy of immigration.

What were the ramifications of this incident?

→ The events of the SS *St Louis*

The SS *St Louis* left Germany for Cuba in May 1939 with 930 Jewish refugees on board. On arrival at Cuba's capital, Havana, the refugees were not permitted to disembark. After several days, the ship was told to leave Cuba and it then sailed for the US coast. The ship sailed along the Florida coast but US authorities did not allow it to dock. There were several attempts to persuade the US government to provide sanctuary for the refugees, including a personal telegram from the passenger committee on board the *St Louis* to President Roosevelt, which received no reply. The ship had to return to Europe, where records indicate that about 30 per cent of the passengers eventually perished in Nazi concentration camps.

SOURCE C

Jewish refugees aboard the *St Louis* arriving in Belgium in June 1939 after having been turned away from Cuba and the USA.

Why were many Americans unhappy about the publication of the photograph in Source C?

SOURCE D

Excerpt from part of a letter from Bishop James Cannon of Richmond, Virginia, to the *Richmond Times-Dispatch* after the *St Louis* returned to Europe. Quoted in *Roosevelt and the Holocaust*, by R. Beir and B. Josepher, published by Barricade Books, USA, 2006, page 142.

Our government in Washington made no effort to relieve the desperate situation of these people but on the contrary gave orders that they be kept out of the country … The failure to take any steps to assist these distressed persecuted Jews in their hour of extremity was one of the most disgraceful things which has happened in American history and leaves a stain and brand of shame upon the record of our nation.

What does Source D tell you about the SS *St Louis* case?

One year after the *St Louis* case, the SS *Quanza*, a Portuguese ship carrying 80 Jewish refugees, tried to dock at Veracruz, Mexico. The Mexican government would not let the refugees disembark and the ship then sailed to Norfolk, Virginia, USA, to collect coal. Eleanor Roosevelt then took up the refugees' cause and pressured the **State Department** to allow them to land. Eventually the refugees were granted visas.

As the situation for Jews in Europe worsened after 1940, further attempts to help from within the USA also met with little success, but attitudes eventually changed as the full events of the Holocaust were brought to light.

 **KEY TERM**

State Department The US government department in charge of foreign affairs.

The SS *St Louis* case
- May 1939: SS *St Louis* left Germany with 930 Jewish refugees
- Refused permission to land in Cuba
- Refused permission to land in USA despite pleas
- Returned to Germany
- Many of the 930 perished in concentration camps during the war
- 1940 SS *Quanza* with 90 Jewish refugees refused permission to dock in Mexico
- Pressure from Eleanor Roosevelt on US State Department – refugees landed in USA and granted visas

SUMMARY DIAGRAM

The SS *St Louis* case

The US reaction to Nazi policies during the war

▶ *Key question: How did the US react to Nazi anti-Jewish policies during the war?*

In the early years of the war, immigration policy shifted in the USA. There was a fear of spies and **fifth columnists** which led to a reduction in quotas of immigrants from countries under German or Italian control. However, as news of the Holocaust filtered through from 1943 onwards, there were more attempts to allow more refugees to enter the USA.

> Why was there a fear of spies and fifth columnists?

 ## Spies and fifth columnists

In January 1940, Roosevelt appointed Breckinridge Long as Assistant Secretary of State. Part of Long's job included passports and visas. Following a spy scandal in May of that year there was a fear of fifth columnists and spies in Washington and Long, in his official capacity in the State Department, decided to curb immigration into the USA. Long was especially concerned that Germans and Russians would be able to enter with refugees.

Tyler Kent and the spy scandal

In May 1940, Tyler Kent, a 29-year-old American code clerk at the US embassy in London, was arrested by British authorities. Tyler Kent was charged with having taken 1929 US embassy documents, some of which included secret correspondence between Franklin Roosevelt and Winston Churchill. Some of the documents were damaging to Roosevelt because they showed him trying to help the UK when the USA was still neutral. Kent was accused of stealing the documents for a pro-German organization. He was tried and imprisoned for ten years.

SOURCE E

Excerpt from a memo sent by Long to all sections of the State Department, June 1940. Quoted in *Roosevelt and the Holocaust*, by R. Beir and B. Josepher, published by Barricade Books, USA, 2006, page 156.

We can delay and effectively stop for a temporary period of indefinite length the number of immigrants into the United States. We could do this by simply advising our consuls to put every obstacle in the way and to require additional evidence and to resort to various administrative devices which would postpone and postpone and postpone the granting of the visas.

How useful is Source E as evidence of the State Department's attitude to immigration?

 **KEY TERM**

Occupied territories Those countries which had been taken over by Nazi Germany.

Final Solution The name given to the Nazi policy to kill all the Jews in Europe. About six million were killed under this policy. The term 'Holocaust' is now used to describe this act of genocide.

World Jewish Congress (WJC) An international federation of Jewish communities and organizations set up in Switzerland in 1936.

Polish underground The Polish movement dedicated to the overthrow of the Nazi occupying forces.

Long's memo was implemented and immigration reduced, despite the fact that immigration quotas had not been met before his appointment as Secretary of State. His policies ensured there was a sharp decline in immigration after 1940. Ninety per cent of the quota places available to immigrants from countries under German and Italian control were never filled. Roosevelt has been criticized for appointing Long and allowing him to remain in office. Many people have alleged that Long was an anti-Semite because he obstructed Jewish immigration to the USA. Henry Morgenthau, Secretary of the Treasury, openly discussed this with Long and tried to minimize Long's influence.

In June 1941, Germany's consulates were closed in the USA and then Germany expelled US consuls, thus making official emigration to USA impossible. By October 1942, immigration from Germany and its **occupied territories** had ended.

As relations between the USA and Germany deteriorated in 1941, the situation for Jews in occupied Europe became untenable. Their treatment worsened and the Nazis began to embark on the **Final Solution**.

The Final Solution 1942–5

By the summer of 1942, stories of Nazi atrocities had flooded into the offices of the **World Jewish Congress (WJC)** in Switzerland. Gerhart Riegner, the WJC representative in Geneva, received information about massacres in Poland and the Ukraine, indicating that thousands of Jews were being systematically murdered. Indeed, on 2 July 1942, the *New York Times* reported mass killings in Chelmno, Poland, which were based on sources from the **Polish underground**. However, the article was placed on page six and hiding such stories became a common occurrence with the paper for the rest of the war. (The *New York Times* was owned by Arthur Sulzberger, a Jew, who believed that Jewishness meant solely religious belief – not ethnicity. He was an American first and did not wish to be seen as promoting any Jewish concern above that of any other religion.)

← **What was the Riegner Report and how did it contribute to exposing the Final Solution?**

The Riegner Report 1942

Riegner informed the US consul in Geneva of the persecution, transportation and mass murders and the report was sent to Sumner Welles, the under-secretary at the State Department in the USA, in early August. He also informed the British Foreign Office, which contacted Sidney Silverman, a British member of parliament, who was chairman of the British section of the WJC. Silverman then contacted Rabbi Stephen Wise, the president of the WJC (Wise was perhaps the foremost spokesperson for American Jews).

Almost a month after the State Department received the Riegner Report, Wise informed Welles what was happening in Europe. Wise did not know that Welles had had the information for almost a month. Welles asked Wise not to publish any information from Riegner and Wise agreed. However, at Wise's request, Roosevelt was told of the Report's details by Supreme Court Judge Felix Frankfurter, a US Jew. Roosevelt said that any transportation being carried out was only for the purposes of forced labour.

Wise held meetings with the State Department in November and was informed by Welles that the USA now had documents which confirmed Wise's claims of events in Europe. Wise then held press conferences in Washington and New York and spoke openly about the events in Europe.

? Study Sources F and G. Can you suggest reasons why there was no huge public outcry in the USA after Murrow's broadcast and the Declaration of the United Nations?

SOURCE F

Excerpt from a radio broadcast in the USA by Edward R. Murrow, a CBS journalist, 13 December 1942, quoted from the Holocaust Survivors and Remembrance Project (http://isurvived.org/Frameset_folder-4DEBATES/-FDR-Holocaust.html).

Millions of human beings, most of them Jews, are being gathered up with ruthless efficiency and murdered ... It is a picture of mass murder and moral depravity unequalled in the history of the world. It is a horror beyond what imagination can grasp ... The Jews are being systematically exterminated throughout all Poland ... There are no longer 'concentration camps' – we must speak now only of 'extermination camps'.

Wise met Roosevelt in December and in a further press conference explained how the president had been shocked by the reports of Nazi actions against Jews. On 17 December, the United Nations (at this time, those countries fighting Nazi Germany and its allies) issued a declaration condemning the Nazi atrocities.

SOURCE G

Excerpt from the joint declaration of the United Nations, 17 December 1942, quoted from the Germanic Migration Archives (www.germanicmigration.info/index.php?t=Joint+Declaration+by+Members+of+the+United+Nations).

From all the occupied countries Jews are being transported in conditions of appalling horror and brutality to Eastern Europe. In Poland, which has been made the principal Nazi slaughterhouse, the ghettos established by the German invader are being systematically emptied of all Jews except a few highly skilled workers required for war industries. None of those taken away are ever heard of again. The able-bodied are slowly worked to death in labour camps. The infirm are left to die of exposure and starvation or are deliberately massacred in mass executions. The number of victims of these bloody cruelties is reckoned in many hundreds of thousands of entirely innocent men, women and children ... Those responsible for these crimes will not escape retribution.

Attempts to help the Jews

Jewish organizations kept the issue of Nazi atrocities in the public eye. On 1 March 1943, Wise organized a rally at Madison Square Gardens, New York, under the slogan 'Stop Hitler Now'. Thousands attended and, afterwards, Wise sent a letter to Cordell Hull, Secretary of State, saying how disappointed he was that despite the United Nations' declaration of December, little or nothing had been done to carry out its aims. He also asked for action 'which may aid in saving the Jewish people from utter extinction'.

Further reports about continued Nazi atrocities were sent by Riegner to the US State Department and Wise. Riegner's plan was to save some 70,000 Jews in France and Romania by bribing some Nazi officials to move them to Hungary where Jews were, at that time, not experiencing atrocities. In order to carry out his plan, Riegner needed to transfer funds from the USA and had to secure permission from the State and Treasury Departments. Wise met Roosevelt again in July 1943 and discussed Riegner's plan. No money was set aside. Roosevelt then met Jan Karski, who brought more news about the extermination of the Jews in Poland. The information given to Roosevelt and Wise led to presidential action but this was six months later, in January 1944, when Roosevelt set up the War Refugee Board.

Bermuda Conference on refugees, April 1943

As concern grew about the treatment of refugees in Nazi Europe, public opinion and Jewish organizations in the USA and the British Commonwealth pressured Allied governments to rescue the victims of the Nazi regime. As a result, the Anglo-American Conference on Refugees was convened by the British government. The conference opened on 19 April and achieved little. It was decided to remove the 21,000 refugees who were stranded in Spain and send them to Allied-occupied North Africa. There were about 4000 Jews among this group. A final communiqué indicated that a number of recommendations had been discussed and were being considered, but little else. Jewish organizations were bitterly disappointed that no plans were drawn up to help those being persecuted in Nazi-occupied Europe.

Roosevelt tried again in October 1943 to help the Jewish refugees when he spoke to the IGCR (see page 161) meeting in Washington, DC. He stated that he was attempting to receive support from Pope Pius XII in the development of a suitable area to admit Jewish refugees in unlimited numbers. The British and French objected to Roosevelt's proposal, using Roosevelt's own argument that the best way to help the Jews was to focus on winning the war as soon as possible. The papacy rejected Roosevelt's idea because it feared retaliation by the Nazis against the Catholic Church in Germany.

The Gillette–Rogers Resolution

In November 1943, Will Rogers and Joseph C. Baldwin introduced a resolution into the House of Representatives that called on President Roosevelt to create a commission to rescue the Jews of Europe. Guy Gillette and 11 other senators introduced an identical measure into the Senate. The resolution called for 'the creation by the President of a commission of diplomatic, economic, and military experts to formulate and execute a plan to save the surviving Jewish people from extinction'. The resolution proposed the setting up of camps in Turkey, Sweden, Switzerland, Spain, Portugal and Morocco, where Jewish refugees would be housed temporarily.

Breckinridge Long opposed the resolution and gave evidence to the Foreign Affairs Committee claiming that everything that could be done to save the Jews was being done. Long said that the majority of 580,000 refugees admitted from Europe since the beginning of Hitler's rule were Jewish. In fact, there had been only about 476,000 immigrants since 1933 and about 165,000 were European Jews. Long resigned from the State Department in 1944 when it was found that he had deliberately lied about the statistics.

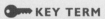

Why was the work of the War Refugee Board important in helping Jewish refugees?

The War Refugee Board

In January 1944, Treasury Secretary Henry Morgenthau Jr met Roosevelt to discuss the Riegner Plan (see pages 168–9) to save Jewish refugees. He had the documents ready for Roosevelt to sign which would establish the body that would begin the rescue. Morgenthau explained that Breckinridge Long and the State Department had delayed, slowed and even obstructed measures to allow Jewish refugees into the USA. Six days after the meeting (and two days before the Senate vote on the Gillette–Rogers Resolution), Roosevelt signed Executive Order 9417. This established the **War Refugee Board (WRB)**.

SOURCE H

Extract from Executive Order 9417 setting up the War Refugee Board, 22 January 1944, quoted from the American Presidency Project (www.presidency.ucsb.edu/ws/index.php?pid=16540).

The functions of the Board shall include without limitation the development of plans and programs and the inauguration of effective measures for (a) the rescue, transportation, maintenance, and relief of the victims of enemy oppression, and (b) the establishment of havens of temporary refuge for such victims. To this end the Board, through appropriate channels, shall take the necessary steps to enlist the cooperation of foreign Governments and obtain their participation in the execution of such plans and programs.

> What do the instructions in Source H suggest about future actions of the USA with regard to refugees?

There was delay in appointing an executive director of the WRB but eventually John Pehle, assistant to Morgenthau at the Treasury, was chosen. The WRB received about $1.6 million from the US government and about $16 million from private Jewish organizations in the USA.

Pehle and his team put forward plans for moving Jewish refugees to neutral countries and then setting up camps for them. In the USA, Roosevelt allowed 1000 Jewish refugees to be admitted from Italy and placed them in Fort Ontario, an army camp. Roosevelt was criticized by Congress for circumventing the quota system and many people wrote to newspapers expressing their anger at allowing Jews into the USA.

The WRB sent representatives to the neutral countries of Europe – Portugal, Spain, Switzerland, Sweden and Turkey – in order to help refugees escape from the occupied territories. The WRB helped to set up escape routes, prepare fake documents and provide cash for bribery purposes. Some 27,000 refugees (20,000 Jews) escaped to Switzerland as a result of the WRB's work and about 7000 Jews were able to reach Turkey, some of whom moved on to Palestine. Others eventually reached Spain, Sweden and Portugal.

The work of Raoul Wallenberg

Hungary had joined the Axis powers in 1941 and its forces had helped Germany to invade Yugoslavia and the USSR. It had remained independent until early 1944 and was occupied by Germany in March 1944, when it became clear that Hungary was making peace moves towards the UK and the USA. In the two months after the German occupation, more than 400,000 Jews were sent from Hungary to their deaths at Auschwitz concentration camp.

In July 1944, the WRB appointed Raoul Wallenberg as its representative in Budapest, Hungary. Wallenberg was a businessman from neutral Sweden who was to be based at the Swedish embassy in Budapest.

By the time of Wallenberg's appointment, there were still some 250,000 Jews left in Hungary and he began his efforts to save as many of these as possible. Wallenberg devised various methods of saving Jews in Hungary. He issued some 20,000 Swedish passports and set up 'safe houses' which he said were Swedish territory and had diplomatic immunity and could not therefore be entered by German or Hungarian authorities. His authority became so strong that eventually he simply issued passes which contained his signature and these gave protection to the owner.

Wallenberg's most significant act was to prevent the massacre of the 70,000 Jews in the Budapest ghetto. As Soviet forces advanced on Budapest in late 1944, Wallenberg informed General Schmidthuber, the Nazi commander, that there should be no assault on the ghetto. If one took place, Wallenberg said that Schmidthuber would be hanged as a war criminal after the war. The planned attack on the ghetto did not take place. It is thought that Wallenberg saved about 100,000 lives in Hungary. Wallenberg was detained by Soviet forces in January 1945 in Hungary and transported to Moscow, Russia. He was never heard from after this, and was reported to have died in 1947. The reasons for his arrest, disappearance and death have never been fully explained.

It has been estimated that by the end of the war, the WRB saved about 250,000 lives.

Proposals to bomb the concentration camps

The WRB became so concerned at the plight of the Jews in Europe that it asked the War Department to bomb the concentration camp at Auschwitz, Poland. Some Jewish leaders such as Chaim Weizmann, head of the **Jewish Agency**, and Nahum Goldmann of the WJC sought attacks on the camps. These leaders asked for the railway lines that brought hundreds of thousands to their deaths to be bombed, but the US military stated that they would be soon repaired. However, there were some Jewish leaders, such as Leon Kubowitzki, head of the Rescue Department of the WJC, and David Ben Gurion, head of the Jewish Agency in Jerusalem, who were horrified at the suggestion that the camps be bombed because it would mean Jewish casualties.

> ### Nazi concentration camps
> When the Nazis came to power in 1933, they set up concentration camps to imprison opponents of their regime and these were gradually used to confine large numbers of Jews. When the Final Solution began, many camps were used to exterminate the Jewish inmates. The Nazis systematically murdered the Jews by such means as gas chambers, mass shootings and medical experiments. The corpses were disposed of in huge crematoria.

On 20 August 1944, 127 bombers dropped thousands of pounds of high explosives on the factory areas of Auschwitz which were less than five miles (8 km) from the gas chambers. On 13 September 1944, 96 Liberator bombers attacked factories in Auschwitz; two bombs accidentally fell near the Auschwitz crematoria and one actually damaged a railway line leading to the gas chambers: 15 SS men died and about 40 prisoners were killed. Between 7 July and 20 November 1944, 2500 bombers struck targets within a 35-mile (56-km) radius of Auschwitz. This clearly showed that it was possible to bomb Auschwitz itself, yet the decision to target Auschwitz as a matter of policy was never made.

SOURCE I

Excerpt from a letter from John J. McCloy, Assistant Secretary of War, to John W. Pehle, Director, War Refugee Board, concerning the request to bomb Auschwitz, 18 November 1944. Quoted from *The Encyclopaedia of World War II: A Political, Social and Military History*, by Spencer Tucker and Priscilla Roberts (editors), published by ABC-CLIO, USA, 2004.

What does Source I tell you about the War Department's attitude to the bombing of Auschwitz?

In consideration of this proposal [to bomb Auschwitz] note the following points:

a. *Positive destruction of these camps would necessitate precision bombing, employing heavy or medium bombardment, or attack by low flying or dive bombing aircraft, preferably the latter.*
b. *The target is beyond the maximum range of medium bombardment, dive bombers and fighter bombers located in United Kingdom, France or Italy.*
c. *Use of heavy bombardment from United Kingdom bases would necessitate a hazardous round trip flight unescorted of approximately 2,000 miles [3200 km] over enemy territory.*
d. *At the present critical stage of the war in Europe, our strategic air forces are engaged in the destruction of industrial target systems vital to the dwindling war potential of the enemy, from which they should not be diverted. The positive solution to this problem is the earliest possible victory over Germany, to which end we should exert our entire means.*

Based on the above, as well as the most uncertain, if not dangerous effect such a bombing would have on the object to be attained, the War Department has felt that it should not, at least for the present, undertake these operations … We have been pressed strongly from other quarters and have taken the best military opinion on its feasibility, and we believe the above conclusion is a sound one.

What were the results of the US liberation of the concentration camps?

KEY TERM

Slave labour camp A concentration camp where people worked under duress and threats.

? What did Murrow mean in Source J when he said the inmates were 'Men from the countries that made America'?

The US liberation of the concentration camps

Exposure

US Army units were the first of the Western allies to discover concentration camps, when, on 4 April 1945 they liberated the **slave labour camp** at Ohrdruf, Germany. However, the first one that US forces liberated with inmates was Buchenwald concentration camp near Weimar, Germany. They entered Buchenwald on 11 April 1945, rescuing about 20,000 prisoners. The soldiers were confronted with heaps of the dead and dying, as well as emaciated and diseased survivors.

SOURCE J

Excerpt from a news report by CBS reporter Ed Murrow, broadcast 15 April 1945. Murrow broadcast his first-hand account of what he had seen at Buchenwald on 12 April 1945, the day after the concentration camp was liberated by American troops. Quoted from the Jewish Virtual Library (www.jewishvirtuallibrary.org/jsource/Holocaust/murrow.html).

In another part of the camp they showed me the children, hundreds of them. Some were only 6 years old. One rolled up his sleeves, showed me his number. It was tattooed on his arm. B-6030, it was. The others showed me their numbers. They will carry them till they die ... I could see their ribs through their thin shirts ... The children clung to my hands and stared. Men kept coming up to speak to me and to touch me, professors from Poland, doctors from Vienna, men from all Europe. Men from the countries that made America.

General Patton, one of the leading US generals, compelled many ordinary German civilians of Weimar to visit the Buchenwald concentration camp to show them the horrors of the Nazi regime. Patton had been revolted by the conditions that he found in Buchenwald.

SOURCE K

Excerpt from the US newspaper *Oregonian*, 20 April 1945, describing the enforced visit of Weimar citizens to Buchenwald.

The doors of the crematoriums were opened, exposing burned and semi-burned bodies of the victims. On being marched past these ovens some Germans tried not to look at the spectacle, but the American officers, on Patton's orders, compelled the Germans to turn their heads toward the scene.

? According to Source K, why did General Patton force German citizens to visit Buchenwald?

US armed units also liberated the German camps of Flossenburg, Dachau and Matthausen. Dachau concentration camp was liberated on 29 April 1945, one week before the end of the war in Europe, by two divisions of the US Seventh Army.

The Dachau massacre

Shortly after US soldiers entered Dachau concentration camp, they shot some of the German SS guards in what has become known as the Dachau massacre. Outside the camp, US soldiers had found several freight-cars which were full of dead bodies. As they went into the camp, they discovered more bodies on open ground and also several rooms which were full of dead bodies. They then discovered a crematorium and a gas chamber. The camp guards had surrendered and were rounded up by the US soldiers. Accounts vary as to what happened – some say that the guards tried to escape and were then shot, others that some inmates killed some of the guards and others that the guards were stood against a wall and then machine-gunned. It is not known how many Germans were killed and figures range from 30 to 560.

Post-war attitudes to immigration

After the war, President Truman made clear efforts to ease US immigration restrictions for Jewish refugees and displaced persons. In December 1945, an executive order allowed 16,000 Jewish refugees to enter the USA during the next three years. There was also a feeling in the USA that something should be done to help the refugees in Europe. In 1948, Congress passed the Displaced Persons Act, as a result of which US authorities granted about 400,000 visas to immigrants above the quota system. Jewish displaced people received some 80,000 of these visas. For Truman, the eventual act did not go far enough and limited numbers but for the first time, refugees became a major factor in US immigration.

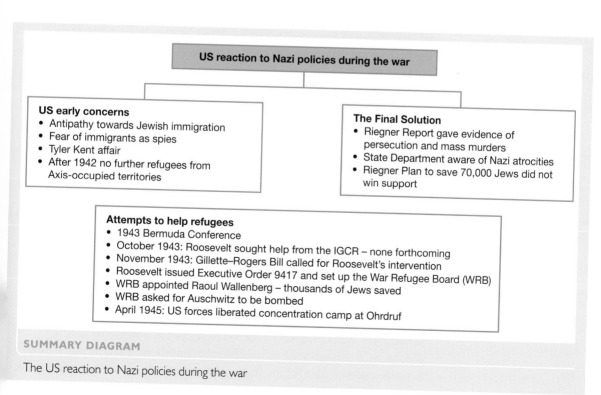

US reaction to Nazi policies during the war

US early concerns
- Antipathy towards Jewish immigration
- Fear of immigrants as spies
- Tyler Kent affair
- After 1942 no further refugees from Axis-occupied territories

The Final Solution
- Riegner Report gave evidence of persecution and mass murders
- State Department aware of Nazi atrocities
- Riegner Plan to save 70,000 Jews did not win support

Attempts to help refugees
- 1943 Bermuda Conference
- October 1943: Roosevelt sought help from the IGCR – none forthcoming
- November 1943: Gillette–Rogers Bill called for Roosevelt's intervention
- Roosevelt issued Executive Order 9417 and set up the War Refugee Board (WRB)
- WRB appointed Raoul Wallenberg – thousands of Jews saved
- WRB asked for Auschwitz to be bombed
- April 1945: US forces liberated concentration camp at Ohrdruf

SUMMARY DIAGRAM

The US reaction to Nazi policies during the war

Key debate

Assessment of Roosevelt's role concerning the Jews during the Second World War and the Holocaust is made difficult by the relative lack of documentation about his thinking. At all times, Roosevelt said that his policy was always to win the war first and that other issues could be dealt with but must not obstruct his primary aim.

Roosevelt's inaction

Some historians have criticized Roosevelt for failing to use his powers and the resources of the Allied armies to save the Jews, especially after there was hard evidence of the Final Solution. Critics have said that his 'win the war' policy did not adequately address the possibility that significant numbers of Jews could be rescued if immediate action had been taken.

Historian David Wyman argued in *The Abandonment of the Jews* (1984) that the War Department's rejection of the proposal to bomb Auschwitz on the grounds that it would divert air support from the war effort was merely an excuse. Wyman's view is that 'to the American military, Europe's Jews represented an extraneous problem and an unwanted burden'. He was even more scathing of Roosevelt when he stated, 'Authenticated information that the Nazis were systematically exterminating European Jewry was made public in the United States in November 1942. President Roosevelt did nothing about the mass murder for fourteen months, then moved only because he was confronted with political pressures he could not avoid and because his administration stood on the brink of a nasty scandal over its rescue policies.'

Going further, William O'Neill clearly stated in *A Democracy at War* (1993) that the US government's policies in the war were racist, anti-Semitic, and responsible for the USA's worst violations of human rights and common decency. Emphasizing the notion of anti-Semitism, Beir and Josepher in *Roosevelt and the Holocaust* (2006) point to people such as Long who were disposed to prevent immigration by ensuring that there were bureaucratic hurdles that people found almost impossible to surmount. Schulzinger in *American Diplomacy in the Twentieth Century* (1990) agrees, saying that the USA 'did next to nothing to help [the Jews'] plight' and criticizes the State Department and the War Department for their refusal to act. Above all, Schulzinger attacks Roosevelt for following public opinion by saying 'Roosevelt, a consummate judge of public sentiment, thought that if he were to make a special plea for the Jews, other Americans would no longer think the war was their fight.'

Saul Friedman makes a similar point as Schulzinger in *No Haven for the Oppressed: United States Policy Toward Jewish Refugees 1938–45* (1973): 'Roosevelt's failure to live up to the Jews' expectations lies not so much with the man but with the people who deified him … Ultimately, however, the blame for inaction lies with the faceless mass of American citizens.'

However, Rubinstein in *The Myth of Rescue* (1997) says that none of the plans put forward in the war would have rescued one single Jew who perished in the Holocaust.

Some of the points these historians use to argue that Roosevelt did not act include the following:

- He adhered to the immigration quotas during the 1930s and did not challenge them after 1941 for fear of losing votes.
- Roosevelt followed the views of the US public. Polls always showed that there was an unwillingness to accept increased numbers of Jewish immigrants even after 1939.
- He did not intervene over the SS *St Louis* case.
- He did not step in when Congress debated the Wagner–Rogers Bill.
- The appointment of Breckenridge Long hindered the rescue of many Jews. Some thought Long was an anti-Semite and some historians have written that the State Department was extremely anti-Semitic, and that there was a climate of racism and anti-Semitism across the whole government, despite senior members being Jewish.
- He was slow to react to the information provided by Wise and Karski and his action on the Riegner Plan (see page 169) showed no urgency.
- He has been accused of not impressing the gravity and urgency of the situation on the papacy.
- In some of his speeches condemning Nazi policies and actions, Roosevelt never promised rescue. He said that actions would be taken 'appropriate with winning the war'.
- He did not press for the bombing of railway lines to the camps or even bombing the camps themselves. In an interview in 1986, McCloy, Assistant Secretary of War 1941–5, said that Roosevelt stopped the idea of bombing the camps.

Roosevelt's action

Other historians and even many Jews have defended Roosevelt, saying that he did as much as was possible under the circumstances. Some leading Jews were concerned that attacks on the concentration camps would lead to more casualties and agreed with Roosevelt that it would give the Nazis the opportunity to accuse the USA of murder.

Henry Feingold in *The Politics of Rescue: The Roosevelt Administration and the Holocaust, 1938–1945* (1970) saw the problems Roosevelt faced and accepted the dilemmas Roosevelt faced: 'I am … aware that there were many factors in the rescue situation which were simply beyond the Roosevelt

Administration's control. Not the least of these was Berlin's determination to liquidate the Jews and the great difficulty of assigning to a modern nation-state a humanitarian mission to rescue a foreign minority for which it had no legal responsibility.' R. Dallek agrees that Roosevelt saw the problems of the Jews and did try to help. In *Franklin D. Roosevelt and American Foreign Policy, 1932–45* (1970) he notes that Roosevelt continued to address the crisis for European Jews by combining the German and Austrian immigration quotas after the *Anschluss*. However, Dallek says there was no effective way to rescue great numbers of Jews from Hitler's Europe while the war raged.

Doris Kearns Goodwin in *No Ordinary Time* (1990) agrees that he did address the problems of the Jews: '[Roosevelt] believed that winning the war was the best means of rescuing the Jews. And there was merit to his belief. By the time the news of the systematic murder of the Jews reached the West in mid-1942, it was too late to mount a massive rescue effort short of winning the war as quickly as possible.'

Robert Rosen has summed up the role of Roosevelt: 'He did not abandon the Jews … Hitler's immediate and seemingly attainable goal was to kill 11 million Jews, not six million. Roosevelt prevented Hitler from achieving his goal.'

Some of the points these historians use to argue that Roosevelt did address the problems of the Jews include the following:

- He appointed Jews to senior positions in his administrations, among them Henry Morgenthau, Secretary of the Treasury, and Felix Frankfurter, a Supreme Court judge. Fifteen per cent of Roosevelt's highest ranking appointees were Jewish, although Jews represented less than three percent of the population at the time.
- Rabbi Stephen Wise, President of the World Jewish Congress, was a personal friend of Franklin and Eleanor Roosevelt. Wise kept Roosevelt informed of events in Europe.
- His reaction to *Kristallnacht* indicates that Roosevelt was appalled by the persecution of the Jews.
- He called the Evian Conference (see page 161) on refugees.
- Despite all the clamour about Jews and mistreatment in the war, many Jewish leaders in the USA endorsed Roosevelt's line that the best way to rescue Jews was to defeat Nazi Germany. This legitimized Roosevelt's policy.
- He pressed the papacy to act but Roosevelt could not be blamed for the Catholic Church's lack of a robust approach.
- He warned that those responsible for atrocities would be punished.
- He set up the War Refugee Board in 1944 by executive order.
- He helped to establish Fort Ontario, New York, as a camp for refugees.

It can be argued that the USA could have done more on behalf of European Jews. How valid are US claims that it was operating under constraints? (Logic, Emotion, Language, Ethics, Social Science – Political Science.)

T
O
K

- From 1942, he constantly warned that those responsible for atrocities would be punished. In a radio broadcast on 24 March 1944, President Roosevelt spoke of the problems facing Jews in all the occupied territories.
- He allowed 1000 refugees into the USA in 1944 outside the quota system.

SOURCE L

Extract from President Roosevelt's statement about victims of Nazi oppression, 24 March 1944. Quoted from Teachingamericanhistory.org (http://teachingamericanhistory.org/library/index.asp?document=2148).

In one of the blackest crimes of all history – begun by the Nazis in the day of peace and multiplied by them a hundred times in time of war – the wholesale systematic murder of the Jews of Europe goes on unabated every hour … It is therefore fitting that we should again proclaim our determination that none who participate in these acts of savagery shall go unpunished. All who knowingly take part in the deportation of Jews to their death in Poland or Norwegians and French to their death in Germany are equally guilty with the executioner. All who share the guilt shall share the punishment.

> Why did Roosevelt say in Source L that 'All who share the guilt shall share the punishment'?

5 Latin America, Canada and the Holocaust

▶ *Key question: How did Latin America and Canada react to the Holocaust?*

Jewish emigration to Latin America

> Why did emigration to Latin America fall in the 1930s?

There were about 150,000 Jewish emigrants to Latin America in the years 1919–33 and during Hitler's time in power, 1933–45, Latin American governments allowed only 84,000 Jewish refugees to settle. In several countries, leaders such as Vargas of Brazil, Alessandri of Chile, Cardenas of Mexico and Batista of Cuba followed anti-immigration policies. These leaders introduced strict immigration laws which were copied by other Latin American states. On 27 November 1941, Argentina, Paraguay, Uruguay, Bolivia and Chile co-ordinated immigration laws which made entrance for refugees from Germany and Axis-occupied countries extremely difficult. These countries required immigrants to have valid passports from their country of origin. In the case of the majority of Jewish refugees such passports were almost impossible to obtain.

There were several reasons why Latin American countries began to limit Jewish immigration. Anti-Semitism was increasing not least because some of those of German descent in Brazil and Argentina did have leanings towards

Nazi racial philosophy. There was also the concern that in the economically strained times, immigrants would take the jobs which might otherwise go to nationals.

Jewish emigration during the Second World War
However, between 1938 and 1941 more than 20,000 Jewish refugees were admitted to Bolivia. This was as a result of the work of Moritz Hochschild, a German-Jewish industrialist who had mining interests in the country. Hochschild secured Bolivian visas for German and Austrian Jews, who sailed to Chile and then completed the journey by train to Bolivia on what became known as the *Express Judío* (Jewish Express). Many of these immigrants eventually moved to Argentina.

However, after 1941 when the Final Solution began, some Latin American governments began to issue passports and visas through their European embassies. Many Jews in Hungary were saved in 1944 because El Salvador issued some 20,000 passports through its consul general in Geneva, José Arturo Castellanos, and these prevented deportation and transportation to concentration camps.

Jewish emigration to Argentina
The immigration laws had immediate effects and Argentina admitted almost 80,000 Jewish immigrants in the years 1918–33 but after 1933 began to impose restrictions on those wishing to enter the country. In the years 1933–43, only 20,000 Jewish immigrants were able to secure entry. However, it has been estimated that another 20,000 moved, illegally, across the borders, from neighbouring countries during that time. (Some did move from Bolivia – see above.)

However, there was some anti-Semitism in Argentina during the Second World War. There were anti-Jewish riots in the province of Entre Ríos where the homes of many Jews were attacked. Many Jews in Argentina were accused of siding with the USA and the UK and were charged in the pro-Nazi press with trying to destroy Argentina's neutrality. There were even calls for a pogrom against the Jews.

Although Jews were allowed to emigrate to Argentina after 1945, there were undercurrents of anti-Semitism and the new leader of the military junta, Colonel Juan Perón, was accused of favouring Nazi Germany. In 1947, Dr Peralta was removed from his position of director of the immigration department having been charged with advocating and following an anti-Jewish policy in selecting immigrants to enter Argentina.

After 1945, the Argentine government enabled many Nazis to escape from Germany and Europe and allowed them to settle in Argentina. Some moved to Argentina and lived under assumed names and others continued to use their own names. Perhaps the two most infamous Nazis to escape to Argentina were Adolf Eichmann and Josef Mengele. Eichmann was an SS officer who had organized the mass deportation of more than 400,000 Jews from Hungary to concentration camps in Poland. Mengele was a doctor who carried out medical experiments on Jews who were sent to Auschwitz concentration camp. He lived in Argentina and Paraguay, and died in Brazil.

Paradoxically, almost 5000 Holocaust survivors were allowed to settle in Argentina in the immediate post-war years.

Jewish emigration to Brazil

Brazil admitted 96,000 Jewish immigrants between 1918 and 1933, but only 12,000 between 1933 and 1941.

Brazil had the largest number of German immigrants in Latin America and almost 100,000 went to Brazil in the years 1900–39. More than 3000 of the immigrants joined the Nazi Party, but this was not a huge number considering the total number of Germans and their descendants in Brazil, However, there was quite broad support for the Nazi regime within the German community. This made President Vargas' position difficult when addressing the issue of Jewish refugees. He had close trading and commercial links with Germany (see page 122) and did not wish to lose a valuable trading partner.

Vargas restricted immigration and did not challenge the growing anti-Semitism in Brazil. Following an attempted coup by communists in 1935, he deported Olga Benário Prestes, the German-born wife of Brazil's communist party leader. She was arrested on arrival in Germany and later died in a concentration camp.

After the war, many former Nazis escaped to Brazil; one of the most infamous was Franz Stangl, commandant of the Treblinka extermination camp.

Jewish emigration after the Second World War

After the end of the Second World War, Latin America became an important destination for survivors of the Holocaust, Nazi officials who were escaping the Allied authorities and also many of the thousands of refugees in Europe.

Many Nazi officials were able to use the chaotic situation and acquire passports and visas from the **International Committee of the Red Cross (ICRC)** and the **Vatican**. During the period 1945–7, there were so many refugees that the ICRC was unable to cope with the situation and did not have the means to check the identities of all those who sought help. Consequently, many Nazis who assumed false names were given passports. Some senior Nazis like Franz Stangl (see above) secured travel papers by means of help from the Vatican with the help of Bishop Alois Hudal.

More than 20,000 Jewish displaced persons left Europe to settle in South America in the years 1947–53. Brazil, Paraguay and Uruguay were also countries which took many survivors.

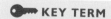 **KEY TERM**

International Committee of the Red Cross (ICRC)
An international movement which has special responsibilities under international humanitarian law.

Vatican The papal government.

How did Canada react
to the Holocaust?

Canada and the Holocaust

Emigration to Canada

Canada had strict immigration policies in the first part of the twentieth century. An immigrant had to be able to contribute to the Canadian economy. Most immigrants were encouraged to move west and become involved in the agricultural sector in order to leave industry to those already living in Canada. By the time of the Depression of the 1930s, there was a fear, just as in Latin America, that any newcomer might compete for the scarce jobs. If an immigrant could not contribute to the economy and became a 'public charge', that is, dependent on the state, then they could be deported. Several thousand immigrants were deported in the 1930s. Immigration and immigrants were not popular in Canada during the 1930s.

Jewish emigration to Canada

At the time when many Jews were seeking to leave Europe and settle elsewhere, Canada was a place that had nearly entirely closed its doors to immigrants. Moreover, as the Depression deepened, Canada expected immigrants to be able to support themselves on arrival. This was almost impossible for Jews who had experienced dispossession of their property. In addition, there was widespread anti-Semitism in Canada and politicians did not like to go against public opinion. In Quebec, Jews were seen by Catholics as posing a threat to the Catholic values of the province.

After *Kristallnacht* (see pages 162–3), the Canadian Jewish Congress guaranteed the financial support of 10,000 Jewish refugees to Canada. However, the government of Canada rejected this proposal, indicating the two major issues within the country: a lack of jobs in a weak economy and anti-Semitism.

In 1940, Canada agreed to the UK's request to accept 'enemy aliens' and prisoners of war. However, when these people arrived in Canada, it was found that there were about 2000 Jewish refugees from Nazism. These refugees had sought asylum in the UK and had been arrested, mistakenly, as spies. They were placed in prison in New Brunswick, Ontario and Quebec alongside political refugees. In some of the camps they were incarcerated with actual Nazi sympathizers. Even though the UK eventually informed the Canadian government of the true status of these Jewish refugees, it was not until the end of 1943 that all had been released from internment. Of the 2000 or more Jewish internees brought to Canada more than half returned to the UK, where they joined the Pioneer Corps or returned to previous occupations, and the others remained in Canada, where they became agricultural workers, students or workers in war industries.

As the war progressed, some Canadian politicians bemoaned the country's immigration policy towards refugees from war-torn Europe, saying that Canada would benefit from the industry and skill of those people.

It has been estimated that about 5000 Jewish refugees settled in Canada during the war and most of these arrived in the first two years of the conflict.

Jewish emigration after the Second World War

After the war, despite the publication of the shocking details of the Holocaust, a poll conducted by the Canadian Institute of Public Opinion showed that 60 per cent of Canadians approved of the exclusion of Jews from Canadian immigration. Canada admitted about 65,000 refugees from 1945 to 1947 but only 8000 were Jews.

Attitudes did begin to change and in 1948, the Canadian government gave permission for 1000 Jewish orphans to immigrate. The children were given assistance by the Jewish community who helped to find foster homes for them. The number of Jewish immigrants began to increase after 1948 because of liberalized legislation regarding the admission of relatives of Canadian citizens. Others arrived as industrial workers under schemes which the Canadian Jewish Congress assisted and encouraged because Canada was experiencing an economic boom and needed labour as quickly as possible.

By 1950, about 40,000 Holocaust survivors had settled in Canada.

Latin America, Canada and the Holocaust

- Immigration to Latin America reduced after 1933
- Jewish immigration restricted generally across Latin America after 1933
- Some countries like Bolivia and El Salvador were exceptions

Argentina
- Immigration restricted
- Anti-Jewish riots in one province
- Both Jews and Nazis settled in Argentina after 1945

Brazil
- Immigration restricted
- Vargas deported Olga Benário Prestes, wife of Brazil's Communist Party leader
- Both Jews and Nazis settled in Brazil after 1945

Canada
- Anti-immigration in the 1930s
- Took in 2000 Jewish internees from the UK
- Some Jews able to reach and settle in Canada during the war
- By 1950, c.40,000 Holocaust survivors settled in Canada

SUMMARY DIAGRAM

Latin America, Canada and the Holocaust

Chapter summary

Reaction to the Holocaust in the Americas

When Hitler embarked on his racial and eugenic policies in the 1930s, the world was suffering from a desperate economic depression. Countries around the world were unwilling to accept floods of refugees seeking better lives, and the Americas were no different. The USA had already restricted immigration in the 1920s, and Canada and Latin America did the same.

President Roosevelt attempted to combat the refugee problem which Hitler created, such as by calling the Evian Conference and setting up the War Refugee Board. Together with the United Nations he issued warnings to the perpetrators of the Holocaust that there would be punishment when the war ended.

However, even after 1945 when the horrors of the Holocaust were universally known, it took some time for attitudes to change in the Americas in order for them to welcome the displaced Jews.

 Examination practice

Below are two exam-style questions for you to practise on this topic.

1 Analyse the effectiveness of US diplomatic efforts in saving European Jews.
  (For guidance on how to answer 'Analyse' questions, see page 49.)

2 Compare and contrast US and Canadian immigration policies during the 1930s.
  (For guidance on how to answer 'Compare and contrast' questions, see page 224.)

CHAPTER 8

Technological developments and the beginning of the atomic age

The Second World War led to many developments in weaponry and tactics, and ultimately the beginning of the atomic age. This chapter looks at these technological advances, especially the development of radar and the importance of aircraft carriers and submarines. It also considers the development of the atomic bomb and the Manhattan Project.

You need to consider the following questions throughout this chapter:

✪ How did technology affect military capability in the Second World War?

✪ In what ways did the war change industry?

✪ What was the impact of the war on medicine?

1 The impact of the war on military technology

▶ *Key question:* How did technology affect military capability in the Second World War?

The Second World War brought many changes to how fighting took place. The war against Japan ended because of the USA's use of the atomic bomb, a product of scientific and technological advances. In most instances, the war accelerated the development of technology and improved such things as radar and weaponry. Importantly, the USA was able to increase its existing mass-production technology to provide huge numbers of goods for itself and its Allies, all of which contributed to victory over the Axis powers.

Radar

Radar (Radio Detection and Ranging) was developed in the 1930s by various countries in order to detect distant objects. This acronym was first used by the United States Navy. As radar was developed, it became possible to determine not only if there was an object but also its position and speed by analysing the reflected radio waves. During the Second World War, radar eventually became an invaluable weapon for all combatant nations because it could target ships and aeroplanes and could be used in all types of weather, in daylight and the dark.

> **Why was radar important during the war?**

KEY TERM

Battle of Britain A series of air battles between Britain and Germany fought over the UK from August to October 1940.

Friendly fire Injuring or killing a member of one's own armed forces or an ally.

Depth charge An anti-submarine bomb that explodes at a pre-set depth under water.

Radar was crucial in the **Battle of Britain** because it gave early warning of incoming German air raids. It meant that planes did not have to be airborne and wait for attacks. Above all, the defensive response could be matched to the size of the incoming raid, thus increasing the chances of success.

Shared technology

During 1940, the UK decided to offer its existing technology secrets to the USA in exchange for access to related US secrets and its manufacturing capabilities, in order to acquire assistance in maintaining the war effort. The result of the exchange led to improvements in the development of radar. The USA then created its own radar research unit at the Massachusetts Institute of Technology which eventually employed more than 4000 people. The USA also developed research departments which looked into counter-measures to radar, and methods of identifying 'friend or foe' craft which would prevent **'friendly fire'** incidents. Several million dollars was spent on radar research.

In addition, radar was important to the Battle of the Atlantic (see page 71). Air-to-surface vessel (ASV) radar was used widely in the Battle of the Atlantic by US and British aircraft on German submarines. If a submarine surfaced or even just the periscope of a submerged submarine was detected by radar, the radar operator guided the aircraft pilot to it, then **depth charges** could be deployed. For night-time bombing, aircraft carried a powerful fixed searchlight aimed forward, lit only in the last few seconds – early enough for the pilot to actually see the target on the water ahead, yet too late for the submarine to dive to safety.

Allied bombers also used H2S, a ground-mapping or scanning radar, for both navigation and targeting in long-range missions. This new targeting radar was designed to fit in a specially designed dome on the fuselage of a bomber, where the radio antenna would rotate to scan the terrain and feed the reflections to a display unit. This would produce a map of the land below the bomber and could be used to locate town shapes, lakes and rivers, thus helping to pinpoint targets. The system was of great help in the US and British bombing of the German cities of Hamburg and Berlin after 1943.

As the war progressed, the Allies used radar in many ways. It was used to help direct searchlights, anti-aircraft fire and guns on board ships where it was used to navigate at night and through fog, to locate enemy ships, aircraft and buried landmines, and to direct gunfire. Eventually, military meteorologists used radar to track storms and predict their route.

Radar detectors

Naturally, anti-radar devices were also developed. The two most common devices used by the USA and the UK were:

- 'chaff': thin, light metal strips dropped from a plane, causing the radar operators to see a large cloud on the screen rather than individual targets

- 'jammers': these transmitted strong radio waves on the same frequency as the radar, with the result that the weaker signal of the real target could not be seen.

The impact of radar

Radar has been seen as one of the decisive factors behind the victory of the Allies because of its ability to provide an early warning system, which was demonstrated in crucial battles, such as the Battle of Britain in 1940, the Solomon Islands campaign in 1942, the Battle of Midway in 1942 and the Battle of the Atlantic, 1939–45. Although the Axis powers had radar, neither Germany nor Japan introduced improvements and innovations as quickly as the USA. Moreover, Japan did not use it effectively in its navy and suffered for this in the Pacific theatre of war.

Aircraft carriers

Aircraft carriers enabled a naval force to project airpower great distances without having to depend on local bases for staging aircraft operations. They developed slowly in the 1920s and 1930s and played a significant role during the Second World War, especially in the Pacific theatre. At the beginning of the war, Japan had ten aircraft carriers, making it the largest and most modern carrier fleet in the world. The USA had six.

> **Why were aircraft carriers important during the war?**

SOURCE A

Photograph of the aircraft carrier USS *Enterprise*, 1939.

> How helpful is Source A as evidence of the importance of aircraft carriers? ?

Japan's attack on Pearl Harbor in 1941 clearly demonstrated the tactical use of aircraft carriers. Both the US and Japanese navy thus required a large fleet of carriers if successful attacks were to be made on the hundreds of islands scattered over the vast expanses of the Pacific Ocean. The carriers' aircraft could support the amphibious landings and keep enemy aircraft at bay. Using aircraft carriers brought an end to the age of the battleship. Before the widespread use of aircraft carriers, whoever possessed the most and biggest battleships – each with huge guns and armour plating – would control the seas. However, it was extremely difficult for the battleship to escape aerial attack if an aircraft carrier was in the vicinity. Even though a battleship could outgun a carrier, the carrier would always be out of range of the battleship's guns, yet the latter would be at the mercy of the carrier's aeroplanes. The two biggest ever battleships, the *Musashi* and *Yamato* (72,500 tons each (65,770 tonnes)), were sunk in the Pacific by US carrier aircraft in October 1944 and April 1945, respectively.

The impact of aircraft carriers on the outcome of the war

The war in the Pacific made these the foremost vessel in any navy. After the Japanese used them to attack Pearl Harbor, the defeat of the Japanese navy after 1942 hinged upon the use of US carriers.

There are several US–Japan battles where aircraft carriers made a significant impact:

- The Battle of the Coral Sea, May 1942 (see page 58) was the first naval battle where neither side's ships sighted the other. Although the USA lost more ships and aircraft than Japan, the battle is viewed as a victory for the USA because it prevented the attack on Port Moresby and the isolation of Australia.
- At the Battle of Midway, June 1942 (see page 59), the Japanese lost some 250 aircraft, four aircraft carriers and several of its best trained pilots. Losing so many carriers meant that the Japanese could not support, defend or resupply their troops on the ground. These losses were unsustainable and thus made Midway the turning point of the war in the Pacific. (The USA lost one carrier.)
- The Battle of the Philippine Sea, June 1944, saw the largest aircraft carrier battle of the war. Japan lost three aircraft carriers and three were damaged. In addition, only 35 operational aircraft remained out of the initial 430. (The USA lost just over 120 aircraft and suffered damage to one of its battleships.)

During the war, Japan built only four additional aircraft carriers whereas the USA built 17. Hence, Japan's losses at Midway and the Philippine Sea were unsustainable. The USA now had control of not only the sea but also the air.

Submarine warfare

Immediately after Pearl Harbor, the US submarine fleet was commanded to attack any Japanese vessel on sight. This broke the London Naval Treaty of 1930 which stated that submarines had to inform merchant vessels of an intended attack so that non-combatants could abandon the ship.

However, US submarines did not possess radar at the beginning of the war and could only go where they thought there would be enemy vessels, then surface and attack if they located any. Moreover, the US Navy was aware that in clear waters, a submarine could be detected to depths of about 100 feet

(30 m) so all US submarines were required by orders to remain submerged within 500 miles (800 km) of an enemy airfield. This greatly restricted US submarine action until radar was fitted.

US submarines also faced problems with their torpedoes. Many submarine commanders complained of torpedoes that did not detonate. One submarine commander claimed that during one attack, 13 out of 15 torpedoes failed to detonate. Eventually, it was discovered that the firing-pins were faulty and a better design was fitted.

It was only in 1943 that the US Navy began to use the newly developed SJ radar, a surface search system, to detect Japanese ships and aircraft at night and in bad weather. When searching for enemy ships, SJ radar could detect an enemy destroyer six miles (10 km) away. The system allowed aggressive submarine commanders to infiltrate Japanese convoys and attack using the element of surprise.

By the end of 1943, the US submarine fleet in the Pacific had sunk 1.5 million tons (1.4 million tonnes) of Japanese merchant shipping, which was crucial in degrading the Japanese ability to wage war. By 1944, US submarines were sinking an average of 50 Japanese merchant ships per month, many of which were oil tankers. Japan began to find it difficult to supply its navy and land forces. Importantly, the introduction of radar and the diminishing number of ships in the Imperial Japanese Navy meant that US submarines could attack vessels in the Sea of Japan. Radar meant that minefields were less of an obstacle and continued defeats at sea resulted in fewer Japanese naval patrols near the home shores.

During 1944 and 1945, US submarines curtailed Japan's ability to import crucial goods to sustain its war effort. Japan lost almost 10 million tons (9 million tonnes) of merchant and military shipping; 54 per cent was sunk by submarines.

Anti-submarine warfare

The German U-boat threat to food and armament supplies became critical by early 1943. The convoys were crucial not only for feeding Britain but also for stockpiling items for the D-Day invasion. After 1940, technological developments gradually overcame the threat, especially the British **ASDIC** system, which the UK shared with the USA after 1940. The system located underwater objects by transmitting an acoustical pulse of energy, then listening for any echoes returned from that object. If conditions were ideal, a target at a range of 3000–4000 yards (2700–3700 m) could be detected.

In March 1943, the Atlantic convoys lost 95 vessels against the destruction of only 12 U-boats. In May the Allies lost just 34 ships and sank 38 U-boats. The Germans could not sustain such losses. The threat to the convoys began to diminish and, by early 1944, U-boat losses were so heavy that by May 1944 North Atlantic operations had virtually ceased.

 **KEY TERM**

ASDIC Named after the Anti-Submarine Detection Investigation Committee which began development during the First World War.

How did technology help the US soldier?

Rockets

The USA developed the bazooka, a rocket-propelled, anti-tank hand-held weapon. It came into operation in 1942. The bazooka could destroy a tank at 200 yards (180 m) and could also destroy fortified positions from 750 yards (690 m), but it was not always accurate. It was first used by US troops in the North Africa and Sicily campaigns. However, it was less effective in the Pacific campaign against sand emplacements, because these softer defences often reduced the force of the rocket's impact. The bazooka was quite successful when used against Japanese tanks and armoured vehicles because of their thin armour plate.

Some soldiers disliked using the bazooka because the smoke from firing it betrayed their position to the enemy.

How did aircraft technology develop during the war?

Jet aircraft

A key development was the jet engine. This type of engine burned fuel internally and then pushed out the resulting hot air and gases at the back of the engine at high speed, which forced the engine forward. Jet fighters were much faster than the conventional propeller engine aircraft. Although the war came to an end just as they were being introduced, by that time almost 2000 such aircraft had been built.

The first operational Allied jet aeroplane was the British Gloster Meteor and more than 200 were built. The USA developed the Lockheed Shooting Star and about 50 were in operation before the end of the war. The Germans introduced the first operational jet during the war, the Messerschmitt 262, and built more than 1400. They also built more than 300 of the Heinkel 162. Both German aeroplanes were much faster than the Allied ones.

Jet fighters had a negligible impact on the outcome of the war. However, the technology developed provided the foundations for new models after 1945. Because German scientists and aeronautical engineers had developed more advanced aerospace technology, the USA encouraged many of them to work for the USA after the war. In some cases, the USA created false records to hide how these people had been Nazis. Perhaps the most famous of these was Wernher von Braun, Nazi Germany's top rocket scientist, who went on to help the USA land men on the moon.

Why did the USA develop the atomic bomb?

The atomic bomb

The atomic bomb in the Manhattan Project was the most significant new technology used in the war. In August 1939, Roosevelt received a letter from the physicist Albert Einstein, which informed him that recent developments in splitting uranium atoms could lead to 'extremely powerful bombs of a new type' by means of nuclear fission. Such a bomb would be far more destructive than any that had been built before. Einstein recommended that the USA should consider research into this new field.

> **Nuclear fission**
>
> Nuclear fission is the process whereby the central part of an atom, the nucleus, absorbs a neutron, then breaks into two equal fragments. In certain elements, such as plutonium-239, the fragments release other neutrons which quickly break up more atoms, creating a chain reaction that releases large amounts of heat and radiation. The atomic bomb harnesses this chain reaction.

The Manhattan Project

Roosevelt, concerned that Germany might develop similar technology and thereby gain a huge military advantage, gave permission for research to start. He appointed an Advisory Committee on Uranium, which met for the first time on 21 October 1939 and included both civilians and representatives of the military. The emerging atomic research project was given the name Manhattan Engineering District (later known as the Manhattan Project), and placed under the command of Army Brigadier General Leslie Groves. Groves recruited American physicist J. Robert Oppenheimer as scientific director. In June 1942, Roosevelt and Churchill agreed to pool all information and work together regarding the development of an atomic bomb. By the time of the first atomic bomb test in July 1945, more than 130,000 people were working on the project and it had cost more than $2 billion.

Three main research establishments were set up at Oak Ridge, Tennessee; Hanford, Washington; and Los Alamos, New Mexico. Almost 90,000 workers were involved in the construction of the Oak Ridge and Hanford sites and two towns grew up around them. The population of Oak Ridge grew from about 3000 in 1942 to about 75,000 in 1945. Hanford grew to a size of 50,000. In all there were some 30 smaller sites working on the project.

Security for the project

Once the project was fully running, the various research sites operated in secret and in isolation and most workers did not know to what end they were working. Those who worked in the laboratories were forbidden to discuss any aspect of the project with friends or relatives. Security in the surrounding areas was very severe and restrictions were placed on workers. Some workers were not permitted to use telephones and many worked under false names. Military security personnel guarded the grounds and monitored communications between the research teams.

Official communications outside Los Alamos, especially to the other Manhattan Project sites, were coded and enciphered. Mail was permitted, but heavily censored. Security was similar to the other two major centres and all residents were confined to the project area and surrounding town.

Yet, despite all the security, the Manhattan Project was infiltrated at Los Alamos by spies from the USSR. These were Klaus Fuchs, Theodore Hall and David Greenglass. As a result of the espionage, Stalin was aware of US technology in the atomic field. When Truman informed Stalin at the Potsdam Conference (see pages 100–3) that the USA possessed a powerful weapon, Stalin had to feign surprise. The espionage also permitted the USSR to catch up on atomic technology, eventually testing its own bomb in 1949.

The work at Los Alamos

As at the other major facilities, physicists, chemists, metallurgists, explosive experts and military personnel worked simultaneously. However, at Los Alamos, the quality of the scientists is evidenced by the attendance at meetings, on many occasions, of six Nobel Prize winners.

On 16 July 1945, the first atomic bomb was tested at the Alamogordo Test Range, New Mexico. The test was codenamed Trinity. Its power surpassed the expectations of the scientists who had been working for so long on the project. Oppenheimer and his colleagues now knew that a single bomb could devastate an entire city and kill thousands of people.

> **The explosion of the test bomb at Alamogordo**
>
> It has been estimated that at the instant of the explosion, the temperature at the core of the bomb was 60 million °C (140 million °F) and that the initial explosion was brighter than the sun. The bomb's cloud rose at 5000 feet (1500 m) a minute. The explosion was the equivalent of 22,000 tons (20,000 tonnes) of conventional explosives. To deliver the equivalent payload, 5000 bombers would have been needed. The explosion created a crater 1200 feet (360 m) in diameter and 25 feet (8 m) deep. The brilliant light created by the explosion was seen 180 miles (290 km) away.

SOURCE B

Excerpt from an interview in 1965 with J. Robert Oppenheimer. The interview was first broadcast as part of the television documentary _The Decision to Drop the Bomb_. Here he expressed his thoughts after seeing the first test of the atom bomb on 16 July 1945.

We knew the world would not be the same. A few people laughed … A few people cried … Most people were silent. I remembered the line from the Hindu scripture the Bhagavad Gita; Vishnu is trying to persuade the prince that he should do his duty, and to impress him takes on his multi-armed form, and says, 'Now I am become death, the destroyer of worlds.' I suppose we all thought that, one way or another.

?
What did Oppenheimer mean in Source B when he said 'We knew the world would not be the same'?

The attacks on Hiroshima and Nagasaki, August 1945

By the end of July, President Truman had decided to use the atomic bomb against Japan (see pages 61–4). Hiroshima was the target because it had not been bombed yet and it was an industrial and military centre. The bomb, nicknamed 'Little Boy', was dropped on 6 August 1945. It has been estimated that there were about 60,000 killed on the day and more than 100,000 deaths afterwards from the lasting effects of the explosion, such as radiation sickness. Japan was asked to surrender and refused to do so. Three days after Hiroshima, another bomb was dropped on Nagasaki, killing about 70,000 people. On 14 August, the Japanese government surrendered.

SOURCE C

Extract from *Hiroshima Diary*, by Michihiko Hachiya, published by University of North Carolina, USA, 1995. Hachiya, who lived in Hiroshima, wrote an account in his diary of the day the atom bomb was dropped on 6 August 1945.

Hundreds of people who were trying to escape to the hills passed our house. The sight of them was almost unbearable. Their faces and hands were burnt and swollen; and great sheets of skin had peeled away from their tissues to hang down like rags or a scarecrow. They moved like a line of ants. All through the night, they went past our house, but this morning they stopped. I found them lying so thick on both sides of the road that it was impossible to pass without stepping on them.

What are the values and limitations of Source C?

SOURCE D

Excerpt from an interview with an American soldier who fought against the Japanese, from *The Good War*, by Studs Terkel, published by Pantheon Books, USA, 1984.

I was in Hiroshima … [that] I saw deformities that I'd never seen before. I know there are genetic effects that may affect generations of survivors and their children. I'm aware of all this. But I also know that had we landed in Japan, we would have faced greater carnage than Normandy. It would probably have been the most bloody invasion in history. Every Japanese man, woman, and child was ready to defend that land. The only way we took Iwo Jima was because we outnumbered them three to one. Still, they held us at bay as long as they did. We'd had to starve them out, month after month after month. As it was, they were really down to eating grass and bark off trees. So I feel split about Hiroshima. The damn thing probably saved my life.

How useful is Source D as evidence of the US decision to bomb Hiroshima and Nagasaki?

Technological developments	**Atomic bomb**	**Naval warfare**
• Radar – helpful in Battles of Britain and Midway • ASV radar used in the Battle of the Atlantic • Radar detectors developed in response to radar • ASDIC developed to detect submarines	• Manhattan Project: $2 billion spent • Test was equivalent to 22,000 tons of conventional explosives • 6 and 9 August 1945: bombs dropped on Hiroshima and Nagasaki	• Radar developed for submarines • Widespread use of submarines by Germany in the Battle of the Atlantic and the USA in the Pacific War • Development of the aircraft carrier – invaluable in the Pacific War • Critical contribution at Battles of Midway, Leyte Gulf and Philippine Sea

SUMMARY DIAGRAM

The impact of the war on military technology

The war and changes in US industry and technology

▶ *Key question: In what ways did the war change industry?*

The scale of the Second World War was such that by 1945 all aspects of US industry had undergone revolutionary changes. The war meant that civil construction of aircraft, ships and automobiles was given over to military production. Changes in these key industries meant that other industries, such as rubber and plastic, had to amend their approach and move to mass production. In addition, the war meant that there were developments in such fields as computing.

Industry

Why was the work of the War Production Board important to the war effort?

To have any chance of success in the war, it was imperative that the warring nations maximized their industrial capacity and increased output accordingly. Roosevelt called the USA 'the arsenal of democracy' and ensured that US industry met the demands of the war by establishing the War Production Board (WPB). Not only did the USA equip its own forces from a low base in 1941, it also supplied the UK and the USSR with huge amounts of *matériel* via Lend–Lease (see pages 41–2).

The work of the WPB

The USA began to experience shortages of key materials during 1940–1. The impact of the war in Europe and the US decision to begin some rearmament led to shortages of steel, rubber and aluminium. Moreover, having signed the Lend–Lease Agreement on 11 March 1941 (see pages 41–2), the USA had to ensure that there were enough ships to carry the materials to the UK. The British were losing huge amounts of merchant ships at the hands of German U-boats. As soon as the war with Japan began, Roosevelt established the WPB.

The WPB was formed on 16 January 1942 to ensure that there was some overall control of production and that the needs of the country in wartime were met. It had 12 regional offices and 120 field offices throughout the country. Its head was Donald Nelson, who had worked for Sears Roebuck and for the government in the Office of Production Management. Other leading members of the WPB were all key figures in US industry such as C. Wilson, President of General Electric, W. Murphy, President of Campbell Soup, and T. Fitch, President of Washington Steel.

The WPB had to ensure that the peacetime industries made the transition to wartime production, that production would be at its maximum and that goods would be produced in the shortest time possible. This meant that there would be controls in a country which did not enjoy governmental interference. Under its aegis, the WPB oversaw the conversion of factories to wartime production. Those that had manufactured silk ribbons produced parachutes; factories which had made upholstery nails produced cartridge clips for rifles; typewriter companies converted to machine-gun production; undergarment manufacturers sewed mosquito netting; and in one case, a rollercoaster manufacturer converted to the production of bomber repair platforms.

The automobile industry

More than three million cars had been produced during 1941, but as soon as the WPB took control, the major companies had to convert to military production. The WPB halted the manufacture of private cars. Chrysler made fuselages for aeroplanes, General Motors made aeroplane engines, guns, trucks and tanks, and Packard made Rolls-Royce engines for the Royal Air Force.

One of the most astonishing changes came at the Ford factory at Willow Run in Michigan. Ford constructed this factory in 1941–2 and it was used to manufacture the B-24 long-range bomber via assembly line production. The aircraft was assembled under one roof and required 500,000 parts as well as 300,000 rivets in 500 different sizes. At its peak, the Willow Run plant produced 650 B-24s per month in 1944. Production was such that pilots and aircrew slept at Willow Run in order to be able to fly the B-24s to their designated bases. This example of production was replicated in other factories across the USA.

The shipbuilding industry

Shipbuilding was another industry which experienced rapid and startling changes during the war. Production techniques developed so much that the speed at which a ship could be produced was hugely improved.

Henry Kaiser, a leading industrialist, introduced mass production methods and new techniques. He dispensed with riveting and relied on welding because it was easier and required less training for his workers. At the height of production in the Second World War, work could be accomplished in four to six days in Kaiser's shipyards.

In the 1930s, shipyards in the USA built only 23 ships but in the five years after 1940, they built 4600 ships. In 1941, a typical steel vessel took 12 months from laying the keel to completion. US shipyards turned out tonnage so fast that by the autumn of 1943 all Allied shipping sunk since 1939 had been replaced. The Axis powers could not compete with this, nor could they compete with the construction of new naval vessels.

Synthetic rubber

After the Japanese captured 90 per cent of the world's rubber trees in South-east Asia in 1942, the Allies' supply of rubber virtually ended and the USA found that it was desperately short. Rubber was needed both for both domestic and military use, such as tyres, hoses, seals, valves and covers for electrical wires. (For example, each Sherman tank contained half a ton of rubber (450 kg) and most warships contained 20,000 rubber parts.) Of all raw materials, rubber was in the shortest supply. It was estimated that in 1942 the USA had only one year's supply of rubber and thus action was urgent. Roosevelt himself recognized its importance and he called it a 'strategic and critical material'.

A recycling programme began and people handed in more than 450,000 tons (408,000 tonnes) of rubber goods, but this did not solve the shortage. Rationing was applied (see pages 152–3) and, although there had been some developments in producing synthetic rubber before the war, the USA produced only 200 tons (180 tonnes) of it in 1941.

The Rubber Reserve Company (RRC) was established to stockpile natural rubber and regulate synthetic rubber production. The WPB then ensured that the major rubber companies such as Firestone, B.P. Goodrich, Goodyear and US Rubber, together with the petrochemical industry and scientists, worked to solve wartime rubber needs. Progress had to be fast. By 1944, a total of 50 factories had been built to manufacture synthetic rubber, and had an output which doubled that of the world's natural rubber production before the beginning of the war. In 1943, 234,000 tons (212,000 tonnes) were produced and this increased to 800,000 tons (725,750 kg) in 1945, far exceeding the German production figures.

The impact of the WPB

The work of the WPB was vital to the success of the US war effort. It helped to mobilize industry as well as the civilian population. Factories worked double shifts and many worked around the clock. The entrepreneurial and innovative spirit that the USA had been famous for before the Depression came to the fore once again.

During its wartime existence, the WPB directed a total production of $185 billion worth of armaments and supplies. US industrial production doubled. This was a phenomenal achievement. Source E shows the industrial output of the USA in comparison with other combatant nations.

> According to Source E, how did US war production compare to that of other nations?

SOURCE E

War production of combatants during the Second World War.

	USA	UK	USSR	Germany	Italy
Tanks	88,500	30,000	105,000	67,000	2,500
Aircraft	300,000	130,000	145,000	120,000	11,000
Artillery units	257,000	125,000	500,000	160,000	7,200
Trucks	2,400,000	480,000	200,000	345,000	83,000
Machine guns	2,700,000	–	1,500,000	675,000	–
Submarines	200	170	–	1,100	28
Surface warships	1,200	730	–	42	15
Merchant shipping (tons)	34,000,000	6,300,000	–	–	1,500,000
Coal (tons)	2,100,000,000	1,400,000,000	590,000,000	2,400,000,000	17,000,000
Iron ore (tons)	400,000,000	120,000,000	71,000,000	240,000,000	4,000,000
Oil (tons)	830,000,000	91,000,000	110,000,000	33,000,000	0

The dash indicates that data are not available.

SOURCE F

Excerpt from a speech by Vice President Henry A. Wallace in New York, 8 May 1942.

If we really believe that we are fighting for a people's peace, all the rest becomes easy. Production, yes — it will be easy to get production without either strikes or sabotage; production with the wholehearted cooperation between willing arms and keen brains; enthusiasm, zip, energy geared to the tempo of keeping at it everlastingly day after day. Hitler knows as well as those of us who sit in on the War Production Board meetings that we here in the United States are winning the battle of production. He knows that both labor and business in the United States are doing a most remarkable job …

> What does Source F suggest about the US war effort?

The war and changes in US industry and technology

War Production Board (WPB)
- Set up in January 1942 to ensure that there was some overall control of production and that the wartime needs of the USA were met
- Ensured the smooth transition from peacetime manufacture to wartime manufacture
- Automobile industry was converted to make aircraft, tanks, aero-engines and military *matériel*
- Shipbuilding streamlined to mass production methods
- Synthetic rubber produced to meet natural shortages
- USA industry out-produced its Allies in key areas such as aircraft, trucks, naval vessels, coal, oil and iron ore

SUMMARY DIAGRAM

The war and changes in US industry and technology

③ Medicine and the war

▶ *Key question: What was the impact of the war on medicine?*

When the war began, there was some hope that the many deaths from injury that had been experienced in the First World War could be avoided. Rather than new discoveries, the mass production of items such as penicillin and blood plasma eventually saved the most lives. Once again, US industry made a prodigious contribution to the war effort.

→ # Developments in the treatment of casualties

How did medical developments improve the treatment of casualties?

The development of penicillin

Although **penicillin** had been discovered in 1928 by Alexander Fleming, it was produced only on a very small scale. It was the war and the work of Howard Florey and Ernest Chain that pushed the production of the drug to an industrial scale. The WPB assisted in the development of the drug and from a position in 1943 where only a handful of soldiers could be treated, the USA manufactured more than 600 billion units in 1945. The drug was available for use on D-Day and was particularly effective in combating gangrene, helping to save countless lives.

Blood plasma

The war hastened the increased production of dried **blood plasma**. Plasma was given to soldiers suffering from loss of blood or from shock in order to help maintain adequate blood pressure. Since plasma can be dried and stored in bottles, it can be transported almost anywhere, ready for immediat

🔑 KEY TERM

Penicillin An antibiotic drug used to treat or prevent a wide range of infections, especially gangrene.

Blood plasma The yellowish fluid portion of the blood in which the corpuscles and cells are suspended.

use. Plasma can be given to anyone, regardless of blood type. By the end of the war, the American Red Cross had collected over 13 million units of blood and converted nearly all of it into plasma. This development was invaluable on the battlefield to keep soldiers alive.

DDT

In addition, US soldiers were able to use dichlorodiphenyltrichloroethane (DDT), which had been developed as an insecticide before the war. Before the introduction of DDT, insect-borne diseases such as malaria, typhus, yellow fever, bubonic plague and others killed millions of people worldwide. During the Second World War, the use of DDT became common among US troops who used it to control these illnesses, especially in Italy and in tropical regions like the South Pacific.

The morphine syrette

During the war, the Squibb pharmaceutical company developed a way for medics and soldiers to administer a controlled amount of morphine, an opiate used in cases of extreme pain, to wounded soldiers. Squibb introduced a morphine syrette – a collapsible tube with an attached hypodermic needle containing a single dose which could be readily injected into the wounded soldier.

The war and changes in medicine

- Mass production of penicillin during the war
- Widespread use of blood plasma – saved lives on the battlefield
- DDT – saved soldiers from suffering from diseases such as malaria and typhus
- Morphine syrette used to ease pain and lessen shock

SUMMARY DIAGRAM

Medicine and the war

Chapter summary

Technological developments and the beginning of the atomic age

Warfare, technology and industry changed dramatically during the Second World War. With such technological developments as radar, the advantage would be with the country that developed the best system of detection. Through sharing their expertise under the Roosevelt–Churchill agreement, the USA and the UK were able to secure the advantage. This, together with the wealth of the USA, ensured that the Manhattan Project was successful. The end result of the project – the development and deployment of the atomic bomb – was to end the war and place the USA as the most powerful nation in the world. The War Production Board (WPB) helped to mobilize the USA so that factories and shipyards were built at a fantastic rate. Technological developments allowed the USA to make rapid progress in such areas as synthetic rubber and computers. Yet, as the WPB showed, it was also the US capacity to mass produce goods which brought success.

Developments in medicine, such as more extensive use of penicillin, the use of plasma and the morphine syrette, meant that casualties could be treated more easily and had a better chance of survival.

 Examination practice

Below are two exam-style questions for you to practise on this topic.

1 To what extent did US manufacturing production help win the Second World War?
(For guidance on how to answer 'To what extent' questions, see page 82.)

2 Assess the effectiveness of new technologies created during the war.
(For guidance on how to answer 'Assess' questions, see page 106.)

CHAPTER 9

The economic and diplomatic effects of the Second World War on the Americas

This chapter examines the economic effects of the war on the USA and how its government mobilized industry and people for the conflict. It looks at how the economy moved into peacetime and the issues this created in the USA. The changing relationship between the USA and the USSR during the war and how alliances realigned after the war is discussed. Finally, the chapter moves on to consider the economic and diplomatic effects of the war on Brazil and Canada.

You need to consider the following questions throughout this chapter:

✪ How did the war affect the US economy?
✪ Why did the US economy face problems after 1945?
✪ Why did relations between the USA and the USSR change during the war?
✪ How did the Second World War affect Brazil?
✪ How did the Second World War affect Canada?

1 The economic effects of the Second World War on the USA

▶ Key question: How did the war affect the US economy?

 **KEY TERM**

The Second World War enabled the USA to expand its **industrial and military complexes** on a huge scale. By the end of the war it had emerged as the most powerful economy in the world. The war had given the USA immense advantages over both its allies and its enemies. The dark days of the Depression had become a distant memory in a country where, by 1945, there were more jobs than applicants.

Industrial and military complexes The aggregate of a nation's armed forces and the industries that supply their equipment, materials and armaments.

As seen in Chapter 8, the War Production Board (WPB) was instrumental in bringing about huge changes during the war. US industry was able to expand as a result of the Lend–Lease programme (see pages 40–1) when huge amounts of aid were given to the UK, the USSR and Latin America (especially Brazil). In addition, US industry and agriculture were able to cope with labour shortages by adopting the Bracero Program (see page 137).

What was the impact
of the war on
unemployment in the
USA?

Employment in the USA during the war

The end of the Depression

The economic crisis and period of low business activity in the USA began at the time of the stock market crash in October 1929 and continued throughout the 1930s (see Chapter 1). President Roosevelt tried to stem the rise in unemployment by introducing the New Deal and was successful to a degree, with unemployment falling to 16.9 per cent in 1936. However, a further recession in 1937–8 pushed the figure back up to 19 per cent. The war in Europe, then US participation in the conflict, ended the Depression and returned the country to full employment.

SOURCE A

A table showing civilian unemployment during the Second World War.
Source: Bureau of Labor Statistics, 'Employment status of the civilian non-institutional population, 1940 to date' (www.bls.gov/web/empsit/cpseea01.htm).

Year	Civilian labour force (millions)	Unemployed (millions)	Percentage unemployed as a total of workforce (%)
1940	55.6	8.1	14.6
1941	55.9	5.5	9.9
1942	56.4	2.6	4.7
1943	55.5	1.1	1.9
1944	54.6	0.6	1.2
1945	53.8	1.0	1.9

The mobilization of US industry

How did the USA
mobilize industry for
the war?

Equipping US industry

As the US economy began to improve after 1939, it became clear that for industrial output to increase, new factories would have to be built and existing ones re-equipped with new machinery. The main problem for US industry in the years 1940–1 was the shortage of **machine tools**. The actual manufacturing of machine tools had diminished during the 1930s, even though these were indispensable for the production of *matériel*. This meant that war *matériel* production would initially slow while the tools were being made before full-scale production could occur. The situation was so grave that Roosevelt banned the export of machine tools in 1941.

🔑 **KEY TERM**

Machine tools Power-driven machines, such as lathes, millers or grinders, used for cutting, shaping and finishing metals or other materials.

The shortage of machine tools was overcome by phenomenal work and organization, although it was only in late 1941 that factories moved beyond one shift per day. Factories came to operate 24 hours a day, seven days a week to produce new machines and to recondition old machines. By 1944, production of machine tools began to slow because US industry was performing at maximum efficiency.

The government played a key role in maximizing and regulating production of war *matériel*, with Roosevelt establishing several new organizations during the war.

Office of Production Management

The USA began to increase its production of defence items from 1939 to 1941. However, at the same time, civilian industries continued to produce for the home market. Hence, there was an internal competition for basic materials. This was an inefficient approach for the preparation of the country for war and therefore, on 7 January 1941 Roosevelt established the Office of Production Management (OPM) by Executive Order 8629. The OPM regulated the production and supply of materials required for national defence and co-ordinated the work of all departments engaged in the country's defence.

The OPM became crucial, especially after the Lend–Lease agreement (see pages 40–1) with the UK in March 1941 when demand for war *matériel* increased greatly. It had to ensure that the UK was supplied with *matériel* but at the same time be certain that the US forces were not denied any of their own demands. Furthermore, when the USSR and other countries were granted Lend–Lease aid, US industry had to meet almost impossible demands not only for its own armed forces but also for those countries fighting Germany.

Supplies Priorities and Allocation Board

However, the OPM did not always regulate supplies effectively. Some companies were able to acquire more raw materials, for example, Henry Kaiser's shipbuilding (see Chapter 8, page 196) and this meant that if there were bottlenecks in supplies then some factories would have to close down. There was also a debate over whether some car companies were still manufacturing too many civilian vehicles and ought to be producing more military vehicles. To combat this in August 1941 Roosevelt stepped in and created the Supplies Priorities and Allocation Board to serve as the co-ordinating centre 'for the execution of the powers and activities of the several departments and agencies relating to priorities of materials' and oversee the OPM. After the Japanese attack on Pearl Harbor, Roosevelt was forced to create a single body to direct mobilization. This was the War Production Board (WPB). The WPB was able to increase US war production but could not always ensure a constant flow of raw materials such as aluminium. Furthermore, the debate with the army and navy over the necessity of civilian production continued. The success of government organizations in increasing wartime production can be seen in Source B. The figures in the table are percentage increases from 1939 to 1944.

? What might explain why growth of some manufactures according to Source B was faster than others?

SOURCE B

Federal Reserve indexes of certain manufacturing industries in the USA, 1939–44 (1939 = 100 per cent output). Source: *War, Economy, and Society, 1939–1945*, **by Alan S. Milward, published by University of California Press, USA, 1979, page 69.**

Manufacture	1940	1941	1942	1943	1944
Aircraft	245	630	1706	2842	2805
Munitions	140	423	2167	3803	2033
Shipbuilding	159	375	1091	1815	1710
Aluminium	126	189	318	561	474
Rubber	109	144	152	202	206
Steel	131	171	190	202	197

? How useful is Source C as evidence of US wartime production?

SOURCE C

Photograph of the Chrysler assembly line at Detroit Arsenal Tank Plant, February 1942.

The scale of US production

In 1945, at the end of the war, it was clear that the scale of US industrial output had been immense. For example:

- By 1944, the USA produced 25 per cent of the UK's military equipment.
- By 1945, half of the world's manufacturing took place in the USA.
- The US **gross national product** grew from about $200 billion in 1940 to $300 billion in 1950.

The conversion from a peacetime economy to a wartime one was necessarily quick and production rose at astonishing rates. A key contributory factor was ensuring that there were enough workers with the requisite skills to work in the factories.

The recruitment of workers

War Manpower Commission

The War Manpower Commission (WMC) was set up on 18 April 1942 by Roosevelt to establish a clear policy about the wartime labour force. There was tension between the military, which sought to recruit huge numbers of men, and industry, which required vast numbers of workers. To cope with the shortage of skilled and trained workers, the WMC established the Training Within Industry (TWI) department. This helped to provide training services for unskilled workers to cover the shortfall of those who had enlisted. The TWI was able to help to overcome the skills shortage and more than 1.5 million workers were given training during the war.

Although US workers complied with many of the regulations and requests from employers and the government, there were strikes and disputes brought about by economic changes after the war. Workers were most concerned about rising prices and rents.

Inflation during the war

Office of Price Administration

During the First World War, retail prices in the USA rose by more than 60 per cent. To combat inflation during the Second World War, Roosevelt set up a specific body, the Office of Price Administration (OPA), to control prices and rents. By 1945, the OPA had placed a ceiling on 90 per cent of retail food prices and residential rents. Prices did remain relatively stable throughout the war years and the OPA kept inflation to an average of 3.5 per cent in the years 1942–6. Workers generally received wage rises well above the inflation rate and therefore had more disposable income. However, there were few goods to purchase, and so the government was able to encourage people to save and buy **war bonds** which helped the government to finance the war. By 1945, about 85 million Americans had purchased almost $200 billion worth of war bonds mostly through automatic deductions from their wages and salaries.

 **KEY TERM**

Gross national product
The value of all the goods and services produced, plus the value of imported goods and services, less exported goods and services.

How were workers recruited and trained during the war?

How did the US government combat inflation?

KEY TERM

War bonds Securities sold by the US government to its citizens to finance military operations during the war. The war bonds took money out of the economy and thus prevented inflation from becoming too high.

Why did demand for US goods grow after 1945?

→ US domestic and foreign markets

Importantly, the US domestic market proved to be much more buoyant than had been anticipated. The millions of US citizens who had purchased war bonds now began to cash them in and this amounted to almost $200 billion. Ordinary Americans wanted to leave rationing behind and buy consumer goods. The demand for consumer goods enabled US industry to convert to peacetime production with relative ease and this helped to contribute to continued and sustained economic growth.

Economic aid to Europe

The strength of the US economy can be seen by its actions in Europe after 1945. The UK borrowed more than $4 billion and the loan was made with very low interest, to be paid off in 50 annual repayments starting in 1950. Loans and gifts were also made to other European nations but in 1947, when the plight of Europe was fully realized, George Marshall, Truman's Secretary of State, announced details of the European Recovery Program (ERP or Marshall Plan). Financial aid was offered to Western European governments to assist economic recovery and by 1951, the total given amounted to $13 billion.

The impact of the Cold War

Moreover, as the **Cold War** developed after 1947, the rise in defence spending helped to sustain economic growth. It had been thought that much of the US defence industry would be run down after 1945 with the advent of peace. However, deteriorating relations with the USSR and a fear of future conflict meant that defence spending remained high. US forces remained in Germany and Japan, and the USA had built 14 more atomic bombs by March 1947. In 1948, the US defence budget was about $11 billion.

World trade

Importantly, world markets began to open up now that the seas were free and demand for consumer good began to rise. The USA anticipated that there would be an **open trading system** when there were no tariffs or trading restrictions. Because US industry had not been damaged by air attacks, it meant that the USA had a clear advantage over the European countries which had been ravaged and devastated by war. Demand from Europe and other markets helped to keep US production high.

KEY TERM

Cold War A tense strategic and ideological confrontation between the USA and USSR after the Second World War. It was 'cold' as there was never a direct war between the two powers.

Open trading system Trading between countries when there are no tariffs and restrictions.

SOURCE D

An excerpt from 'Mobilization and militarization' by M. Sherry, in *Major Problems in American History*, by C. Gordon (editor), published by Houghton & Mifflin, USA, 1999, page 438.

America's economic leverage allowed it to arm-twist allies dependent on American assistance into accepting tariff and monetary agreements that pried open much of the world, especially Europe's colonial empires, to American trade and investment.

What does Source D show you about the USA's attitude towards its allies?

The USA met the challenges of the war and as a result unemployment fell to minimal levels and industry coped with the needs of the USA itself as well as those of Lend–Lease. The economy remained buoyant after 1945 with strong domestic and foreign markets but there were still issues to be faced and problems to be solved in the early years of peace.

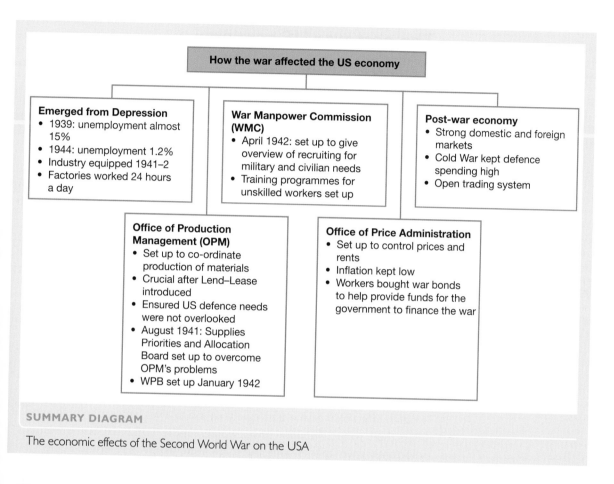

SUMMARY DIAGRAM

The economic effects of the Second World War on the USA

② The problems of the US economy after 1945

▶ *Key question: Why did the US economy face problems after 1945?*

Towards the end of the war, Congress anticipated a depression in the aftermath of peace and worked on legislation to avoid a repetition of the 1930s. Many people believed that huge military spending had been the main cure for US economic ills after 1939. They thought that the federal government would have to ensure that US soldiers would not return home to a country without jobs or opportunities. Almost 10 million service people were looking for jobs in civilian life in 1945 and 1946. There were also issues of what to do with the women who had taken on men's jobs during the war, as well as what to do with workers who, now the war was over, demanded better working conditions. The government realized that it had a central role to play in peacetime economic affairs.

How did the government deal with economic issues?

The post-war US economy

The GI Bill of Rights

One of the most important preparations for peacetime was the GI Bill of Rights, officially known as the Servicemen's Readjustment Act of 1944. This was designed to provide federal aid for the millions of returning war veterans and was to help make the transition to work easier. It helped servicemen to start businesses and go to college. Almost eight million took advantage of the educational opportunities offered by the bill. The GI Bill also offered low-interest mortgages and this in itself created employment by contributing to a construction boom. Aid from the GI Bill amounted to almost $14 billion by 1951.

In 1946, the Employment Act was passed. It stated that the federal government, assisted by industry, labour, and state and local governments, was responsible for promoting maximum employment, production and purchasing power.

Women after the war

During the war, women took on traditionally male jobs such as lathe operators, welders and carpenters which were often higher paid than the employment they had been used to. At the end of the war, because of the mass of returning soldiers, the government and owners of industry urged women to 'go back home' and 'give your job to a vet [veteran]'. By the end of 1946, there were 2.5 million fewer women in the workforce. Some women reluctantly gave up their jobs, but many were happy to return to being homemakers and housewives. However, in the post-war years, women were forced back into traditional patterns of employment in low-paying jobs such as clerks, secretaries, waitresses and textile workers. (See pages 138–42 for more about the impact of the war on women.)

Strikes

There was often an undercurrent of dissatisfaction among workers during the war and although there were strikes, the vast majority of workers refrained from demanding huge and outrageous demands for higher wages or better working conditions. Most labour unions made a no-strike pledge for the duration of hostilities.

However, once the war was over, issues which had been fermenting during the war now came to the surface. The situation was compounded because the power of the unions had grown as a result of the growth of membership.

n 1945, unions had more than 14 million members. As price controls ended and workers saw that they could spend their disposable income they demanded more consumer goods. Not only did they demand consumer goods, they demanded wage increases, pensions and health insurance. Wage increases had matched inflation during the war and most workers had experienced rises above inflation. However, after price controls were removed, the USA saw inflation rise rapidly and workers were unhappy with this. Their demands were rejected and strikes across all types of industries followed in the autumn of 1945. In 1945, there were 4750 strikes involving 3,470,000 workers for 38 million days, and in 1946 there were 4985 strikes involving 4,600,000 workers for 116 million days.

SOURCE E

Major strikes in the USA from 1945 to 1946. Source: Bits of News (www.bitsofnews.com/content/view/6638/).

Date of strike	Industry	Number on strike
September 1945	Petroleum	43,000
	Coal	200,000
October 1945	Lumber	44,000
	Haulage (Teamsters)	70,000
	Machine tool operators	40,000
November 1945	Automobile	250,000
January 1946	Electrical	174,000
	Meatpacking	300,000
	Steel	750,000
April 1946	Coal	350,000
May 1946	Railway	250,000

What does Source E indicate about labour unrest after the Second World War?

In early October 1945, Harry S. Truman, who had become president on the death of Roosevelt in April 1945, broke the petroleum strike by directing the navy to seize half the refining capacity of the USA. The steel workers went on strike in January 1946, seeking improved wages and benefits. With some 750,000 refusing to work, the prospect of a long and bitter dispute looked certain. However, President Truman put pressure on the steel companies to accede to the demands of the workers and the strike soon ended.

It was in April and May 1946 when industrial relations worsened. The United Mine Workers went on strike and fuel shortages resulted. Truman seized control of the mines and forced a settlement on the miners. He then threatened to conscript striking rail workers into the army and force them to run the trains (see Source F on page 210). This pushed the railroad union to come to a settlement.

Looking at Source F, how did President Truman try to discredit the railroad strike?

SOURCE F

An excerpt from President Truman's speech to Congress, 24 May 1946, quoted from History Matters (http://historymatters.gmu.edu/d/5137).

For the past two days the nation has been in the grip of a railroad strike which threatens to paralyze all our industrial, agricultural, commercial, and social life. The strike will spare no one. It will bear equally upon businessmen, workers, farmers and upon every citizen of the United States. Food, raw materials, fuel, shipping, housing, the public health, the public safety – all will be dangerously affected. Hundreds of thousands of liberated people of Europe and Asia will die who could be saved if the railroads were not now tied up … unless the railroads are manned by returning strikers I shall immediately undertake to run them by the Army of the United States. I assure you that I do not take this action lightly. But there is no alternative. This is no longer a dispute between labour and management. It has now become a strike against the Government of the United States itself.

The Taft–Hartley Act

Following the wave of strike activity, Congress passed the Taft–Hartley Act (named after the two Republican Party sponsors, Senator Robert Taft and House of Representative Fred Hartley). This allowed employees the right not to join unions and required advance notice of a strike, authorized an 80-day federal injunction when a strike threatened national health or safety, narrowed the definition of unfair labour practices, specified unfair union practices, restricted union political contributions, and required union officials to take an oath pledging that they were not communists.

SOURCE G

According to Source G, why was the war important for the US economy?

An excerpt from *War, Economy, and Society, 1939–1945*, by A. Milward, published by University of California Press, USA, 1979, page 63.

The United States emerged in 1945 in an incomparably stronger position economically than in 1941 … By 1945, the foundations of the United States' economic domination over the next quarter of a century had been secured … [This] may have been the most influential consequence of the Second World War for the post-war world.

The government was surprised and concerned by the number and extent of strikes after the war finished and President Truman wanted to ensure that the strikes caused minimal disruption to the USA. He was keen to impress on the US people that such actions damaged the USA domestically and that they could damage the USA's position in the world.

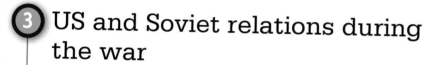

Problems of the US economy after 1945

Concerns over US economy
- Fear of unemployment and depression
- 10 million in armed forces to be demobilized
- Strikes in 1945–6 in major industries
- GI Bill of Rights
- Taft–Hartley Act

SUMMARY DIAGRAM

The problems of the US economy after 1945

3 US and Soviet relations during the war

▶ **Key question:** *Why did relations between the USA and the USSR change during the war?*

The war in Europe soon had consequences for US foreign policy. The USA was committed to grandiose ideals because it had signed the Atlantic Charter (see pages 44–5), which meant that it could no longer shirk involvement in world affairs. The attack on Pearl Harbor ended any pretence that the USA had about fighting the Axis powers and thus ended the policy of isolationism. The war brought the USA closer to the USSR. Importantly, the war pushed the USA into becoming a member of the international organization the United Nations (UN), which meant that the policy of isolation could not be resurrected after the cessation of hostilities.

The USA and the USSR: a rollercoaster relationship

Were the USA and USSR really allies?

Pre-war rivalry between the USA and the USSR

There had been tension between the USA and the USSR throughout the 1920s and early 1930s. This went back to the Bolshevik revolution in 1917 because the Bolsheviks believed in world revolution and sought to spread communism. At the heart of the rivalry were the conflicting belief systems of the two sides: **communism** and **capitalism**. The vast majority of Americans believed in free trade and free enterprise. The idea that a government might take control of land, property and industry, as advocated by communism, was abhorrent to them and any threat to the US system had to be countered. The fear of the spread of communism was evident when, in 1918 and 1919, forces from the USA, the UK, France and 12 other countries invaded Russia

🔑 **KEY TERM**

Communism A theory that society should be classless, private property abolished, and land and business owned collectively.

Capitalism A system under which businesses are owned privately and people are able to make a profit.

in support of the **Whites**. The aim was to remove the Bolsheviks. However, foreign intervention failed and the Bolsheviks were able to establish their regime.

The US government did not extend diplomatic recognition to the Bolshevik regime and continued to view it as an outlaw state. However, when Roosevelt became president, he began to reconsider the US position. He saw that the USSR could be a trading partner and might also be an ally against the growing threat of Japan. Diplomatic relations between the USA and the USSR were finally established in November 1933, after Roosevelt negotiated a new trade agreement between the two nations. However, relations between the USA and the USSR cooled after the Nazi–Soviet Pact in 1939 and then worsened when Roosevelt criticized the Soviet invasion of Finland and even considered offering the Finns help against the USSR.

The US–Soviet relationship during the Second World War

The relationship between the two countries changed when Hitler invaded the USSR in June 1941. Roosevelt immediately promised Stalin Lend–Lease aid. The situation changed once again following the Japanese attack on Pearl Harbor when the two countries became allies against Hitler. The USSR and Japan remained at peace as a result of their Neutrality Pact of April 1941 (see page 20). Now that there was a coalition of the USA, the UK and the USSR, relations became more complex because finding a compromise between them in a difficult situation would not be easy.

Roosevelt, like Churchill and Stalin, was focused on the defeat of the Axis powers, but he was also intent on creating a stable post-war system which would eliminate war. He clashed with Churchill about the maintenance of the British Empire after the cessation of hostilities and saw Stalin as an ally in ensuring that European colonial empires would be dismantled.

Roosevelt knew that some members of his administration were antipathetic towards Stalin and therefore he appointed Harry Hopkins, a trusted adviser, as his chief envoy to Moscow. Moreover, Roosevelt ensured that promises of aid to the USSR were kept. In March 1942, he wrote to all US war agencies on the importance of the shipments to the USSR, saying he 'wished all material promised to the Soviet Union to be released for shipping at the earliest possible date regardless of the effect of these shipments on any other part of the war program'. He saw that he needed to win Stalin's trust and began to believe that he could make a close friend of Stalin. Roosevelt needed Stalin for any possible help against Japan in the future and wanted to ensure that friendship would help in the post-war settlement.

Importantly, the USA and USSR were able to establish a framework for what became known as the United Nations Organization at the Dumbarton Oaks Conference in August to October 1944. However, there was much wrangling about membership and the use of the veto (see pages 97–8) and these issues were solved at later conferences. Yet, even these discussions about peace and a peacekeeping body created tension between the two major powers.

The Tehran, Yalta and Potsdam Conferences

Relations were not always smooth because of the delay in opening the Second Front (see pages 87–8) and Roosevelt found himself fending off Churchill's demands for invasions in south-east Europe and Stalin's demands for immediate action in western Europe. At the Tehran Conference in 1943 (see pages 91–3), Roosevelt stayed in the Soviet embassy and met Stalin away from Churchill. He made jokes at Churchill's expense and in full discussions positioned the USA between the UK and the USSR.

Tension grew among the Big Three about the future of Germany and there was a fear that the USSR might take advantage of a dismembered Europe. However, at the Yalta Conference (see pages 95–7) in February 1945, Roosevelt was happy to guarantee friendly governments on the USSR's borders and accepted Stalin's promise to hold free elections in the territories liberated by Soviet forces. The Soviet army was already occupying Poland, and Roosevelt wrote to his Chief of Staff, William Leahy, 'It's the best I can do for Poland at this time.'

At Yalta, Roosevelt succeeded in gaining a commitment from Stalin to enter the war against Japan after hostilities with Germany ceased and he felt that the USSR's participation in the Pacific War would also help to strengthen relations between the two countries. Although the agreements made at Yalta were fraught with problems, Roosevelt and Churchill saw the main one being whether Stalin would allow free elections in liberated territories.

Churchill, unlike Roosevelt, grew more suspicious of Stalin's motives in eastern Europe as the war drew to a close. He was convinced that Soviet troops would remain in the countries they liberated from German occupation. Yet, it was not difficult to understand Stalin's rationale behind creating a **buffer zone** in eastern Europe. The USSR had been invaded from the west by Germany on two occasions, in 1914 and 1941, and had suffered huge casualties during the ensuing wars. Stalin sought to create a zone of 'friendly' or, better still, Soviet-controlled states in eastern Europe as protection against future invasions. Moreover, Stalin harboured fears, even up to April 1945, that the USA and the UK might make a separate peace with Germany. He was transfixed by the need to secure the USSR's borders.

However, Roosevelt was convinced that his personal friendship and rapport with Stalin would ensure solutions to the problems facing post-war Europe. He believed that relations with the USSR would be good after the war and he viewed the USSR as one of 'the four policemen' who would keep peace after the cessation of hostilities. (The UK, the USA and China were the other three 'policemen'.) Stalin's fears for the future defence of the USSR and his aims in eastern Europe did not change after the Yalta Conference. They resurfaced at the Potsdam Conference (see pages 100–3).

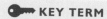 **KEY TERM**

Buffer zone A neutral area between hostile or belligerent forces that serves to prevent conflict.

SOURCE H

Stalin speaking about the takeover of eastern Europe in April 1945. Quoted from *Conversations with Stalin*, by Milovan Djilas, published by Harcourt Brace International, USA, 1963, page 90.

This war is not as in the past. Whoever occupies a territory also imposes on it his own beliefs and social system. Everyone imposes his own system as far as his army has power to do so. It cannot be otherwise. If now there is not a communist government in Paris, this is only because Russia has no an army which can reach Paris in 1945.

? What does Source H show you about Stalin's view about the victors in this war?

President Truman and the USSR

When President Roosevelt died in April 1945, his successor, Harry S. Truman, had opposing views about Stalin, the USSR and communism. President Truman disliked communism and was determined to be tough on Stalin and the USSR at Potsdam (see pages 100–3). Yet, at Potsdam, Stalin was not cowed by Truman or the 'weapon of awesome destruction'. Truman's decision to use the atomic bomb has been seen as a means of intimidating Stalin (see pages 65–8) because it gave the US military superiority and therefore co-operation with Stalin was no longer needed.

SOURCE I

An extract from the *Pelican History of the United States of America*, by Hugh Brogan, published by Penguin Books, UK, 1987, page 601.

No peace settlement in Europe was ever agreed; new spheres of influence were claimed and appropriated by East and West, new crises erupted, and before long a new arms race was developing. It was a confirmation … that great alliances rarely survive the shock of victory, and that great powers usually behave as rivals rather than as partners.

? How helpful is Source I in understanding international relations after 1945?

Growing US–Soviet rivalry

Post-war rivalry

By the summer of 1945 it was clear to see that there was some animosity between the two great powers. The ideologies which had caused suspicion in the inter-war period surfaced once more after 1945. Even the establishment of the United Nations Organization (see pages 97–8) showed tension between the two powers when there was disagreement about the veto and membership. The USSR's establishment of satellite states in eastern Europe after the war and refusal to allow democratic elections exacerbated the communist threat. This division of Europe into an Eastern bloc and a Western one led Winston Churchill to make his '**iron curtain**' speech in Fulton, Missouri, in 1946. The situation had deteriorated so much that in 1947, President Truman issued what became known as the '**Truman Doctrine**' and then established the Marshall Plan (see page 206).

How did rivalry develop after 1945?

🔑 KEY TERM

Iron curtain The military, political and ideological barrier established between the Soviet bloc and Western Europe from 1945 to 1990.

Truman Doctrine Truman's policy of providing economic and military aid to any country threatened by communism or totalitarian ideology.

Changing alliances

Stalin was convinced that there would be a future conflict with the capitalist world. His establishment of communist dictatorships in eastern Europe in the years after the war convinced the USA that he sought to spread communism across the globe. Truman had to act and secure allies, and he told his aides: 'It means the US is going into European politics.' It then became the aim of the USA to establish a coalition against the USSR to contain the spread of communism.

Following the Truman Doctrine and the Marshall Plan, the USA signed the North Atlantic Treaty in April 1949 which led to the North Atlantic Treaty Organization (NATO) being formed. NATO comprised the USA, the UK, Canada and nine other European states, and they made it plain that an attack on any NATO member would be considered as an attack on the whole alliance. It was a clear signal to the USSR.

During the same period, the USSR developed its own network of agreements. In September 1947, the Communist Information Bureau (COMINFORM) was established. This was a Soviet-dominated organization of communist parties. Then, in January 1949, in response to the Marshall Plan, the USSR established the Council for Mutual Economic Assistance (COMECON). COMECON's aims were to co-ordinate economic development and facilitate trade between its members. The alliance of the war had now broken and there were two distinct blocs in the world.

The USA was also determined to ensure that any threat from the USSR anywhere in the world, especially in the American hemisphere, was minimized. Canada joined NATO and the USA wanted to maintain the close links, which had been developed during the war, with countries such as Brazil and Mexico.

US and Soviet relations during the war

- Ideological antipathy pre-1941
- USA immediately offered USSR help after the German invasion
- Tension grew over delay in opening the Second Front
- Roosevelt felt he could manage Stalin
- Tension at Yalta over reparations, elections and Poland
- Truman anti-communist and anti-Stalin
- Rivalry clear at Potsdam
- Use of atomic bombs ushered in a new phase of the US–Soviet relationship
- Truman Doctrine, Marshall Plan and NATO
- COMINFORM and COMECON

SUMMARY DIAGRAM

US and Soviet relations during the war

Brazil and the Second World War

> ▶ *Key question: How did the Second World War affect Brazil?*

The Second World War had a tremendous impact on Brazil. Initially, Brazil followed a policy of neutrality and then entered the conflict on the side of the Allies in 1942 (see pages 104–5). The three years of neutrality brought improvements in Brazil's international trading status. Even though some of its exports to Europe were now limited, Brazil's exports to the rest of the world rose quite substantially, for example, Brazil's textile exports to Argentina and South Africa rose very quickly and, in 1942, Brazil's exports were valued about $388 million, which was more than double the 1941 figure.

Brazil's developing links with the USA

What were the aims of President Vargas?

🔑 **KEY TERM**

Estado Novo 'New State': Getúlio Vargas' 1937 dictatorial regime.

Import substitution A trade and economic policy advocating replacing foreign imports with domestic production.

The aims of President Vargas

Getúlio Vargas, the leader of Brazil, having announced his *Estado Novo*, wanted to follow a policy of **import substitution** and state-managed industrialization and sought to move away from Brazil's dependency on the export of coffee, textiles, sugar and beef. He saw that the government would have to take an active role in stimulating key industries such as mining, oil, steel, electricity and chemicals. He was aware from the late 1930s, and in the early part of the European war, that the most realistic hope to develop an industrial base was to seek assistance from the USA despite growing exports and links to Germany. Vargas' main problem was how to promote his idea of economic nationalism but at the same time allow some foreign investment.

Brazil's links with Germany

In the century before the Second World War, Brazil had experienced a large influx of German and Italian immigrants. Their descendants had been assimilated into Brazilian society and held important positions in government and the military. By the late 1930s, there were some 900,000 people of German descent and 1.5 million Italians living in Brazil.

Germany became the second most important trading partner of Brazil and Hitler sought to develop a strategic commercial bond with Brazil. Brazil exported raw materials to Germany and imported manufactured goods from Germany. Moreover, the Brazilian government sought to buy arms from Germany rather than rely on US munitions. The value of trade between the two countries more than quadrupled in the 1930s (see page 122). In 1938, Brazil was the biggest non-European consumer of German products and ranked ninth among Germany's trading partners overall.

The USA and the Brazilian economy

During the first two years of the European war, 1939–41, the USA sought to divert Brazil away from its relationship with Germany (see pages 104–5). Vargas gradually realized that it could only be the USA that would provide investment to help accelerate industrialization in Brazil. He saw the USA as a better, more accessible market for Brazilian goods after 1940. The USA was keen to bring Brazil closer into its orbit. One way it achieved this was through offers of investment, aid and loans to Vargas. First, in the spring of 1940, following lengthy negotiations, the USA loaned almost $70 million to Brazil. In addition, in September 1940, the USA offered Brazil credit to construct the Volta Redonda steel mill. The mill became the symbol for Brazil's industrialization but, importantly, the agreement firmly cemented links with the USA, leading to Brazil declaring war on the Axis powers in 1942 (see page 105).

When Brazil declared war on Germany, Roosevelt was able to give Lend–Lease aid (see pages 41–2), which enabled Brazil to modernize its armed forces, especially its navy. Brazil emerged from the war as the principal military power of South America with modernized armed forces. By the end of the war, 70 per cent of all Latin American Lend–Lease aid had been given to Brazil.

The aid from Lend–Lease meant that the USA could now rely on Brazil's natural supply of iron ore, chrome, manganese, nickel, bauxite, tungsten and industrial diamonds which was critical to the US war effort. Later in the war, the US imported quartz crystals to use in military communications equipment and then monazite sands were imported because they contained thorium which was used in the atomic programme (see pages 191–2).

The USA was desperate to import rubber, one of the most important raw materials, following the Japanese capture of the Asian rubber plantations. Brazil agreed to supply the USA with rubber and this meant increasing its annual production from 18,000 to 45,000 tons (16,300 to 41,000 tonnes) and resulted in 100,000 workers being recruited to the industry in the Amazon basin. At the end of the war, the rubber industry declined dramatically.

Brazil's economy after the war

At the beginning of the war, Brazil's manufacturing had been limited largely to textiles and food. However, by 1945, there were some 70,000 small- and medium-sized factories employing more than a million workers. Brazil had developed a range of industries and Vargas had established the National Motor Factory which made engines for trucks and aircraft.

Involvement in the war provided Brazil with huge amounts of US aid, which enabled the development of Brazil's infrastructure. In addition, the war furthered import-substitution processes and made Brazil the strongest power in Latin America. The industrialization spurred by the war 'propelled Brazil during a single generation from the age of the bull-cart to that of the internal combustion engine', according to historian Frank McCann.

In what ways did
Brazil's diplomatic
position change?

The diplomatic effects of the war on Brazil

Brazil had strong trading links with Germany in the 1930s but expansion of
trade became difficult in the naval war after 1939. The USA offered a bigger
market and above all was offering to invest in Brazil and make loans available.
Moreover, at the Rio de Janeiro Conference in January 1942, Brazil agreed
with other American republics to co-ordinate defence policies in the Western
Hemisphere. The delegates at Rio unanimously adopted a resolution which
called for all of the American states to sever diplomatic relations with the
Axis powers. Brazil duly broke off relations with the Axis powers.

When several Brazilian ships were sunk by German U-boats in 1942, war
against the Axis powers was the only option. The war permitted Brazil to
make a tremendous contribution to the Allied victory (see pages 122–3).
Brazil had become the strongest country in Latin America and looked
forward to playing an increasing role in world politics. Furthermore, the war
brought Brazil much closer to the USA not only as a trading partner but as
an ally. The USA could now rely on Brazil as a key Latin American ally and
was able to influence politics in that country.

Brazil in the aftermath of the war

At the end of the war, Vargas was under pressure for various reasons. He had
intimated that there would be a return to democracy and the military leaders
did not wish to see his rule continue. Furthermore, the USA did not like his
dictatorship and nationalist economic policies. In addition, there were some
in Brazil who saw the contradiction of having lived in a country with a
dictatorship fighting dictatorships in Europe.

Following free elections in 1945, Vargas was replaced by Eurico Dutra, who
moved away from the *Estado Novo* (see page 216). Dutra encouraged private
companies, especially those from the USA, to invest in Brazil. Dutra followed
US foreign policy closely. He outlawed the Brazilian Communist Party in
1947 and broke off relations with the USSR.

Brazil and the Second World War

- Brazil and Vargas developed import substitution and economic
  nationalism
- Close links with Germany and USA initially
- USA offered credit for the Volta Redonda steel mill
- Brazil declared war on Germany in 1942
- USA gave Lend–Lease and Brazil increased trade in raw materials
- By the end of the war, US aid had improved Brazil's infrastructure and
  greatly helped in the development of industry
- 1945: Brazil was the most powerful country in Latin America
- 1945: Vargas was replaced by Dutra who followed US diplomatic and
  economic policies
- Brazilian Communist Party banned in 1947 and relations with
  USSR severed

SUMMARY DIAGRAM

Brazil and the Second World
War

Canada and the Second World War

▶ *Key question: How did the Second World War affect Canada?*

During the Second World War, Canada's economy was able to recover from the depredations of the Depression and looked forward to peacetime optimistically from a position of strength. Canada's government ensured that agriculture and industry were able to face the demands of the war – the UK was supplied with $1.2 billion worth of goods by 1944 (food, especially wheat, raw materials, military hardware). In addition, Canada provided the USSR and China with essential war supplies. By 1945, Canada's war production was fourth among the Allied nations, less only than that of the USA, the USSR and the UK. Only some 30 per cent of this was needed for Canada's armed forces, the remainder went overseas. (For Canada's military contribution, see pages 110–16.)

Canada's developing economy

How did Canada's industry contribute to the Allied war effort?

Government intervention

Although Canada was partially industrialized, it did not have a strong base to produce large quantities of war *matériel*. The challenge to expand and convert Canadian industry was met by the government and its people and, by 1945, Canada's contribution to the Allied victory was remarkable. When the war started, the government became involved in building production plants, training a workforce, controlling wages and prices, managing labour disputes, and regulating the movement of employees seeking to change jobs. To do this, two important bodies were set up:

- The Department of Munitions and Supply, in 1940, which co-ordinated all purchases made by British and other Allied governments for all the military materials manufactured by Canada.
- The Wartime Industries Control Board, in the spring of 1940, and which applied tough wage and price controls in 1941. The Board issued the National Selective Service Regulations, which prohibited employers from advertising for workers except through National Selective Service offices. In addition, employees were prohibited from seeking other employment without a permit.

Shipbuilding

By mid-1940, the UK was losing merchant vessels to the German U-boat fleet and needed to have replacements as quickly as possible. In addition, the UK needed more naval escort ships for the Atlantic convoys and placed orders with Canada for destroyers and minesweepers. These British demands and Canada's own naval requirements meant a rapid expansion in its shipbuilding industry. In 1939, Canada had three shipyards employing about 4000 men but by the end of the war, there were some 90 plants on the east and west coasts, the Great Lakes and even inland. These shipbuilding plants employed more than 126,000 people.

As in the US shipbuilding industry, the speed of construction improved substantially when assembly-line techniques were adopted. In 1941, the first 10,000-ton (9000-tonne) merchant ships were taking an average of 307 days to build, but by 1942, the average production time had dropped to 163 days.

In all, Canada's shipyards built:

- 4047 naval vessels
- 300 anti-submarine warships
- 410 cargo ships.

Aircraft construction

Aircraft construction during the war was perhaps Canada's greatest industrial achievement. Canadian factory space for the production of aircraft increased from 500,000 square feet (46,500 m^2) for eight small companies before the war to 14,000,000 square feet (1,300,000 m^2) during the war. Employment in the industry rose astonishingly and by 1945, there were some 120,000 workers, 30,000 of whom were women.

In 1939, the Canadian aircraft industry manufactured about 40 aeroplanes. By 1945, almost 16,500 aircraft had been manufactured, mainly for the UK and the USA. There were also many built for use by the Royal Canadian Airforce and the British Commonwealth Air Training Plan (see page 111). There was great co-operation between different companies in the construction of aircraft. For example, when the British ordered 1100 Mosquito fighter-bombers, General Motors made the fuselages, Massey Ferguson made the wings, Boeing made the tailplanes, the flaps were made by Canadian Power Boat Company, and the undercarriages were constructed by OTACO. They were then all assembled at the De Havilland plant. President Roosevelt praised Canada as the 'aerodrome of democracy'.

Military *matériel*

Canadian industry also expanded to meet the demand for goods for its own and the Allied armies. One of the most important features was the production of almost a million trucks and more than 45,000 tanks and armoured vehicles. Canadian factories also produced 1.7 million rifles, submachine guns, light machine guns, anti-tank guns and anti-aircraft guns, 43,000 25-pounder (11-kg) artillery pieces and more than two million tonnes (2.2 million tons) of explosives.

Military technology

The war also resulted in Canada becoming a leader in several areas of military technology, including radar to counter German air attacks and ASDIC apparatus for submarine detection (see page 189).

It is important to remember that Canada supplied uranium for the atomic bomb programme and allowed the UK to run an atomic laboratory on its soil during the war. Experience in this field led to Canada being the first country after the USA to set up a nuclear reactor.

Canada's economy after the war

Canada provided supplies to the Allies to the value of about $2000 million and its total annual exports rose from $573 million to $1323 million. The war had resulted in Canada becoming the third largest trading nation in the world and just as in the USA, the shadow of the Depression had been removed. The extent of Canada's economic power can be seen in 1946 when it loaned the UK $1.25 billion and signed a wheat contract ensuring cheap grain for the 'mother country'.

The government established the Department of Reconstruction in June 1944 to guarantee industrial output and maximize employment during the move from war to peace. In 1948, unemployment was still at a minimum. Canada's steel mills were exceeding their wartime capacity and the demand for aluminium continued.

Canada experienced a consumer boom after 1945 which was generated by the needs of a rapidly growing population which required homes, schools, hospitals, roads and factories. In addition, Canada's exports continued to grow as a supplier of goods to Europe via the Marshall Plan (see page 206).

SOURCE J

An excerpt from 'Our factories grow' in the *Hamilton Spectator*, a Canadian newspaper, 22 November 1945.

The nation has, in brief, graduated from an 'assembly line' industrial set-up – in which parts are imported from other nations – to a 'production' basis, where we make those parts ourselves, and turn out the finished goods for consumers. This is a marked step ahead; and the industrial vitality that Canada showed in wartime should not be checked or injured by the changeover to peace.

How useful is Source J as evidence of Canada's industrial progress? **?**

Diplomatic effects on Canada

The people of Canada made a tremendous contribution to the war effort both at home and on the front lines, and in doing so Canada earned the respect and admiration of its allies and the world. More than a million Canadian men and women served in the armed forces out of a population of 11.5 million. Some 42,000 died, and there were more than 55,000 wounded, indicating that Canada suffered disproportionately in comparison with its western allies. Thus, the war raised Canada's international profile and placed it among one of the most powerful countries in the world. It was one of the founding members of the UN and was a key figure in the **British Commonwealth**. (See pages 117–20 for further details about Canada's diplomatic role in the war.)

In what ways did Canada's diplomatic position change?

**KEY TERM**

British Commonwealth An association of nations consisting of the UK and several former colonies that had become sovereign states but still paid allegiance to the British Crown.

Canada and the USSR

Canada's foreign policy before 1939 had been rather similar to the USA. It followed an isolationist line but after 1945 began to play a more visible role in international affairs.

As a result of the destruction of much of Europe, and the political weaknesses on that continent, it was thought that Canada, as a major contributor to the war and a nation that had not suffered domestic damage, would play a significant part in post-war international relations. However, the Gouzenko affair in 1945 immediately threatened diplomatic relations with the USSR and strengthened them with the USA.

The Gouzenko affair

As a result of Canada's involvement in the atomic programme (Canada had provided uranium for the atomic bombs and had allowed British scientists to establish atomic laboratories in Montreal) the USSR established a spy network in Ottawa. Igor Gouzenko was a clerk at the Soviet embassy in Ottawa. He defected and offered the Canadian government 109 Soviet documents which gave details of the espionage being conducted in Canada. As a result of the evidence he provided, 22 local agents and 15 Soviet spies were arrested. The evidence Gouzenko offered was vital to the discovery of Soviet spies in several organizations, including MI5, Britain's **counter-intelligence** organization.

Canada's status in the world

Canada's status as an independent country, only recently established, was beyond doubt after 1945. Its role in hosting several major international conferences during the war was testimony to its pivotal link between the USA and the UK. After the war, Canada's important position can be seen when, in 1948, it held one of the rotating UN Security Council seats (one of the six non-permanent members who held a seat on the Council for two-year terms). However, Canada's Prime Minister King was pessimistic about the role of the UN and saw that the veto (see pages 97–8) would denude the organization of teeth.

The modest nature of Canada's international position can be seen when it joined NATO in 1949 with the USA and ten European nations. This was a clear recognition that Canada needed allies and had to remain close to the USA to counter the threat of the USSR.

Canada and the Second World War

Economic effects of the Second World War on Canada

Diplomatic effects of the war on Canada

- Won respect and admiration from Allies
- Founding member of the UN
- Key figure in the British Commonwealth
- Gouzenko affair soured relations with the USSR – several spies arrested
- 1948: held one of the rotating seats on the UN Security Council
- Joined NATO in 1949

The role of government
- Aware of the devastating effects of the 1930s depression
- Established the Department of Munitions and Supply in 1940
- Set up the Wartime Industries Control Board
- Supplied goods to Allies

Canada's wartime production
- Ships – more than 4000 constructed
- Aircraft – more than 16,500 built
- *Matériel* – thousands of rifles and guns
- Technological assistance – contributed to the development of radar and ASDIC

Post-war Canada
- Strong economy
- Low unemployment
- Production at peak wartime levels
- Exports grew

SUMMARY DIAGRAM

Canada and the Second World War

Chapter summary

The economic and diplomatic effects of the Second World War on the Americas

The war made the USA the strongest power in the world. Its economy and industry had expanded enormously and without the huge military aid given to the UK and the USSR, Hitler could not have been defeated. Moreover, fighting a second war in the Pacific had added to the USA's economic and military power. However, the war had also made the USA realize that

it could not pursue a policy of isolation in the future and it was recognized that it would have to participate in world affairs, hence its membership of the United Nations Organization. Nevertheless, as peace was made the scene was set for disharmony and rivalry as relations with the USSR quickly deteriorated.

For Brazil and Canada, the war had similar outcomes. Both experienced huge industrial change and Canada emerged as one of the strongest economies in the world. Brazil emerged from the war as the strongest power in South America having received aid via Lend–Lease.

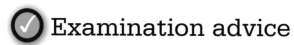

✓ Examination advice

How to answer 'compare and contrast' questions

For <u>compare and contrast</u> questions, you are asked to identify both similarities and differences. Better essays tend to approach the question thematically. It is best not to write half of the essay as a collection of similarities and half as differences. Finally, a straight narrative should be avoided. To score in the highest mark band you need to write an essay that contains a structured framework, and includes analysis as well as some evaluation of different interpretations.

Example

> <u>Compare and contrast</u> the economic effects of the Second World War on two countries in the region.

1 It helps to provide historical context. What was taking place nationally and internationally that led to specific governmental actions and with what results? You could discuss the economic effects on two countries during and immediately after the war. If you choose to write solely on the economic effects either during or after the war, state this in your introduction. Finally, choose two countries from the Americas only. The USA and Canada are two possible countries, although if you have studied other countries in depth and you have enough supporting historical evidence, then feel free to write an essay using them as your two examples.

2 When answering a 'compare and contrast' question like this one, you should create a list that illustrates the similarities and differences between these two. Take five minutes to do this before writing your essay.

USA/Canada similarities:
- Both mobilized industry for meeting wartime needs.
- By end of war, both nations were economically powerful.
- Women in large numbers entered workforce; many left workforce after war.
- Both governments played key roles in organizing economies.
- Huge increases in production of planes, ships, produce.
- Prices controlled.
- Both trained workers to meet new industrial demands.
- Consumer boom after war.

USA/Canada differences:
- USA was already heavily industrialized at beginning of war, Canada less so.
- Wartime Industries Control Board in Canada controlled hiring of workers.

- Canada entered war more than two years before USA and was major supplier to the UK. Recovered from Great Depression earlier.
- Workers in USA joined unions at faster rate.
- Department of Reconstruction (Canada) created to ensure industrial output and maximize employment after war.
- US GI Bill of Rights.
- Canada began to produce finished goods after war; USA had already been doing this.
- Scale differed between the two.

3 In your introduction, state briefly and clearly how the effects of the Second World War for the USA and Canada were similar and different and why. An example of a good introductory paragraph for this question is given below.

The Great Depression had ravaged global economies resulting in shuttered factories and millions out of work. When war broke out in Europe in 1939, Canada began to shift its mostly agriculturally based economy to a more industrial one; the USA would not enter the war until more than two years later, and while it was already an industrial powerhouse, it still had to shift its factories from producing mostly consumer goods to military items. Both governments actively intervened in their respective economies and both enacted a series of measures meant to control prices, thereby keeping inflation rates low. Another economic effect of the Second World War was that women entered the workforce in large numbers. At the war's conclusion in 1945, many would leave the factories and focus on raising families. It is important to keep in mind that one area of difference between the two countries was that of scale. The USA had a much larger economy and population than Canada's and when it went to war in December 1941, it had greater resources to bring to bear. Nonetheless, because neither country's industrial and agricultural infrastructure had been damaged during the war, both came out of it in a much stronger economic position, especially in relation to former European and Asian powers. Pent-up consumer demand exploded after 1945 and this helped ease the transition from a heated wartime economy to a peacetime one. That said, there were a whole series of large strikes that affected the USA unlike what took place in Canada. Finally, in the USA, the government created the GI Bill of Rights. Former soldiers had the opportunity to go to university and receive loans. In Canada, as its population grew so did the need for new schools and roads which meant that there were plentiful work opportunities for the newly demobilized soldiers.

4 In the body of the essay, discuss each of the points you raised in the introduction. This also means adding supporting historical evidence. Make sure the reader knows you are explaining similarities or differences. You will probably also find many of the similarities and differences are not exactly the same, or even polar opposites. Explain the extent to which they are similar or different. Your answer should be a balance between comparisons and contrasts even though you are not expected to have an exact 50–50 breakdown of the two. Essays that explain *why* there were similarities and differences between the economic effects on the USA and Canada will receive higher marks than ones that only compare and contrast.

5 In your conclusion, summarize your findings. This is your opportunity to support your thesis. Remember not to bring up any evidence that you did not discuss in the body of your essay.

6 Now try writing a complete answer to the question following the advice above.

 # Examination practice

Below are two exam-style questions for you to practise on this topic.

1. Assess the effectiveness of the US government's economic response to the outbreak of war in 1941.
   (For guidance on how to answer 'Assess' questions, see page 106.)

2. Analyse the ways in which Canada's diplomatic and economic position changed as a result of the Second World War.
   (For guidance on how to answer 'Analyse' questions, see page 49.)

Timeline

1929	October	Wall Street Crash
1931	September	Japan invaded Manchuria
1932	November	Franklin Roosevelt elected president of the USA
1933	March	President Roosevelt's inauguration
	December	Inter-American Conference, Montevideo
1934	April	Nye Committee set up
1935	May	Italian invasion of Abyssinia
	August	First Neutrality Act
	September	Nuremberg Laws
1936	February	Second Neutrality Act
	July	Beginning of the Spanish Civil War
	November	Roosevelt re-elected president of the USA
	December	Conference for the Maintenance of Peace, Buenos Aires
1937	January	Third Neutrality Act
	May	Fourth Neutrality Act
	July	Start of the Sino-Japanese War
	October	Roosevelt's Quarantine Speech
	November	Vargas declared *Estado Novo* in Brazil
	December	USS *Panay* sunk by Japanese planes
1938	March	Hitler annexed Austria (*Anschluss*)
	July	Evian Conference
	September	Munich Conference
	October	Hitler gained the Sudetenland from Czechoslovakia
	November	*Kristallnacht*
	December	Pan-American Conference, Lima
1939	March	German invasion of Czechoslovakia
	August	Nazi–Soviet Non-aggression Pact
	September	Germany invaded Poland
		UK declared war on Germany
		USSR invaded eastern Poland
	October	Hemisphere Neutrality Belt established
	November	Fifth Neutrality Act
1940	May	Committee to Defend America established
	June	Greater East Asia Co-prosperity Sphere announced by Japan
	July	Act of Havana
	September	America First Committee established
		'Destroyers for bases' deal
		Peacetime conscription in the USA
		Three Power Pact (Germany, Italy and Japan)
	November	Roosevelt re-elected president of the USA
1941	January	Four Freedoms Speech
	March	Lend–Lease passed in Congress

	April	Soviet–Japanese Non-aggression Pact signed
	May	Robin Moor incident
	June	Germany invaded USSR
		Executive Order 8802 established Fair Employment Practices Commission
	July	USA extended Lend–Lease to USSR
	August	Atlantic Charter signed
	November	US Neutrality Act amended
	December 7	Japan attacked Pearl Harbor
	December 8	USA declared war on Japan
	December 11	Germany declared war on USA
		Washington Conference
1942	January	Declaration of the United Nations
		Rio de Janeiro Conference
		War Production Board set up
	February	Internment of Japanese Americans began
	May	Battle of the Coral Sea
	June	Battle of Midway
	August	Dieppe Raid
		Brazil declared war on the Axis powers
	November	Operation Torch (Allied invasion of Morocco and Algeria)
1943	January	Casablanca Conference
		Germans surrendered at Stalingrad
	April	Bermuda Conference on refugees
	May	Washington Conference
	June	'Zoot suit' riots in California
		Race riots in Detroit
		Bracero Agreement
	July	Operation Husky (Allied invasion of Sicily)
	August	Quebec Conference
	December	Tehran Conference
		USA captured the Solomon Islands
1944	January	War Refugee Board set up
	February	US troops captured the Marshall Islands
	June	D-Day (Operation Overlord – Allied invasion of France)
	August	Battle of the Philippine Sea
	September	Quebec Conference
	October	Battle of Leyte Gulf
	October 9–19	Moscow Conference
1945	January	Germans defeated in the Battle of the Bulge
	February	Yalta Conference
		US forces recaptured Manila
	March	Iwo Jima captured by US forces
	April	Death of Roosevelt, suicide of Hitler
	May	Surrender of Germany
	June	US forces captured Okinawa
	July	Atomic bomb tested
		Potsdam Conference
	August 6	Atomic bomb dropped on Hiroshima
	August 9	Atomic bomb dropped on Nagasaki
	September 2	Formal surrender of Japan

Glossary

Aircraft carrier A warship with an extensive flat deck space for the launch and recovery of aircraft.

American republics All the independent republican countries of the Americas.

Amphibious warfare Military operations launched from the sea against an enemy shore.

Anschluss The union of Germany with Austria, March 1938.

Anti-Semitic Prejudiced against Jews.

Armada A large naval force.

ASDIC Named after the Anti-Submarine Detection Investigation Committee which began development during the First World War.

Atlantic Charter The joint declaration issued by Roosevelt and Churchill which set down the principles to guide a post-war settlement.

Atomic bomb A type of bomb in which the energy is provided by nuclear fission.

Axis The alliance of Germany, Italy and Japan.

B-29 Superfortress bomber An advanced heavy bomber used in the US campaign to bomb mainland Japan in the final months of the war. It was used to carry out the bombing of Hiroshima and Nagasaki.

Balance of payments The difference in value between total payments made to a country and total payments received from that country in a given period.

Battle of Britain A series of air battles between Britain and Germany fought over the UK from August to October 1940.

Beachhead An area on a beach that has been captured from the enemy and on which troops and equipment are landed.

Belligerent A country engaged in war.

Blackout The hiding of artificial light visible to an enemy attack from the air.

Blood plasma The yellowish fluid portion of the blood in which the corpuscles and cells are suspended.

Bocage Thick hedgerows 10–13 feet (3–4 m) high which tanks and infantry found almost impossible to negotiate.

Bridgehead An advanced position seized in hostile territory.

British Columbia A province of western Canada on the Pacific coast.

British Commonwealth An association of nations consisting of the UK and several former colonies that had become sovereign states but still paid allegiance to the British Crown.

Buffer state A small and usually neutral state between two rival powers.

Buffer zone A neutral area between hostile or belligerent forces that serves to prevent conflict.

Buying on the margin Purchasing stocks and shares by putting up only a part, or a margin, of the purchase price and borrowing the remainder.

Capitalism A system under which businesses are owned privately and people are able to make a profit.

Capital ships The largest and most heavily armed ships in a naval fleet.

Casus belli The Latin phrase for an event or act which is used to justify a declaration of war.

Civil disobedience A non-violent way of protesting in order to achieve political goals.

Civil rights movement A movement that attempts to secure equality in social, economic and political rights.

Cold War A tense strategic and ideological confrontation between the USA and USSR after the Second World War. It was 'cold' as there was never a direct war between the two powers.

Combat zone An area of military fighting.

Combined Chiefs of Staff The supreme military staff of each of the Western Allies working together in one group.

Communism A theory that society should be classless, private property abolished, and land and business owned collectively.

Concentration camp A camp where civilians, enemy aliens, political prisoners and sometimes prisoners of war are detained and confined under harsh conditions.

Congress US legislature consisting of the Senate and the House of Representatives.

Consulates The premises of officials appointed by countries to protect their interests and citizens in a foreign city.

Counter-intelligence Keeping sensitive information from an enemy, deceiving that enemy, preventing subversion and sabotage, and collecting political and military information.

D-Day The selected day for the start of Operation Overlord, 6 June 1944.

Dachau concentration camp The first concentration camp opened by the Nazis, initially for political prisoners.

Danzig crisis The demand by Germany in the summer of 1939 that the city of Danzig should be returned to Germany. (Now Gdańsk, Poland.)

Depth charge An anti-submarine bomb that explodes at a pre-set depth under water.

Direct action The use of acts, such as strikes, marches and demonstrations, to achieve a political or social end.

Duce 'Leader', the title assumed by Mussolini in 1922 as dictator of Italy.

Dunkirk evacuation The evacuation of British and some French forces from mainland Europe.

Ellis Island The immigration processing centre in New York from 1892 to 1954.

Estado Novo 'New State': Getúlio Vargas' 1937 dictatorial regime.

Estancieros The large landowners who were the élite of the nation.

Executive decision A decision made by the president without consulting Congress.

Fifth columnists People working secretly within a country to further an invading enemy's military and political aims.

Final Solution The name given to the Nazi policy to kill all the Jews in Europe. About six million were killed under this policy. The term 'Holocaust' is now used to describe this act of genocide.

Fireside chat Informal talks that President Roosevelt made on the radio. They were so called because it was intended that people could sit at home and listen to the president.

Flying Fortress The Boeing B-17 bomber aircraft which had so many machine guns it was given this name.

14 Points The principles drawn up by President Wilson for ending the war.

Free French The military units led by General Charles de Gaulle after the fall of France in 1940.

Freezing assets The suspending of access to property, money and investments.

French resistance Anti-German groups that were based within France which organized fighting for liberty while under German occupation.

Friendly fire Injuring or killing a member of one's own armed forces or an ally.

Gallup poll A public opinion poll originated by Dr George Gallup in the 1930s.

Gentlemen's Agreement Whereby the USA would not impose restrictions on Japanese immigration and Japan would not allow further emigration to the USA.

Good Neighbor Foreign policy adopted by Roosevelt to mend and improve relations with Latin America.

Government-in-exile A political group which claims to be a country's legitimate government but is unable to exercise legal power and instead resides in a foreign country.

Gross national product The value of all the goods and services produced, plus the value of imported goods and services, less exported goods and services.

Hemisphere Neutrality Belt Roosevelt declared that the Atlantic, 300 miles (500 km) out from the eastern US coast, was part of the Western Hemisphere and therefore neutral.

Hemispheric Relating to the western or eastern or northern or southern part of the world. In this case, it refers to North and South America.

Hispanic American A person of Spanish ancestry, particularly Latin American, living in the USA.

Hunger winter The famine in the Netherlands during the winter of 1944–5.

Import substitution A trade and economic policy advocating replacing foreign imports with domestic production.

Incendiary bombs Bombs designed to start fires.

Indochina The region of South-east Asia which was a colony of France.

Industrial and military complexes The aggregate of a nation's armed forces and the industries that supply their equipment, materials and armaments.

Infamous Decade The period following Uriburu's coup which was characterized by rural decline, electoral corruption and economic dislocation.

International Committee of the Red Cross (ICRC) An international movement which has special responsibilities under international humanitarian law.

Internationalist An advocate for co-operation and understanding between nations.

Internment camps Places where people were imprisoned or confined without trial.

Interventionist Someone who advocates becoming involved in foreign affairs, in this case, the war in Europe.

Iron curtain The military, political and ideological barrier established between the Soviet bloc and Western Europe from 1945 to 1990.

Isolationism The policy of avoiding involvement in conflicts and alliances with other nations.

Issei First generation of Japanese immigrants to the USA.

Jewish Agency Established at the 16th Zionist Congress in 1929 to promote Jewish settlement in Palestine.

Jim Crow army Segregated African American army units. 'Jim Crow' referred to US laws that permitted segregation.

Kristallnacht 'Night of Broken Glass', the name given to the violent anti-Jewish riots that began on the night of 9 November 1938 and continued through the day of 10 November.

Laissez-faire The theory that an economy should be run without government interference.

Landing craft A vessel used for landing troops and equipment on beaches.

Latin America The countries of the Americas whose official languages are Spanish and Portuguese.

Luftwaffe The German air force.

Machine tools Power-driven machines, such as lathes, millers or grinders, used for cutting, shaping and finishing metals or other materials.

Manoeuvres Military exercises simulating actual wartime situations.

Marines Originally a branch of the US armed forces using the navy to deliver combined forces.

Matériel Military equipment.

Mediterranean campaign The Allied attacks on Sicily and mainland Italy.

Merchant fleet The ships engaged in a nation's commercial shipping.

Militarism The tendency to regard military efficiency as the supreme ideal of the state and to subordinate all other interests to those of the military.

Monroe Doctrine The principle of US foreign policy which opposes the influence or interference of outside powers in the Americas and US involvement in internal European affairs.

Moral embargo The partial or complete prohibition of commerce and trade in goods with a particular country based on the notion that trading in those goods does not accord with accepted humanitarian standards.

Munich Agreement Agreement between the UK, Germany, France and Italy, September 1938, which ceded the Sudetenland to Germany.

Munich crisis The crisis over the Sudetenland in Czechoslovakia. Hitler demanded this German-speaking area and was awarded it after the conference in Munich, September 1938.

Nationalized Placed under state control.

Native Americans The indigenous people of the USA.

Neutrality Act An act passed to limit US involvement in possible future wars.

New Deal The domestic policies of Franklin Roosevelt for economic and social reform.

Nikkei Kanadajin Canadians of Japanese ethnicity.

1911 trade treaty A treaty to improve trade and commerce between the USA and Japan.

NIRA The National Industrial Recovery Act, part of Roosevelt's New Deal. It aimed to increase productivity in US industry.

Nisei The children of first generation Japanese immigrants (*Issei*).

Nuremberg Laws A series of measures aimed against the Jews in Germany in 1935. They included the Reich Law on Citizenship, which stated that only those of German blood could be German citizens. Jews lost their citizenship, and the right to vote and hold government office. The Law for the Protection of German Blood and Honour forbade marriage or sexual relations between Jews and German citizens.

Occupied territories Those countries which had been taken over by Nazi Germany.

Officers' commission Being granted the position of an officer.

Open-door policy The practice by which one country grants opportunities for trade to all other nations equally.

Open trading system Trading between countries when there are no tariffs and restrictions.

Partisans Members of armed resistance groups within occupied territory.

Peacetime draft The selection of people for service in the military. The draft had been compulsory in the First World War but this was the first time the USA had had conscription in peacetime.

Penicillin An antibiotic drug used to treat or prevent a wide range of infections, especially gangrene.

Platt Amendment The amendment added to the Cuban constitution of 1901, which affected Cuba's right to negotiate treaties and permitted the USA to maintain its naval base and intervene in Cuban affairs for the preservation of Cuban independence.

Pogrom An organized massacre of an ethnic group.

Polish underground The Polish movement dedicated to the overthrow of the Nazi occupying forces.

Primaries Preliminary elections in which the voters of a state choose a political party's nominee for president.

Prisoners of war Members of the armed forces captured by an enemy in time of war.

Protectionist A policy which placed tariffs/taxes on imports to protect US industry from foreign competitors.

Puppet state Nominally a sovereign state but controlled by a foreign power.

Purple Heart A decoration awarded to members of the US armed forces for a wound incurred in action.

Québecois A French-speaking native or inhabitant of Quebec.

RAF Royal Air Force – the British air force.

Ratify To give formal approval.

Regular army The permanent standing army of a nation or state.

Reparations Compensation payable by a defeated country to the victors.

Rugged individualism The idea that individuals are responsible for their own lives without help from anyone else. An individual has to stand or fall by his or her own efforts.

Sanctions Punishments against a country for breaking international law.

Second Front Stalin's wish for the USA and the UK to open another theatre of war in France against the Germans in order to take the pressure off the Soviet forces on the Eastern Front.

Sink on sight' policy Any ship that was seen was immediately attacked without warning, whether the country the ship belonged to was at war with Germany or not.

Sino-Japanese War War between China and Japan from 1937 to 1945.

Sit-in A form of civil disobedience in which demonstrators occupy a public place and refuse to move as a protest.

Slave labour camp A concentration camp where people worked under duress and threats.

Sorties Operational flights of military aircraft.

Spanish Civil War The war (1936–9) in which the Nationalists, led by General Franco, overthrew the Republican government.

Stalemate Situations in which two opposing forces find that any further action is impossible or futile.

Stars and Stripes flag The national flag of the USA.

State Department The US government department in charge of foreign affairs.

Status quo A Latin term meaning the existing state of affairs.

Stock market A place where stocks and shares are bought and sold.

Surface raiders Ships of the German navy used against Allied merchant vessels.

Tariffs Duties or taxes imposed on items of overseas trade.

Tenentes Army lieutenants in Brazil.

Three Power Pact This pact, between Germany, Italy and Japan, was signed on 27 September 1940. It is also called the Tripartite Pact.

Totalitarianism When political regimes suppress political opposition and control all aspects of people's lives.

Treaty of Versailles The treaty signed between the Allies and Germany in June 1919, after the end of the First World War.

Tribal reservations Areas of land managed by Native American tribes.

Truman Doctrine Truman's policy of providing economic and military aid to any country threatened by communism or totalitarian ideology.

U-boats German submarines.

Ultra The British project which successfully decrypted German codes.

Unconditional surrender Surrender without conditions, in which no guarantees are given to the country that is surrendering.

United Nations Originally, those countries that had signed the Atlantic Charter. The term was later used for the international organization of nations replacing the League of Nations from 1919. It would promote peace, international co-operation and security.

US General Staff The senior officers who advise in the planning and execution of military policy.

USAAF United States Army Air Forces – the USA's air force during the Second World War.

USSR The Union of Soviet Socialist Republics was the name given to Russia after the Bolshevik Revolution. It was also known as the Soviet Union.

Vatican The papal government.

Vichy government The puppet government of France after Germany defeated and occupied it in 1940.

Voluntarism The principle of depending on volunteers to join the armed forces.

War bonds Securities sold by the US government to its citizens to finance military operations during the war. The war bonds took money out of the economy and thus prevented inflation from becoming too high.

War Refugee Board (WRB) An independent agency established to take all measures to rescue victims of enemy oppression in imminent danger of death.

Western Hemisphere The part of the world containing North and South America.

Whites Anti-Bolshevik supporters of the former Tsarist government.

World Jewish Congress (WJC) An international federation of Jewish communities and organizations set up in Switzerland in 1936.

Zone of occupation An area of a defeated country occupied by the victors' armed forces.

Zoot suit A suit with a long jacket that reached to the fingertips, heavily padded shoulders, pleated trousers tapered at the turn-ups and long key chains, occasionally with a wide-brimmed hat.

Further reading

Background works

Peter Clements, *Prosperity, Depression and the New Deal: The USA 1890–1954*, Hodder Education, 2008
This is a sound introduction to the history of the USA during this period.

Works on US foreign policy

Hugh Brogan, *The Pelican History of the United States of America*, Pelican, 1985

Robert Dallek, *Franklin D. Roosevelt and American Foreign Policy, 1932–45*, OUP, 1979

Robert A. Divine, *The Reluctant Belligerent: American Entry into World War II*, Wiley, 1979

Robert D. Schulzinger, *American Diplomacy in the Twentieth Century*, OUP, 1990

Daniel Snowman, *America Since 1920*, Heinemann, 1978
Brogan, Schulzinger and Snowman's books give clear analyses and Divine gives a concise account to 1941. Dallek offers a thorough consideration of Roosevelt's problems.

Works on USA, the US economy and industry during the war

Arthur Herman, *Freedom's Forge: How American Business Produced Victory in World War II*, Random House, 2012

Alan S. Milward, *War, Economy, and Society, 1939–1945*. University of California Press, 1979

William L. O'Neill, *A Democracy at War*, Free Press, 1993

Harold G. Vatter, *The U.S. Economy in World War II*, Columbia University Press, 1985
These texts give excellent accounts of the transition to a wartime economy and also of the impact of the war on industry.

Works on the USA's military role during the war

Stephen Ambrose, *Citizen Soldiers*, Touchstone, 1997

Max Hastings, *Nemesis: The Battle for Japan, 1944–45*, Harper Perennial, 2007

Ernie Pyle, *Ernie's War: The Best of Ernie Pyle's World War II Dispatches*, Touchstone/Simon & Schuster, 1986

Andrew Roberts, *Masters and Commanders*, Allen Lane, 2008
These texts cover the war from the viewpoints of leaders to ordinary soldiers in the US theatres.

Works on US society and the Second World War

Tom Brokaw, *The Greatest Generation*, Random House, 1998

Doris Kearns Goodwin, *No Ordinary Time*, Simon and Schuster, 1994

David Kennedy, *Freedom from Fear: The American People in Depression and War 1929–45*, OUP, 1999

William L. O'Neill, *A Democracy at War*, Free Press, 1993

David Paterson, Doug Willoughby and Susan Willoughby, *Civil Rights in the USA 1863–90*, Heinemann, 2001 (Chapters 4 and 5)

Vivienne Sanders, *Race Relations in the USA Since 1900*, Hodder, 2000 (Chapter 3)

Emily Yellin, *Our Mothers' War: American Women at Home and at the Front during World* War Two, Free Press, 2004
These texts give clear accounts of the impact of the war on US society as a whole and the role of women and African Americans in particular.

Works on the Holocaust and the Americas

Robert L. Beir with Brian Josepher, *Roosevelt and the Holocaust*, Barricade, 2006

Henry Feingold, *The Politics of Rescue: The Roosevelt Administration and the Holocaust, 1938–45*, Rutgers University Press, 1970

Robert N. Rosen, *Saving the Jews: Franklin D. Roosevelt and the Holocaust*, Basic Books, 2007

William D. Rubinstein, *The Myth of Rescue*, Routledge, 1997

David Wyman, *The Abandonment of the Jews*, Pantheon, 1984
These books are very thought-provoking and approach the debate from various angles.

Works on Franklin Roosevelt

Conrad Black, *Franklin Delano Roosevelt: Champion of Freedom*, Public Affairs, 2003

H. W. Brands, *Traitor to his Class*, Anchor Books, 2008

Frank Friedel, *Franklin D Roosevelt: A Rendezvous with Destiny*, Little, Brown, 1990

Doris Kearns Goodwin, *No Ordinary Time*, Simon & Schuster, 1994
Biographies are frequently long and tend to offer extremes of views. Black, Brands and Friedel are no exceptions. Goodwin offers an intimate portrait as well as a close analysis of Americans during the war.

Works on Canada

Robert Bothwell, *The Penguin History of Canada*, Penguin, 2006

Robert Bothwell, Ian Drummond and John English, *Canada 1900–45*, University of Toronto Press, 1987

Terry Copp, *No Price Too High: Canadians and the Second World War*, McGraw-Hill Ryerson, 1995
Good texts beginning with an overview and moving to a more detailed analysis of Canada's role in the war.

Works on Latin America

Celso Furtado, *Economic Growth of Brazil: A Survey from Colonial to Modern Times*, University of California Press, 1971

Stanley E. Hilton, *Hitler's Secret War in South America, 1939–1945: German Military Espionage and Allied Counterespionage in Brazil*, Louisiana State University Press, 1999

Thomas M. Leonard, editor, chapters by Joseph Smith 'Brazil: the effects of cooperation' and David Sheinin 'Argentina: the closest ally' in *Latin America During World War II*, Jaguar Books, 2006

Luís Romero, *A History of Argentina in the Twentieth Century*, Pennsylvania State University Press, 2002

Thomas Skidmore and Peter Smith, *Modern Latin America*, OUP, 2005

Edwin Williamson, *The Penguin History of Latin America*, Penguin, 2009

John D. Wirth, *The Politics of Brazilian Development, 1930–1954*, Stanford University Press, 1970
The two texts by Skidmore & Smith and Williamson offer sound overviews and the others give authoritative and scholarly analyses.

Works on medical and weapons developments

Albert Cowdrey, *Fighting for Life*, Free Press, 1998

Francis Gosling, *The Manhattan Project: Making the Atomic Bomb*, University Press of the Pacific, 2005

Mark Stille, *US Navy Aircraft Carriers 1942–45*, Osprey Books, 2007
Cowdrey gives excellent coverage of the medical issues facing the US Army, and Gosling and Stille offer sound accounts of the two key weapon developments of the war.

Internet sources

www.loc.gov/vets/stories/afam-pioneers.html
The US Library of Congress 'Veterans History Project' site. This section is on 'Experiencing War: African American at War: Fighting Two Battles'.

www.thecanadianencyclopedia.com/articles/canada
A useful resource on Canada.

www.fdrlibrary.marist.edu
Roosevelt Presidential Library and Museum.

http://ww2db.com/battle_spec.php?battle_id=225
US and Canadian Japanese in the war.

www.gresham.ac.uk/lectures-and-events/franklin-d-roosevelt-president-1933-1945-foreign-policy
Lecture on Roosevelt's foreign policy from London's Gresham College.

www.lwfaam.net/ww2/
African Americans in the Second World War

http://mashpedia.com/Argentina_in_World_War_II
Argentina in the Second World War.

http://mexconnect.com/articles/678-mexico-forgotten-world-war-ii-ally
Mexico and the Second World War.

http://rosietheriveter.org/memory.htm
The role of US women in the war.

http://tau.ac.il/eial/VI_2/mccann.htm
Analysis of Brazil in the 1930s and its role in the war.

http://WWII.ca
Canada and the Second World War.

Internal assessment

The internal assessment is an investigation on a historical topic. Below is a list of possible topics on the Second World War and the Americas that could warrant further investigation. They have been organized by chapter theme.

Chapter 1: The Americas from peace to the Depression 1919–32

1 How effective were President Getúlio Vargas's measures to combat the Depression?
2 What role did the Republican 'irreconcilables' play in ensuring the USA did not join the League of Nations?

Chapter 2: Hemispheric reactions to the events in Europe and Asia 1933–41

1 What led President Roosevelt to adopt the 'Good Neighbor' policy?
2 What impact did refugees from the Spanish Civil War have on Mexican culture?
3 To what extent was Charles Lindbergh a supporter of Nazi Germany?

Chapter 3: The military role of the USA during the Second World War

1 How did the US Lend–Lease programme contribute to the USSR's victory over the Germans?
2 To what extent was the 1940 Export Control Act successful in hurting Japan's economy?
3 Why did the USA delay opening a second front in Europe?

Chapter 4: The diplomatic role of the USA in the Second World War 1941–5

1 Why was an important conference of Allied leaders held in Tehran?
2 How successful were Nazi espionage rings in Latin America?
3 Why did Roosevelt think that the British Empire was an anachronism?

Chapter 5: The military and diplomatic role of Canada and Brazil in the Second World War

1 How successful was Canada's 1943 Mutual Aid Programme?
2 What role did the Mexican Aztec Eagles play in the Second World War?
3 Why did the Argentine government allow Nazi officials to settle in Argentina after the Second World War?

Chapter 6: The social impact of the Second World War on the USA

1 What consequences did Brazil's declaration of war have on its large Japanese Brazilian population?
2 How did the Bracero Agreement affect Mexican–US relations?
3 To what extent were Victory Gardens successful?

Chapter 7: Reaction to the Holocaust in the Americas

1 Why didn't the US Air Force bomb concentration camps?
2 What led to the deportation of Olga Benário Prestes from Brazil?
3 What role did Mexico play in taking in Jewish refugees during the Second World War?

Chapter 8: Technological developments and the beginning of the atomic age

1 What impact did new medical advances made by the USA during the Second World War have on keeping servicemen alive?
2 How successful were the efforts of the War Production Board in meeting the needs of the USA during the Second World War?
3 To what extent was the Battle of the Philippine Sea a key turning point in the Pacific War?

Chapter 9: The economic and diplomatic effects of the Second World War on the Americas

1 How did President Truman break the 1946 United Mine Workers' strike?
2 What factors led President Getúlio Vargas to declare war on Germany?
3 What impact did the Gouzenko affair have on Canadian–Soviet relations?

Index